"The Earth has given birth to the Sky"

European Folklore Institute

*Bibliotheca Traditionis Europae*

Volume 4

Edited by MIHÁLY HOPPÁL

Kornélia Buday

# "The Earth has given birth to the Sky"

FEMALE SPIRITUALITY IN THE HUNGARIAN FOLK RELIGION

Akadémiai Kiadó
European Folklore Institute
Budapest

ISBN 963 05 8136 1

ISSN 1419-7901

Published for the European Folklore Institute
by Akadémiai Kiadó Member of Wolters Kluwer Group
P.O. Box 245, H-1519 Budapest, Hungary
www.akkrt.hu

Printed in Hungary

To Him

# Contents

# Acknowledgements

I would like to thank all those who opened my eyes to the complexity of religious-cultural tradition (in chronological order):

*From Debrecen:* Ladiszla Maros, Vilmos L. Szabó

*From Szeged:* József Hofher, Béla Somfai

*From Dublin:* Soline Vatinel, Cathy Molloy, Edel O'Kennedy, James Corkery, Sean Fagan, Robert Noonan, David Smith

*From Innsbruck:* Julius Morel, Beáta Hanák, Franz Weber, Gertraud Ladner, Martha Heizer, Ruth, Francis and Davis.

*From Mainz:* Rolf Decot and all co-workers of the Institut für Europäische Geschichte

*From Vienna:* Antonia Himmel-Agisburg

*The experts of Hungarian ethnography:* Zsuzsanna Erdélyi, Tamás Grynaeus, Mihály Hoppál, Imola Küllős, Gábor Limbacher, Éva Pócs

Special thanks to *Birgit Heller,* professor of the Institut für Religionswissenschaft – Universität Wien, for her understanding and support from the very beginning. Her constant guidance and encouragement has motivated me to enter areas related to the Hungarian divine figure of the Happy Woman I would not have thought to explore.

Without the financial support and other resources offered by *the Deutsche Akademische Austauschdienst (Mainz/D), the Sacred Heart Sisters (Dublin/IRE), the Franciscan Missionaries of Mary (Dublin/IRE), the Barmherzige Schwestern (Innsbruck/A) and Alexandre Gánóczy (Dauphin/F),* this work would have never been able to get off the ground.

Last but not least thanks a lot, *Lucy Hunyár,* for your generosity, because, as a non-native English speaker, I could not have managed properly without your help.

# Introduction

*"Revival is an interesting and important aspect of traditional culture [...] "*[1]

The revival of tradition is such an obvious process of our so-called modern, civilised reality that it sets scholars of different scientific areas simultaneously in action. It has particular significance not only for ethnochoreologists, but also, amongst others for researchers of religion and gender. In gender studies, but in particular in women studies there have been materials explored and published on re-visioned tradition of a respectable quantity all over the world.[2] We might ask, *"why to invest a good deal of energy in order to revive something that is dead and seems to have nothing to do with our modern and late- or post-modern reality?"*[3] –, at the same time knowing, that it is indeed worthy to revive our traditions, namely, the silenced, but unconsciously always present and definitely influential deep level of our personal and communal identity.

Practising traditional acts even in today's world does not call forth automatically and necessarily scientific questioning of certain details, but rather presumes full personal involvement and engagement. In the past this process was strongly determined by the local community. Belonging to a certain communal tradition and practising its undeclared rules based on common consent has been actually a kind of supporting power for the individual, in which one was able to define his or her social roles at the same time. Our generation has virtually nothing to experience from this traditionally interpreted, communally defined self. It does not mean however

[1] Felföldi, László – Buckland, J. Theresa (eds.): *Authenticity. Whose tradition?* (The volume presents papers of the conference of Revival Sub Study Group of the Study Group on Ethnochoreology of International Council for Traditional Music held from 16–22 July 1999 in Szekszárd, Hungary.), European Folklore Institute, Budapest. 2002, vii

[2] See e.g. Chung, Hyun Kyung: *Schamanin im Bauch – Christin im Kopf. Frauen Asiens im Aufbruch,* Kreuz Verlag, Stuttgart, 1992

[3] Felföldi – Buckland 2002, vii

complete liberation from determining effects of the modern era. Yet members of the younger generation devoted to re-discovery of their ancient roots are motivated by inner search and convinced choice rather than by externally given communal expectations (although their interest is often stimulated by different forms of resistance to precisely those social expectations of modernity). Instead of living in a *"value vacuum"*[4] they make an attempt *"to hear the voice of the traditions that warn us to carry on our continuities"*.[5]

When we listen to and ask questions about the issue, we should not forget the possible dualism simultaneously conceivable among the concepts of folk tradition and of the modernist turn aiming to investigate, recreate and define the past correctly. In this way the two separate groups of (1) *collectors* (and/or interpreters) and of (2) the *folk* can be described with the aid of the following distinguishable features. While the former is usually urban, young, literate, reflexive, sophisticated, high cultured, cosmopolitan, pluralist, rootless and increasingly secular (without traditional background), the latter is rural, old, illiterate, unreflective, simple, rooted in the past, tradition bearer.[6]

I would like to avoid the danger of controlling cultural change, namely, of *"doing things to help the folk maintain authenticity, whether they wanted it or not"*.[7] The purpose of the present investigation is rather to re-explore and re-adopt the message of forgotten, but positively strengthening Hungarian traditional female images, overcome by different ideological interests, and to revive them for the coming female (and male) generations as living heritage of our ancestries. The rediscovery and reinterpretation of these ancient images helps to preserve the richness and powerfulness of self-interpretation from the perspective of historical-social-cultural continuity with all the previous generations left behind us.

---

[4] Kapitány, Ágnes – Kapitány, Gábor: *Értékrendszereink* [Our value systems], Kossuth, Budapest, 1983, 226: *"The first signs of the emergence of vacuum situations in value systems can be observed around the first steps of the disintegration of the traditional peasant society."*

[5] Hoppál, Mihály: *Tradition, Value System and Identity: Notes on Local Cultures,* in: Felföldi–Buckland 2002, 1–18, here 15

[6] Cf. Buckland, Jill Theresa: *Multiple Interests and Powers,* in: Felföldi – Buckland 2002, 70–78, here 75

[7] Nettl, Bruno: *Arrows and Circles.* Yearbook for Traditional Music, ICTM, 1998, 7

# PERSONAL EXPERIENCES

My grandmother, who died 20 years ago, was a primary school teacher, well-known in her village, often sang a song to me which she called the *"Hungarian hymn"*:

> *"Happy Woman, our mother, our ancient great protector,*
> *our country is addressing you in its big misery:*
> *Do not forget Hungary, our beloved country,*
> *poor Hungarians."*

The song presented by her can still be heard today, as my mother taped it in 1976.

According to historical research this "hymn" was composed around 1715 by *S. Lancsics Bonifacius OSB*, a Benedictine living in the abbey of Pannonhalma (H)[8]. Even today the folk refers to it [9] as 'The (national) Hymn'[10] in the Hungarian Catholic ritual often sung at the end of the mass, especially on feast days, although it has nothing to do with the officially acclaimed Hymn written by *Kölcsey* in the middle of the 19th century.

Not until I began my research did I first pay close attention to the female figure represented in the text and to its meaning supporting my granny.

Just before Christmas 2001 I met an old countrywoman on the train travelling through Budapest. Gradually I became acquainted with various interesting aspects of her past. She told me that country folk still strongly retain their religious traditions. Even if the people go to mass on Sundays, they never discuss their problems with the local parish priest, but only with the *Wise Woman* (an old woman living in the village as part of the rural community). Then she recited a long prayer about the *Happy Woman* (Boldogasszony[11]) and her son, Jesus. She said that this prayer would never have been prayed in the church, only in the family circle. Finally,

---

[8] Falvay, Károly: *Boldogasszony – A női szerep a magyar hitvilág tükrében* [Happy Woman – The female role in the mirror of the world of the Hungarian belief], Tertia, Budapest, 2001, 220

[9] Cf. my interview with József and Anna Dér in Törökbálint/Hungary on 11th January 2003, in which both the man and woman refer to this song as *the* "Hungarian Hymn".

[10] Volly, István: *Karácsonyi és Mária énekek* [Christmas- and Mary-chants], SzIT, Budapest, 1982, 454, 504

[11] Hungarian BODOG > BOLDOG = happy, joyous, beautiful, pregnant; Hungarian ASZ-SZONY = queen in old Hungarian, married woman today.

she added proudly that she had already taught this prayer to her grand-daughter.[12]

I was actually surprised to hear that ancient prayer from a simple, uneducated rural woman while travelling from a posh town at Lake Balaton to the "enlightened" City of Budapest, but then I realised the background of the situation. Mrs. János Bugóczi, aunt Erzsi, the interpreter of the ancient prayer originally comes from a little village (Hernádkércs) in the county of Borsod-Abaúj-Zemplén (in the north-eastern part of the country), but she moved years ago to be with her son's family who lives in Balatonfüred by Lake Balaton (West-Hungary). Her living female tradition can indeed be discovered much more easily in the north-eastern, poorer region of the country (or even easier beyond the north-eastern and south-eastern borders of Hungary, where ancient tradition was kept even stronger by Hungarian minorities, especially in the last decades, under Slovakian, Rumanian, Ukrainian, Yugoslav political-economic oppression) than in the elite places of Lake Balaton.

The last 14 years of intense relations between rural Hungarians in and out of Hungary (Transylvania, Vojvodina etc., regions of Pre-Trianon [Hungary before 1920]) presented me with experiences of the obvious *living* tradition permeating everyday thoughts and events. This exploration convinced me of the continuous, often unconscious strong influence of traditional communal characteristic features of the area. Acknowledging the fact of the permanent effect of tradition on the individual (also on my individuality) makes me finally aware of my fully engaged personal involvement towards the heritage I was brought up in.

Consequently when I attempt to investigate female images of the Hungarian religious folk tradition, I do it practically not from the perspective of sterile laboratory analyses. I see the system of belief in *comprehensive wholeness*, inseparable from the motivating social background and the living mental-spiritual heritage passed from one generation to another throughout the centuries. The ground of this transformed view is a kind of "scientific empathy" with all those confessing their popular belief in a particularly embracing *circular* time and space, bringing everything into contact with one another.[13] Jumping out of the modern *linear* way of logic of history helps me to come closer to a world that is completely unfamiliar to our modernity. The two quite dissimilar cultural existences seem to be a kind of mere side-by-side neighbourhood, even if their nearness in time and space could offer a good opportunity for respectable dialogue between them.

---

[12] The whole story happened in the early morning on 17th December 2001

[13] Liszka, József: *Ágas-bogas fa* [Branchy tree], Dunaszerdahely, Lilium Aureum, 1992, 20–21

With this revised type of methodology I also explored some important aspects of my own female identity and of the influence of the image of the Happy Woman built deeply into the collective Hungarian national-religious subconscious. At the same time I realised the obvious strong relationship between the figure of the Happy Woman and the power of the Wise Women [spiritual leaders] of the local rural communities, my ancient "mothers" carried in my genes. This exploration leads me to the question that gives me no respite: Why is one song about the Happy Woman respected – also allowed by the clergy – as a national Hymn, while thousands of prayers about the same female figure are forbidden and forced behind the walls of peasant houses, or, presented often only as "museum pieces" by modern ethnographical research?

Putting tradition into showcases within the frames of a museum, is obviously a political decision, in consequence of which powerful images of the past should surely lose real intensity. Their living roots should be considered merely untouchable, fixed, petrified memorials, or, what is even worse, marketable souvenirs of the past and subjects of several disciplines keeping the scientific distance. I would like to lift these vigorous images out of their artificially created conserving environment, while restoring them and replacing them to their original living function to fulfil their everlasting duties.

## THE METHOD OF INTERPRETATION

In the course of examining archaic Hungarian texts I am following the complex method of *Feldtkeller*[14] who focuses on three different but combined aspects of religion in his research:

(a) On the level of the *social system* religion is interpreted as the context of the *inter*personal communication (words, stories, images, objects, gestures, handling). As input it is the horizon of meaning *for* the psychical system; as output it is the manifestation *of* the psychical system.

(b) On the level of the *psychical system* religion is interpreted as religious experience within the context of *intra*personal communication.

(c) The *transcendence* is interpreted as indefinable reality behind all religious systems.

---

[14] Feldtkeller, Andreas: *Im Reich der syrischen Göttin – Eine religiös plurale Kultur als Umwelt des frühen Christentum*, Studien zum Verstehen fremder Religionen, Band 8, Gütersloher Verlagshaus, Gütersloh, 1994, 24–31

As Feldtkeller points out, the connections between religions (religious systems) are never objectively established facts but are always described by the concrete perspective of the individual. This is why all systems need to be defined from the extant connection between the environment and the system itself. This kind of description of the identity is also valid in the case of the personal conviction of the researcher. The result of this argumentation must be kept in my mind continuously: While examining subjectively chosen elements of my own traditional heritage, I should never lose sight of my unexcludable personal involvement and interest in the theme.

Let us have a short look at the most emphasised perspectives of the actual inquiry:

– The perspective of the *cultural-religious selection* will be clarified by concrete *social-historical-theological* features of the developmental process of images in the Hungarian religious folk tradition. The selection, influenced by the prevailing society and by its religious heritage, will be redefined in a revised religious-cultural context.

– The perspective of the *religious view and the religious practice* is the process of comparing actual surrounding religions with present personal and communal religious convictions, and of building and defining relations to those given "alien" religious world views. These views and practices will be examined through concrete attitudes expressed in positive as well as in negative female *images of the Hungarian religious folk tradition.*

– The perspective of the *religious biography* is an understanding of the individual supported by the comparison of religious convictions from earlier points along the path of personal life with the present religious view of the self. Special elements of this process will be pointed out with the help of comparing analysis of the biographies of two Hungarian female peasant visionaries and healers, Klára Csépe (Mrs. László Sánta) and Mária Katona (Mrs. István Karman). Both of these women lived in and after the era of the communist regime in Hungary.

As we shall see, the order of the perspectives cannot be clearly fixed because the different dimensions are mutually influenced by one another, and therefore are in continuous dynamism by means of endless changes and variations of configurations, even if the folklore strongly preserves certain ancient elements of tradition.[15] In this manner they build up a special type of hermeneutic circle of reciprocal dependence of the cultural-historical selec-

---

[15] Cf. Liszka 1992, 20

tion, of the religious views and practices, and of the religious biography. Here I am trying to expose a kind of logic, coherence and cohesion of the previously described hermeneutic circle, while at the same time focusing on religious elements representing female power of textual collections of the Hungarian religious oral tradition, and comparing them simultaneously with their social environment and with their personal manifestation and interpretation in the individual cases of Mrs. Sánta and Mrs. Karman.

In contradistinction to Erdélyi, who takes only *two* different interwoven world views (communism and Christianity) into consideration while describing the phenomenon of modern syncretism in her study,[16] from the point of view of the Hungarian peasantry of the second half of the 20th century I see *rather* three dominating, well separable synchronic ideologies: 1. *Communism* established by the Hungarian state, 2. *Official Christianity* established by the predominating churches of Hungary, 3. *Popular belief* inherited from ancient generations, but assimilated or opposed to both communist and officially accepted Christian ideas.

---

[16] Cf. Erdélyi, Zsuzsanna: *Modern szinkretizmus* [Modern syncretism], in: Horváth, Pál (ed.): Néphit, népi vallásosság ma Magyarországon [Popular belief, folk religion in Hungary today], MTA Filozófiai Intézet, Budapest, 1990, 9–30

# The standpoints of the research

Before we come closer to the examined images and attitudes, I will give a general overview of the social-historical-theological circumstances, which the rich world of the Hungarian folk religion is encased in, so that we are able to see the inherence of certain investigated practices more clearly. Mapping all the numerous sources of these appearances is not the task of the present research. I refer rather to materials of the most typical and, from my particular scientific point of view, the most exciting occurrences of ideas interpreting femaleness in the Hungarian popular religious practice.

## THE SOCIAL-HISTORICAL-RELIGIOUS BACKGROUND

Human outlets commenting on essential phenomena of the elbow-room in a narrower, local and in a wider, cosmological sense are thickened moments of the temporarily and spatially specified network of a combined, but often simplified reality. While understanding and describing particular cultural-anthropological manifestations of femaleness through images of the Hungarian popular belief, several important aspects are to be observed. The roles of women as active participants or as passive objects of the religion are obviously influenced socially, historically and theologically. Here I introduce the most fundamental elements of the centuries old religious socialisation of the Hungarian peasant women.

### SOCIAL BACKGROUND:
### HUNGARIAN PEASANT WOMEN UNDER MULTIPLE OPPRESSION

As we already have seen and shall see, being oppressed, living in any kind of minority of the surrounding society seems to be nevertheless a strong motivation for preserving the treasures of the ancient knowledge transmitted by foremothers (or forefathers). Although oppression can never be interpreted as a positive historical fact, it can play a propitious role in the survival of the otherwise vanishing civilisations.

I am examining three basic aspects of possible oppression of women in Hungary or in Hungarian speaking areas outside of Hungary (elitism, clericalism, patriarchalism). I could have mentioned further standpoints of despotic systems like racism-nationalism to which I have referred earlier as cases of Hungarian minorities beyond national borders. However, later I shall briefly touch on the question of distinguishable male attitudes towards women detectable in expressions of Hungarian speaking gypsy minority groups in the country, while attempting to point out similarities of the culturally-economically connected majority (Hungarian) and minority (Gypsy) male systems. The apparent community of fate between the Gypsy and the Jewish folk[17] would be also interesting aspect of the research, but it is not in the focus of my actual interest at the moment.

---

[17] Cf. Erdélyi, Zsuzsanna: *Hegyet hágék, lőtőt lépék – archaikus népi imádságok* [~ Up to hill, down to vale – archaic folk prayers]. Kalligram, Pozsony, ³1999. In many prayers collected by Erdélyi the Jews are depicted negatively, as torturers and killers of the poor Jesus. (See further more similar examples in Russian religious folk songs, in: Orosz, György: *Nézzetek rám szemetekkel, hallgassatok fületekkel* [Look at me with your eyes, listen to me with your ears], Nyíregyháza, 1996, 34, 40: "cursed Jews") This fact bears witness to a deeply rooted antipathy against the Jews in several local communities. Here however I would like to show an exceptionally positive attitude towards a Jewish person who actually himself is badly affected by the inhumane treatment of Jesus. The usual negative role of the Jews played in the passion, interpreted by Hungarian peasants, turns here to be a positive, compassionate Jewish lad, who suffers together with Jesus, and even he himself seems to criticise the *pagans* for their barbaric attitude towards Jesus – as it is interpreted by a young *gypsy* lad from the county of Szabolcs-Szatmár-Bereg, north-eastern part of Hungary, where there live a massive number of gypsy inhabitants, most of whom are basically unemployed (prayer nr. 249, 750. The numbering of the prayers comes from Erdélyi.):
*"Above the gate there is a golden flag,*
*Under the flag there is a golden chair,*
*There sits a very unhappy,*
*Very unhappy Jewish lad.*
*The Virgin Mary is passing by,*
*Asking about her Holy Son.*
*Where is her Holy Son,*
*The fair-haired, with golden teeth?*
*Your beautiful Holy Son was carried that way*
*By the pagans.*
*He is lashed by iron lash,*
*He is slapped in the face by iron gloves "*

Above all I must call attention to the fact that in the below-investigated social stratum many kind of oppressions had to be endured by *both* men and women. However as it will soon come into prominence, several of the examined female images seem to be simply projections of experienced male powerlessness in the lowest stage of male hierarchy.

## *Elitism versus popular culture*

According to Scannone[18] the expression "folk" refers to *one* collective subject with two distinguishable semantic variants. He defines the notion as follows:

1. It is a community of people sharing common historical experiences, culture, lifestyle and destiny. This characterising cultural-historical collective heritage can be more or less well-recognised in national consciousness.

2. It is however also a collective term defining a group of people owning nothing except common goods. In this stratum, individual characteristics are absorbed into the crowd. This group has no special privileges from the elite point of view. Its socially marginalised members are made blind tools of the welfare of a few.

The two sorts of interpretation belong together, especially on the level of the simple rural people, whose culture and religion reflect most authentically the common heritage of the community.

The metaphorical world of the traditional folk culture was gradually shaped to fit the views of institutionalised hierarchy, characterised by the discursive mind. Already in antiquity there had been tension between metaphorical and discursive approaches in history. The power and role of the subconscious and intuition was repeatedly undervalued and overwhelmed by worldviews built on consciousness and pure logic.[19] In this well-organised, but inhumane, demythologising "high culture" remained no room for the "imperfect", asymmetrical, natural-intuitive spontaneity of the folk.[20]

Even now there is a tendency to consider the irrational manifestations of uneducated rural people childish and primitive. However it is also an interest

---

[18] Rahner, Karl – Modehn, Ch – Göpfert, M. (eds.): *Népi vallásosság* (Hungarian translation of "Volksreligion – Religion des Volkes"), OMC, Vienna, 1987, 31–32

[19] Cf. Durand, Gilbert: *Les structure anthropologiques de l'imaginaire. Introduction à l'archétypologie générale*, Bordas, Paris, 1969

[20] Cf. The asymmetry and disproportionateness in fine arts from the perspective of Hungarian sense of space, in: Lükő, Gábor: *A magyar lélek formái* [The forms of the Hungarian Soul], Táton, Budapest, 2001 (first edition: 1942), 165–190

of certain elite to keep this stratum naive and ignorant, in a status that allows the political-economic decision makers many opportunities to oppress these exhausted and disdained people, whose social position seems to be obviously an unbroken destiny of constant losers of the society. Their settled social role points however unambiguously to the various interpretations of the notion "elite", because the examined social stratum called "folk" is defined always merely *from the perspective of the* contemporarily identified *elite* groups.

The "elite" is not necessarily educated or rich, but somehow is still always above the "folk". As compared with the "folk", the "elite" believes to be "enlightened", freed from any kind of "primitive" tradition. From the perspective of the disdained folk I am defining "elite" as a dominating pragmatic group with a great lack of responsiveness to spiritual-metaphorical dimensions. As we shall see, in this way the scale of variations relating to the oppressing "elite" can be very wide, from the character of a Catholic bishop to the figure of an uneducated tractor-driver, who, let us suppose, becomes the "enlightened" leader of a farmers' co-operative of the socialist era, so that both will be in command of the possible content of local communal traditions. To a certain extent their apparently opposite ideologies motivated by similar interests ambivalently find a common language above the head of the "folk" regarded as barbaric, lacking independence.

*Clericalism versus laity*

*Faith is not an emotion, but conviction,* is claimed by some representatives of modern Hungarian theology. Consequently Christian thought is also dominated by radical intellectual rationalism. This theoretical approach forgets that conviction is actually shaped by everyday experiences and emotional-intellectual responses to them. Within the framework of Christian theology or of any kind of institutionally established religious system, the religion of the folk was and is dogmatically not interpretable, therefore meaningless, indifferent, or even a dangerous enemy. However it seems that those forms of prayers, now rejected or even banned by the church, were originally often influenced and manipulated exactly by the intellectual ideologies of the ecclesiastical authorities.[21]

The religious-cultural traces of the folk were then gradually reinterpreted

---

[21] Pointed out by Tánczos, Vilmos: *Eleven ostya, szép virág – A moldvai csángó népi imák képei* [Live host, beautiful flower – The images of folk prayers of the Hungarian-speaking native of Moldavia], Pro-Print, Csíkszereda, 2000, 37, 60 f.

as "non-professional", "incompetent" and "profane"[22] which is obviously the result of the clerical monopolisation of the "sacred" world. For this reason most of the *"para-liturgical"* acts of the folk are practised separately, not only from the liturgy of the high-class elite, but also of the theologically "highly cultivated" clergy.[23] According to Beinert ecclesiastical attitude follows closely the work of Pope Benedict XIV, *"Opus de Servorum Dei Beatificatione, et Beatorum Canonisatione"*, in which he distinguishes unambiguously the *"revelationes privatae"* from the institutionally declared divine *Catholic revelation*, preserved by the teaching church authorities listening to God's Word.[24]

Christian theologians are inclined to consider magic as a purely mechanical, habitual act without any true religious meaning or emotion, although, as *Tánczos* reminds us, this meaningless type of magical process does not exist at all. Acts of magic have a well-established psychological meaning, and satisfy real human spiritual demands. Within the framework of the symbolic structure of culture, the person practising magic is psychically *always* motivated. The so-called "Christian magic" or the popular religious mind never divides magic and religion as rigorously as the theologians do.[25]

*Patriarchalism versus femaleness*

The fact that we know very little about the everyday life of early peasants is shown by *Morvay's*[26] study. It is tenable that these people often lived under very inhumane conditions. The remaining data describes the humiliating situation most often experienced by the head of the family, usually the male members of peasant communities. The woman, standing beside the man, is left obscured in history.

The members of the family worked under the direction of the eldest man in the household. The woman had no voice in the decision making, nor did

---

[22] In the church of the past the so-called "laity" was officially characterised by the same expressions. The significance of the excluding influence of these words is still perceptible in the ecclesiastical practice.

[23] It is, however, questionable how intensively and from which perspectives theology speaks ("theo-logion" = speaking about God) really about God.

[24] Cf. Beinert, Wolfgang: *Theologische Information über Marienerscheinungen*, in: Anzeiger für die Seelsorge, Herder, Freiburg, 5/1997, 250–258

[25] Cf. Tánczos 2000, 104

[26] Cf. Morvay, Judit: *Asszonyok a nagycsaládban* [Women in the larger family], Akadémiai Kiadó, Budapest, ²1981, 7

she share in the property of her father, or husband. In her husband's family she was sentenced to a lifetime of hard work, for living and for the welfare of her children, in an alien and defenceless position. Nevertheless whatever kind of fate the husband had, his wife's was worse due to a variety of oppression. The wife suffered on account of the bitter destiny of her husband in many ways. If the man went hungry, the woman nearly starved to death; if the man worked, the woman, in addition to her engagements, had to serve him; if the man was bound by his landlord, the burden of the peasant woman increased by her subordination to the man.

The ecclesiastical attitude even confirmed the sad situation of women while legitimising and encouraging male force by claiming unconditional female obedience to all male "superiors", especially to husbands and to local parish priests. In this way the (male) clergy and the male laity spoke the same language, in which basically the common interest of keeping women under control was the strongest motivation. This male concern was (and often is) also supported by several ideologies built on specifically male images of God.

The practice of the dominating Catholic Church in Hungary remained almost unaltered against women till our time. Although there have always been given exceptions (men who themselves suffer from the impersonal ecclesiastical-social system), for the majority of the clergy it seems natural enough to exclude women's voices and the manifestation of female characteristics from expressing personal opinions in the course of making responsible ecclesiastical decisions, and from the active participation in the communal rituals built up by strict, often already only routine-like, lifeless rules.

The Hungarian language however, mirrors an originally more egalitarian attitude of mutuality between man and woman. If we follow the etymology[27] of the Hungarian term "feleség" (= halfness, being half) relating to the English word "wife", we get a clearer picture of the language falling victim to dominating patriarchal mental trends of history. The term "fél" is a polysemantic word. Let us look at some of its meanings, the formed variations of the root "fél". The radical "fél" itself has already both nominal and verbal meanings, but always expressing a kind of RELATION:

---

[27] I used the data of Lükő's excellent article written on the theme: Lükő, Gábor: *Feleim* ("My halves", but the title cannot really be translated synonymously, because the expression has several meanings, see the explanations of the polysemantic term above), in: Medvigy Endre (ed.): Válasz [Reply], Püski, Budapest, 1989, 122–136

1. *"Fél"* as "half": There are several human relations in which I experience myself as "half":

1.1. When I am *"fele"* of someone, it means simultaneously being the "half" or the "companion" of someone. *In the past* both wives and husbands addressed one another mutually in this way.

1.2. I am also *"fele"* of those to whom I "reply", *"felelek"*. In a conversation all participants are involved in talking *"felek"*, "halves". Without *the other* none of them are able to be in communication, because there is no one to listen and to reply to; they are then only isolated halves.

1.3. Even if someone does not agree with me or holds an opposite opinion to mine, this someone is not indifferent to me, but my opponent, "opposite half" ( *"ellenfél"*), natural part of my life.

1.4. All those who agree about the most important basic things, belong to the same "denomination", to the same group of halves, *"felekezet"*.

1.5. In contradiction to most Indo-European languages, the Hungarian and kindred languages describe even the double parts of the body as *oneness* of the two. When one of these twin parts are hurt, the whole person is hurt and maimed to be a "half" human being. This is why the Magyar speaks about half-eyed, half-handed or half-legged instead of *one*-eyed, *one*-handed or *one*-legged living beings. According to Lükő's research the same view is reflected in the linguistic expressions of kindred languages alike:

| (English) | *(half)* | (One-eyed) | (One-handed) | (One-legged) |
|---|---|---|---|---|
| Hungarian | *fél* | *fél*szemû | *fél*kezû | *fél*lábú |
| Vogul | *pál* | szam*pál* | kát*pál* | lagül*pál* |
| Zueryen | *pl* | szin*pela* | kí*pela* | kok*pela* |
| Cheremiss | *pel* | *pel*simdzsán | *pel*kidán | *pel*jolán |
| Finnish | *pieli, puoli* | silmä*puoli* | käsi*puoli* | jalka*puoli* |
| Tsuvash | *herah* | *herah* kuszle | *herah* alelle | *herah* uralle |
| Yakut | *angar* | *angar* hartahtáh | *angar* ililéh | *angar* atahtáh |
| Mongol | *öröszön* | *öröszön* nüdtej | *öröszön* gartaj | *öröszön* hölgüj |

2. *"Fél"* as "fears" or "has fear": We realise the importance of our Other Halves truly only, when we lose them. Being left to ourselves we feel our *half* being. This perception leads often to "fear" ( *"félelem"*). The "half" ( *"fél"*) person "fears" ( *"fél"*).

Let us look at the parallels of some kindred languages, in which the two terms ("half" and "fears") are similar, but not as identical as in Hungarian:

| (English) | (half, one's half) | (fears) |
|-----------|--------------------|---------| 
| Hungarian | *fél*, fele | *fél* |
| Vogul | pál, peel | pili |
| Ostyak | pél, pélek | pelta |
| Zueryen | pl, pv | povni |
| Mordvin | pel, pel'e | pel'emsz |
| Finnish | pieli, puoli | pelätä |
| Yurak | pel'l'e | píl'l'uc |
| Yenisey | fele, ferie | fíebo |
| Tavgi | fealea | filitima |
| Kamas | píl, piél | pimnyem |

The rich content of this Hungarian expression was slowly narrowed down. Especially the meaning explained in 1.1. met the influence of the patriarchal turn of mind. The mutually positive appreciation of wife and husband was overshadowed by the negatively interpreted one-sided term "feleség" ("being half" = "wife"). The reciprocity that existed earlier in the term gradually disappeared, in consequence of which the woman was regarded *merely* as "half" as compared with her husband.

Likewise there is an old Hungarian expression, still extant in certain areas, describing the woman, not surprisingly, as *female animal!*[28] In the prayers collected by Erdélyi the word "animal" is used consistently as a synonym for *the soul* (cf. *animal › anima*/animus!) *of the human being*, of both men and women, or even for *the spirit of God* itself. This means that the concept originally was used in a positive, rather than a negative way.[29]

---

[28] Cf. Falvay 2001, 29

[29] In: Erdélyi 1999, e. g. prayers nr. 119, 156, 182 (*"Oh. female animal, do not worry about the opening of my five deep wounds"* – says Jesus to Mary), 224-supplement (*"How many is God in his/her animals? S/he is in three persons..."* › *animal = person!*). Cf.: Tánczos 2000. 68–69

# HISTORICAL BACKGROUND:
## "ADVANCE" FROM "EAST" TO "WEST"

*"Tradition is living because it is carried by living minds – minds living in time. These minds meet with problems or acquire resources, in time, which lead them to endow Tradition, or the truth it contains, with the reactions and characteristics of a living thing: adaptation, reaction, growth and fruitfulness. Tradition is living because it resides in minds that live by it, in a history which comprises activity, problems, doubts, opposition, new contributions, and questions that need answering.*"[30]

In the past historical moments of humankind usually meant "his-story", the story of politically well situated men, heroes and "creators" of their own destiny. Most often we know them also by name and their acts circumstantially. Their female partners are left though simultaneously in the *shadow* of those historical events. However we do not naively believe, that any of the historical changes could be out of female influence (her-story[31]). Even the denial of female power affecting (salvation-) history shows a kind of possible fear of real female ascendancy. While getting a general view of the Hungarian great migration and conquest in this subdivision, we keep to the fore the life of the many (women and men) who might not have been mentioned in history (his-story), but were influenced by and influenced the happenings esteemed highly.

When the Magyar people entered the land of Europe, they seemed to be a part of the Turkish hordes roaming between South-eastern Europe and Central Asia. Greater evidence points to Asia as the Magyar's original homeland. Exactly what part of Asia has been a matter of dispute for generations, but it is clear that the Magyars came from the East. However, in scientifically interested studies we find very little about the specific female roles played in Hungarian tribal culture in the process of migration.

From a male point of view it seems obvious that the *horse*, even as the national symbol of the Hungarian conquest, was the most important animal to the Magyars. They (presumably man) both travelled and fought on horse-

---

[30] Congar, Yves: *The Meaning of Tradition*, Hawthorne, NY, 1964, 75

[31] Cf. MacHaffie, Barbara J.: *Her Story. Women in Christian Tradition*, Fortress Press, Philadelphia, 1986. The following questions are asked in the survey: *"What roles did women play in leadership structures and in religious ceremonies? What roles did they find for themselves outside 'official' institutional churches or the formalities of worship? How were females (persons who carry out the biological function of women) and the feminine (characteristics assigned by cultural traditions to women) regarded in devotional writing?"*, p. 1.

back during their long migrations from the east and eventually into what is present day Hungary.

The *white horse*[32] is one of the most distinguished elements of the Hungarian national mythology referring mainly to the story of the conquest in 896 AD. The same figure can also be found in several Hungarian folk-tales, like in the story about the *Son of the White Horse, learnt by all Hungarian children* at school. This is a narrative in which the white horse is provided with *maternal* features belonging to the most ancient roots of ideas of Hungarian legendary relating to Turkish parallels. In these narratives the mare transmits the power of surmounting every obstacle, namely immortality, to her son through her lactation that at the same time means her self-sacrifice, which leads to her own powerlessness and death.

It is worth mentioning here that the term *"táltos"* used for describing the magical fictitious steed attributed with special abilities in fairy tales is identical with the Hungarian denomination of a type of community leader initiated in a shamanic way. The role of the "táltos" is synonymous with that of the Hungarian Wise Woman[33] or Man[34] (*"tudós"*), as will become more apparent further on.

We also have numerous archaeological or at least legendary information about the *weapons and style of fighting* of the ancient Magyars, which were identical with those of the Huns, Avars and other mounted nomadic peoples, although the Magyars were surely a distinct group separate from the Huns, Avars and Turks.[35] Who were they then? There are several opinions about and approaches to the question of Hungarian origin. Let me briefly mention here the four (Finno-Ugrian, Orientalist, Magyar-Uygur, Hun-Avar[36]) most prefer-

---

[32] Cf. Lengyel, Dénes: *Régi magyar mondák* [Old Hungarian myths], Móra, Budapest, 1974, 70–73; Komjáthy, István: *Mondák könyve* [The book of myths], Móra, Budapest, 1955, 137–140 etc.

[33] Cf. Limbacher, Gábor: *Egy nógrádi javasasszony életútja és gyógyítóvá válása* [The path of life of a wise-woman from the county Nógrád and her becoming healer], in: A Nógrád Megyei Múzeumok Évkönyve [The yearbook of the museums of the county Nógrád], Balassagyarmat, 1994, 144

[34] The influencing leading role of male wisdom can be explored among others in several Hungarian fairy tales, like "Táltos Jankó" ["John the Táltos"], in: Benedek, Elek: *Világszép Nádszálkisasszony* [The most beautiful reed-miss, Hungarian fairy tales], Móra, Budapest, 1976, 29–34

[35] Cf. Erdélyi, István – Sugár, Lajos: *Ázsiai lovas nomádok* [Equestrian Nomads from Asia], Gondolat, Budapest, 1982, 97–182

[36] For more about these theories see: Balázs, György: *The Magyars*, Corvina, Budapest, 1989, 7–9; Kontler, László: *Millennium in Central Europe: A History of Hungary*, Atlantisz, Budapest, 1999, 38–39; Lázár, István: *Hungary. A Brief History*, Corvina,

able theories of scientific research. According to Éva Schmidt[37] all of these theories are partly true, established and acceptable.

## The Finno-Ugrian Theory[38]

The most widely accepted theory of the Magyar's origin is the Finno-Ugrian concept. Advocates of this theory believe the linguistic and ethnic kinship between the Hungarians and the Finns, Estonians, Ostyaks and Voguls provide evidence for the origin of the Magyars. This relation of the Magyars with the Finns places *the ancient homeland of the Finno-Ugrians on both sides of the southern Ural Mountains.*

The advocates of this theory insist that Magyars came from this group in the Urals, and as the theory explains, it was in about 2000 BC when the Finnish branch broke away to settle in the Baltic area. The Magyars remained on the West Siberian steppes with the other Ugrian people until 500 BC It was then that the Magyars crossed the Urals westward to settle in what is present day *Bashkiria*, north of the Black Sea and the Caucasus. The Magyars remained here for centuries with the various Ural-Altaic peoples such as the Huns, Turks, Bulgarians, Alans and Onogurs. The Magyars soon adopted many cultural traits and customs from these people and it was from the region of Bashkiria that the Magyars started their migration westward toward the *Carpathians.*

After World War II, the Finno-Ugrian theory was challenged by scholars who argued that the Finno-Ugrian theory was *based on linguistics alone,* without support in anthropology, archaeology or written records.

## The Orientalist Theory

Scholars known as orientalists believe that the origin of the Magyars and their language is not found in the Urals, but *in Central Asia* known as the

Budapest 1993, 11–35; Sisa, Stephen: *The Spirit of Hungary. A Panorama of Hungarian History and Culture,* Vista Books, New Jersey, 1995, 1–6

[37] Éva Schmidt is a well known Hungarian travelling researcher, an expert of cultures of those existing Asian tribal groups kindred with that of Hungarians at present.

[38] Cf. Korompay, Bertalan: *Finn nyomokon I–II.* [On Finnish tracks, vol. 1–2], private edition, Budapest, 1989, vol. 1, 291–308

*Turanian Plain or Turkestan* which stretches *from the Caspian Sea eastward to Lake Baykal.* Ancient history has traditionally called this region *Scythia*.[39] Folklore holds that the Magyars are related to the Scythians who built the great empire of the 5th century BC. After the Scythian Empire dissolved, the Turanian Plain witnessed the rise and fall of empires built between the first and ninth centuries AD by the Huns, Avars, Khazars and various Turkish peoples, including the Uygurs. The Magyars subsequently absorbed much of the culture and tradition of these peoples and many Onogur, Sabir, Turkish, and Ugrian people were assimilated with the Magyars, resulting in the Magyar amalgam, which entered the Carpathian Basin in the later half of the ninth century AD.

Fig. 1. Old letters of the Seklers[40]: Cuneiform writing

Scholars of Far Eastern history believe that the Magyars were also exposed to the *Sumerian culture* in the Turanian Plain. Linguists of the 19th century, including Henry C. Rawlinson, Jules Oppert, Eduard Sayous and Francois Lenormant found that knowledge of the Ural-Altaic languages such as Magyar helps to decipher Sumerian writings. *Cuneiform writing* (Fig. 1.) was found to be used by the Magyars long before they entered the Carpathian

---

[39] Cf. Thuróczy, János: *A magyarok krónikája* [The chronicle of Hungarians], Európa, Budapest, 1980, 16–35

[40] Sekler = Székely: Hungarian of Eastern-Transylvania

Basin. The similarity of the two languages has led orientalists to form a Sumerian-Hungarian connection.[41] The orientalists speculate that a reverse of the Finno-Ugrian theory may be possible.

The theory holds that if the proto-Magyars were neighbours of the proto-Sumerians in the Turanian Plain, then the evolution of the Hungarian language must have been a result of *Sumerian rather than Finno-Ugrian influences*. The theory in turn holds that rather than being the recipients of a Finno-Ugrian language, it was the Magyars who imparted their language to the Finns and Estonians without being ethnically related to them. What scholars cite for added evidence for this theory is the fact that the Magyars have always been numerically stronger than their Finno-Ugrian neighbours combined. The theory believes that the Finns and Ugors received linguistic strains from a Magyar branch that had broken away from the main body on the Turanian Plan, and migrated to West Siberia.

## The Magyar-Uygur Theory

The connection between the Magyars and the Uygurs tie Hungarians even closer to Asia. The *Uygurs* are people who *live in the Xinjiang province of China*. The Uygurs are Caucasian in appearance and maintain a Turkish language. To the north of the Uygar's border stretches the *Dzungarian Basin,* which has a striking similarity to the word *Hungarian*. Northeast of Dzungaria lies the Altai Mountain Range, a name used by linguists to define the Ural-Altaic language group to which the Magyar language belongs. Further up to the north stretches the Lake Baykal region where first the Scythians, then the Huns emerged to conquer the Turanian Plain. The Magyars, Uygurs and Turks may also have started their migrations *from the north-eastern part of the Baykal area.*

Further anthropological, archaeological and linguistic research must be conducted on this theory, but is limited by the little access the Chinese government grants foreigners to the region. There are, however, many Asiatic influences seen among Hungarians today. Hungarian *legends and folk tales* are strikingly similar to those of Asian peoples. The structure of Magyar *folk music*, which uses the *pentatonic scale*, also points to *Asian origins*.

---

[41] Badiny, Ferenc Jós: *The Sumerian Wonder,* School for Oriental Studies, University of Salvador, Buenos Aires, 1974; Bobula, Ida: *Origin of the Hungarian Nation,* Danubian Press, Astor, Fla., 1982

The Chinese believed that there were five cardinal directions, the fifth being "the centre of the universe", China itself. Each of the five directions was symbolised by a colour. The central point, China, was indicated by yellow, for the gold that befit His Imperial Highness. The North, shrouded in dark Arctic nights, was black. The West was designated as white, a colour that reflected the blinding white sands of the vast deserts on the western horizon. Red represented the sun of the South, and the East was symbolised by blue, the colour of the ocean eternally washing China's eastern shores.

Based on these colour symbols, the *White Magyars* (or White Uygurs) represented the Western branch of their race. According to ancient Russian chronicles, the White Magyars appeared in the Carpathian Basin as early as 670–680 AD, first with the Bulgarians, and later with the Avars. The second branch of Magyar tribes – called *Black Magyars* in ancient Russian chronicles – took a different route. The directions of that route are still debated by Finno-Ugrian and orientalist theorists, but the end result was that the Black Magyars became *connected with peoples belonging to the Ural-Altaic groups*. These included a range of *peoples from Manchuria to Turkey*.

Among these groups the Finno-Ugrian Magyars drew closest to the Turks, who were warriors with a talent for stagecraft. This association with the Turks created a new blend of Magyar: *Finno-Ugrian in language but Ural-Altaic in culture*. This was the strain of Magyars that in *895 AD* rode into the Carpathian Basin under Árpád – following the footsteps of the White Magyars who appeared in the Carpathian Basin in the *670s AD*. Árpád's tribe has been termed by some modern historians as the second wave in a two-phased conquest of the Hungarian homeland. Whether this theory is correct or not, it seems fairly certain that the Szeklers (székelyek) had been long-time inhabitants of Transylvania before the Magyars arrived. The Szekler people living in Székelyföld (the land of the Szeklers) is still one of the most conscious Hungarian folk of its own values in Transylvania/Rumania.

### The Hun-Avar Theory[42]

Much of this theory has been perpetuated by *folk tale*. Most Hungarians even today can tell the story of the Legend of the *"Miraculous Stag"*[43]. The story describes how two sons of Nimrod, *Hunor and Magor*, were lured for days

---

[42] Cf. Dümmerth, Dezső: *Az Árpádok nyomában* [On the track of the Árpáds], Panoráma, Budapest, ²1977, 11–209

into a new land by a fleeing white stag. The stag suddenly vanishes without trace. But the disappointed young hunters hear laughing and singing. The two dismount and follow the sound of laughing until they come across a lake in which two beautiful maidens are splashing. The two hunters take the maidens as wives. The Huns are Hunor's descendent, and the Magyars are Magor's descendants. (Table I. / Fig. 8.)

There are variations on the folk tale including *Simon Kézai's* version in his *1283* chronicle, *Gesta Hungarorum*. The same mythical tale takes on a slightly sombre and more realistic approach. Hunor and Magor are Chief Ménrót's grown up sons who had reached maturity and had moved into a separate tent. One day it happened that, as they were going out to hunt, a *hind* suddenly appeared in front of them on the plains, and as they undertook to pursue her, she fled from them into the Maeotian marshes. Since she completely disappeared from sight, they searched for her a long time but could find no trace of her. After having traversed the said marshes, they decided the marshes were suitable for raising livestock. They returned to their father, and securing his consent, they moved into the Maeotian marshes with all their animals to settle down there.

The region of Maeotis is a neighbour of Persia. Apart from a very narrow wading place, the sea everywhere encloses it. It has absolutely no streams, but it teems with grass, trees, fish, fowl, and game. Access to and exit from it is difficult. Thus after settling in the Maeotian marshes, Hunor and Magor did not move for five years. In the sixth year they wandered out, and by chance came upon the wives and children of Belárs sons, who stayed at home without their men folk. Quickly galloping away with them and their belongings, they carried them off into the Maeotian marshes. It so happened that among the children they seized were the two daughters of Dula, the Prince of the Alans. Hunor married one and Magor the other. According to the chronicle all the Huns descend from these women.

From Hunor came the great and dreaded leader *Attila*.[44] After the kingdom of Attila fell apart shortly after his death, further waves of people moved in to the Carpathian Basin but were all crushed by the *Avars*, a quickly emerging *branch of the Ural-Altaic group*. The Avars founded an empire on top of what used to be Attila's – the region between the Danube and the Tisza rivers. The Avars even used a weapon perfected by the Huns,

[43] See its representation e.g.: "Goldener Hirsch (Schildbeschlag) aus Mezőkeresztes-Zöldhalompuszta, Borsod-Abaúj-Zemplén, Ungarn, 8–5. Jahrhundert v. Chr.", in: Egg. Markus – Pase, Christopher: *Die Metallzeiten in Europa und im Vorderen Orient. Die Abteilung Vorgeschichte im Römisch-Germanistischen Zentralmuseum*, Kataloge Vor- und Frühgeschichtlicher Altertümer, Band 26, Verlag des Römisch-Germanistischen Zentralmuseums, Mainz, 1995, Farbtafel XIX

[44] Cf. Komjáthy 1955, 220–299, Lengyel 1974, 12–45

the curved sabre gladicus hunnicus. The Avars downfall, however, was hastened by the development of Charlemagne's Frankish Empire. The Avars and Charlemagne's army went to battle from 796 to 803 AD The Avars were finally defeated by the Frankish troops and most Avar tribes returned to the slopes of the *Caucasian Mountains*. Others stayed and mingled with the Slavs of the area and later with the Magyars. When the Magyar tribes arrived under Árpád, they found a sparse population including many Avars. According to the *Tarih-i-Üngürüsz* chronicle when they arrived in the land, they saw its many rivers teeming with fish, the land rich in fruit and vegetables, and *members of other tribes, some of whom understood their language.*

### Conquest or re-conquest westwards

Although the exact origins of the Magyars are still debated, it seems certain that the Magyars left the region of *Etelköz*, between the lower reaches of the river Don and the Danube on the north shore of the Black Sea, in search of a new permanent homeland. First to shed light on this transition period for the Magyars from their original homeland and their arrival in the Carpathian Basin were the *chroniclers of the Khazar Empire*, mainly Arab and Persian travellers. In the middle of the tenth century, the Byzantine Emperor Constantine VII (Porphyrogenitus) wrote of the Magyars that they lived together with the Khazars for three years, and fought together with them in all their wars. The interpretation of "living together" is controversial, but it is apparent that the Magyars had a tribal alliance in the Khazar Empire.

The peoples of the Khazar Khanate had a more advanced way of life than those of the Central Asian Turkish tribes, whose chief occupation was nomadic animal husbandry. The level of its agriculture and handicrafts industry matched contemporary European standards. In terms of commercial development it even exceeded them. However, the empire was a loosely organised entity, with fluctuating numbers of subjugated peoples rather than fixed boundaries determining its size. The Magyar tribal alliance constituted one such subjugated people.

The Magyars are mentioned in the earliest written records in the West as *turci* or *ungri* – Turks and Onogurs –, the latter giving rise to their name in the main European languages. This is how a Byzantine account from 839 refers to the Magyars, which is the first written account of the Magyars. Since there were no great nomadic migrations in the steppe north of the Black Sea in the eighth and ninth centuries, it was probably due to an internal recovery of strength a result of external pressure that the Magyars separated from the Khazar Khanate and so obtained hegemony over the territory of Etelköz.

In 894, however, the relative tranquillity of the steppe came to an end, with profound consequences for the Magyars. A massive influx of further Turkish peoples from the east compelled the Pechenegs, who had lived between the Urals and the Volga and are supposed to have already waged two 'wars' against the Magyars after the 850s, to cross the Don. Urged by a double motivation, the Pechenegs fell upon the Magyars who, wedged between two hostile forces, immediately looked for a new homeland further west.

RELIGIOUS BACKGROUND:
HUNGARIAN PEASANT WOMEN IN THE INTERSECTION OF TRADITIONS

Similarly to the long distance and interval of prominent historical moments there can be discovered an obvious change also in the history of religious ideas, that has been effected by numerous religious-cultural influences both in time and space. The turn of the Asian nomadic lifestyle into the agriculturally established European way of life called forth the slow disappearance of tribal existence. Simultaneously experiencing the defencelessness of migration and the total co-operation and coherence with the divine sphere of earthly fruitfulness, by giving just as much as was needed, was gradually replaced by artificial guiding of and autonomy above the forces of nature.

Although this autonomy will never be able to completely overcome Gaia and her individuality, there are ceaseless attempts to yield perpetual profit of it, without respecting the circulating female rhythm of it. This predominantly male violent attitude is mirrored more or less in different religious views supported by hierarchically built up human relationships of different cultural backgrounds. The civilisations of the "new world" are no more grown up dynamic wanderers (pilgrims) of the *fertile* Mother Earth, but are stuck to the "skirt" of an unchangeable, "christianised", divined image of an *ever virgin, untouchable* motherhood while rejecting the reality and value of embodied femaleness.[45]

---

[45] "*One has to ask whether elements of male resentment are not built into the matricentric pattern. The matricentric core of human society remains, even under male hierarchies, and continually reproduces the insecure, resentful male, who emancipates himself from his mother by negation of women.*" In: Ruether, Rosemary Radford: *Gaia and God. An ecofeminist theology of earth healing*, Harper, San Francisco, 1992, 169

Here I will try to show the intersection of eastern, tribal, matrifocal and western, governmental, patriarchal traditions interwoven in the worldview and self-valuation of Hungarian peasant women.

## The Happy Woman: The Ancestress of the ancient Hungarian religion

The concept of the Hungarian ancient (often referred to as "pagan") religion usually includes the figure of the *"Happy Woman"* (= Boldogasszony).[46] In Hungarian, this figure has provided the names for plants (e.g. the rose of the Happy Woman = Lychnis coronaria; the slipper of the Happy Woman = Cypripedium Calceolus; the palm of the Happy Woman = Tanacetum balsamita), habitations (e.g. Bol-dogasszonyfa; fa = tree), a month (XI–XIX. c.: January = the month of the Happy Woman) and a day (Tuesday = the day of the Great Happy Woman, cf. St. Anne, mother of Mary). Her figure can also be found in Hungarian children's games and on flags and coins with the title *Patrona Hungariae*.[47] Since the Hungarian translation (before 1583) of the rigorous declaration *Rituale Strigoniensis* (Trent, 1567) the matrimonial oath – "pro more in hac patria usitato"[48] – has been sworn to God and the Happy Woman[49] up to this day.

My conversations with old contemporary Hungarian rural people[50] have strengthened my personal belief, whereas the ordinary daily routine of our earlier generations is permeated deeply by faithfulness to the so-called Happy Woman. Their sense of time is infiltrated by their sense of life supported by and embedded in the living figure of the Happy Woman. When these people speak about the events of their life, they are instinctively connected with female fertility symbolised by the circulating time of nature expressed in feast days[51] of the Happy Woman (who is budding, bearing, reaping) linked with agrarian activities.

---

[46] Ipolyi, Arnold: *Magyar mythologia* [Hungarian mythology], Heckenast, Pest, 1854 and Kálmány, Lajos: *Boldogasszony, ősvallásunk istenasszonya* [The Happy Woman, the goddess of our ancient religion], in: Diószegi, Vilmos (ed.): *Az ősi magyar hitvilág* [The ancient world of the Hungarian belief], Gondolat, Budapest, 1971, 319

[47] cf. Falvay, 2001, 126–140

[48] "in accordance with the national customary law"

[49] Fettich, Nándor: *Vallásos jellegű varázs-szövegek a magyar néphitben* [Religious magic texts of the Hungarian folk belief], in: *Ethnographia*, LXXXII., Budapest, 1971, 63

[50] E.g. conversations (16th, 21st and 25th November 2002) with Mr. József and Mrs. Anna Dér, a Hungarian couple living in Törökbálint, but originating from Adács, near to the place of pilgrimage founded by Klára Csépe mentioned below, in chapter III.

[51] See those dates further on.

We know little about the ancient Hungarian religion, but the linguistic facts mentioned above verify the obvious importance of a powerful female divine figure whose character influenced the whole of the Hungarian culture.[52] It has been historically and ethnographically demonstrated that the majority of Hungarians, before turning to Christianity, lived under a kind of so-called shamanic imagination,[53] although there is a wide hierarchical range of male and female symbols in this system depending on cultural differences. Being a *shaman* is however often a *female* activity of particular Asian regions, even if men also practise shamanic duties in other areas.[54] Nevertheless, the respect of the ancient motherly god and matrifocality surrounding her, even in Hungarian speaking areas beyond and within the national borders is to be noted.[55]

## Women in Christian tradition

In opposition to matrifocal religions, the history of Christian anthropology shows an obviously androcentric[56] tendency. Already in early Christianity, but especially in *medieval* theological[57] approaches, the exegesis of biblical texts depicted a world in which man dominates woman, and he is both morally and spiritually above her. This view was supported by the second creation story (esp. Gen 2:4ff), which glossed the emphasised equality of the first one (Gen 1:27). According to the interpretations of many theologians in the story

---

[52] Cf. several aspects of the recent study of an old Franciscan friar, *Árpád Daczó* from Transylvania. He is engaged with the place of pilgrimage or shrine called Csíksomlyó and with the many legends connected with the *Babba Mária*, the figure of Mary at Csíksomlyó/Transylvania, Rumania. He often refers to the research of Bobula and Badiny, which means that he tries to confirm the Sumerian theory of the Hungarian origin. In: Daczó, Árpád: *Csíksomlyó titka. Mária-tisztelet a néphagyományban* [The mystery of Csíksomlyó. The reputation of Mary in the folk tradition], Pallas-Akadémia, Csíkszereda, 2000

[53] Hoppál, Mihály: *Sámánok. Lelkek és jelképek* [Shamans. Spirits and symbols], Helikon, Budapest 1994, 41, 56, 85; cf. Korompay 1999, 292

[54] In this case the man often wears female clothes. Cf. Falvay, Károly: *A sámánszertartások szimbolizmusához* [To the symbolism of shamanic rituals], Új Magyarország Magazin, Budapest, July 10th 1993.

[55] László, Gyula: *A népvándorláskor művészete Magyarországon* [The art of the period of great migrations in Hungary], Corvina, Budapest, 119–124

[56] male-centred

[57] Notice that theology was basically the only science of medieval universities. Cf. Becker-Cantarino, Barbara: *Der lange Weg zur Mündigkeit. Frau und Literatur (1500–1800)*, Metzler, Stuttgart, 1987, 22

of the Fall, the woman appears morally inferior to the man, which basically confirms the fact that the woman is only the second creature, therefore imperfect[58] and the cause of all bad things in the world. The subordination of women is defined also in several Pauline or pseudo-Pauline quotations of the New Testament.[59] In contradistinction to the Old Testament, even fertility is rejected and rather virginity is praised by Paul,[60] which is, according to recent biblical scholars, merely the result of the dominant eschatological expectations of the era. It created a foundation for dualistic consideration of body and soul, which still exists in Christian thought.[61] According to this worldview the profane body (in particular the female body) is to be ashamed, therefore it is to be hidden behind sacred spheres. (Table I. / Fig. 9.)

## Christianity as an established religion in Hungary and the welcoming of the "alien" God

The controversy between the concept of the *Jewish God* (Yahweh) and the *Goddess of Fertility* (Ashera) was already in the air even prior to the age of

---

[58] Cf. *"Sed mulier est vir imperfectus sive occasionatus"*, the woman is an *imperfect man*, only "derivation" of the "normative" man – according to Thomas Aquinas, the most significant theologian and philosopher of the Middle Ages. Cf. Hufnagel, Alfons: *"Die Bewertung der Frau bei Thomas von Aquin"*, Theologische Quartalschrift 156 (1976) 132–165

[59] *"But I wish you to understand that, while every man has Christ for his Head, woman's head is man, as Christ's Head is God."* (1Cor 11:3); *"As in all congregations of God's people, women should not address the meeting. They have no licence to speak, but should keep their place as the law directs. If there is something they want to know, they can ask their own husbands at home. It is shocking thing that a woman should address the congregation."* (1 Cor 14:34–35); *"Wives, be subject to your husbands as to the Lord; for the man is the head of the woman, just as Christ also is the head of the church. Christ is, indeed, the Saviour of the body; but just as the church is subject to Christ, so must women be to their husbands in everything."* (Eph 5:34–35)

[60] *"The unmarried or celibate woman cares for the Lord's business; her aim is to be dedicated to him in body and spirit; but the married woman cares for worldly things; her aim is to please her husband."* (1 Cor 7:34) Cf. however the radically different interpretation of virginity according to Spinetoli, in: Spinetoli, Ortensio da: *Luca*, Cittadella Editrice, Assisi, ²1986. Besides the biblical story he points out the usual model of divine virgin conception of persons endowed with special attributes in several ancient narratives, which are usually to confirm the power, the binding respect and communal acceptance of the baby coming into the world.

[61] Cf. McLaughlin, Eleonor C.: *Equality of Souls, Inequality of Sexes: Women in Medieval Theology*, in: Ruether, Rosemary Radford (ed.): Religion and Sexism, Simon and Schuster, NY, 1974, 213–266

Deuteronomy.[62] Similarly to the religious conflict between the pagan tribal fertility cult and the officially established religion in Israel, the pre-existing female divine images of the "pagan" Hungarian folk religion have been gradually shaped by the so-called Christian doctrines, actually often in an aggressive manner, since the reign of *St Stephen,* the first king of Hungary (1000–1038). As a result of the law of St Stephen concerning the foundation of churches,[63] the "pagan" Hungarian country folk quickly became acquainted with basic "Christian" doctrines through the mediation of parish priests.

Let us turn our attention to the forms of mediation, which may have taken place in the Middle Ages. Because of the lack of any written Hungarian texts from that period, the parish priests transmitted the primary doctrines of Christianity (retained in Latin) orally to the believers. It is well known from the *Legenda maior* (dated at the beginning of the twelfth century) that seven of the ten missionary friars sent to Hungary preached in Hungarian to the people.[64] On Sundays and on other feast days the congregation was taught the meaning of the "Lord's Prayer" and of the "Creed".

However the worship of this "alien" god[65] was certainly an uncomfortable, unpleasant, unwelcome, and annoying constraint for the inhabitants[66] as is documented in one of the exhortations of St Stephen. All those who, instead

---

[62] Cf. Braulik, Georg: *Die Ablehnung der Göttin Aschera in Israel,* in: Wacker, Marie-Theres – Zenger, Erich (eds.): Der eine Gott und die Göttin, Herder, Freiburg, 1991, 106–136

[63] Each of the ten villages were called upon to build a church at that time.

[64] Érszegi, Géza (ed.): *Árpád-kori legendák és intelmek* [Legends and exhortations of the age of the Árpád-house], Budapest, 1983, 84

[65] According to *recent* ethnographical studies the God of Christianity remained "alien" even for contemporary Catholic believers. Cf. *The leaf of Mary,* a type of mint, is a helpful herb held in the prayer book of some tired faithful of the rural community in order to keep them awake during the mass. *"Because of heaps loads of work the folk is tired on Sunday. And then there is that so good silence, fresh air and rest during sermon that makes the people sleepy.",* told by Tera "nenus" in 1991, Szanda, Hungary, published by Limbacher, Gábor: *Máriácska Káponkája* [The chapel of Mary], in: A Nógrád Megyei Múzeumok Évkönyve [The yearbook of museums of the county Nógrád], Balassagyarmat, 1991, 277

[66] *"In the sky there is a little bird, not a bird, but an angel with wings, under its wings holy altar, in holy altar true faith, in true faith the Happy Woman[...]* Proclaim the holy words coming from my mouth, but denied by the priests[...] "* In: Erdélyi 1999, 460–461, prayer nr. 139

of paying attention to the holy readings had been whispering and gossiping during the mass, and consequently had been rejecting the "food" offered by the Church, were declared sinful and were assigned punishments. Elderly people were "merely" reprimanded in public and chased out of the church; the young ones were publicly bound and whipped in the entrance-hall of the church in order to serve as a deterrent to other members of the congregation.[67]

The treatment described above can be understood more clearly if we first look at the motivations of Stephen for being so strict. When we realise the time and the situation of the king, ruler of a nation with a whole range of ancient eastern customs and the first leader anointed by a Western Christian bishop at the same time, we see his attitude and his laws more objectively. The Hungarian State was established on the 25th December 1000 simultaneously with his anointing. As we have just lived through the endless feasts of the welcoming of the third millennium we can easily imagine the era of the beginning second millennium. That *eschatological period* – different from our age – had been *full of fear* and frustration, influenced by distorted worldviews, which focused on expected cruel, divine judgement, namely punishments. How could Stephen be of a different mind from his contemporaries? Nevertheless he offered the newly established state to the *"Magna Domina Hungarorum"*[68] and the basilica in Székesfehérvár founded by him, but fallen into ruin in the meantime, was called the basilica of the "Happy Woman".[69] This living cult is well represented in the name of medieval Hungary, that is *"the flower garden of the Happy Woman"*.

Generally speaking the priests of the eleventh century knew their "listeners", the country people, quite well, as they themselves originally came from the same villages, afterwards becoming the pastors of their acquaintances. For men of the lower class, priesthood offered the only possibility to receive the new "Western" education and somehow to free themselves from the obligations that bound a peasant to his landlord. The motivation to choose priesthood as a "vocation" was extremely strong. The sudden growth in the number of priests at the time of the newly founded Christian state of Hungary demonstrates this trend.

---

[67] Mészáros, István: *Az iskolaügy története Magyarországon 966–1777 között* [The History of Educational Affairs in Hungary between 966–1777], Budapest, 1981, 36

[68] Cs. Varga, István: *Szent mûvészet II – Tanulmányok költészetünk szakrális vonulatából* [Holy art 2 – Studies from the sacred range of our poetry], Székesfehérvár, 2000, 126–183

[69] See: Marosi, Ernő: *A középkori mûvészet történetének olvasókönyve XI–XV. század* [The reader of the history of medieval art, 11–15th century], Budapest, 1997, 46. Cf Érszegi 1983, 45–48

For the clergy, it was unimportant to put down in writing previously memorised texts used in the sermons. For this reason, no literature of sermons in Hungarian from that time exists. The only written text from the twelfth century is the *Halotti Beszéd* (Funeral Oration) and the attached *Könyörgés* (Entreaty, 1192–1195) that presents a formulation of biblical images in Hungarian, in a language beautifully worked out. The *Ómagyar Mária-siralom (Old Hungarian Mary-lamentation)*, a product of the 13th century's lay female movements, promotes the vibrant cult of Mary in the society. It is a Hungarian, anonymous adaptation of the *Planctus,* a lamentation written by Godefridus de Santo Vittore. Similarly to dramatised Passion-plays deep earthly emotions are expressed here, in the framework of a religious theme. It is composed of three "woes": 1. When the pain of Mary is awakened to the consciousness, 2. When she turns to her son, 3. When she pleads for mercy to her son *at the cost of her own life.*[70]

Following the advice of bishop *Gellért,*[71] in the course of Christian inculturation, the *cult of Mary* soon became a synonym for the *cult of the ancient Happy Woman.*[72] In this way the image of the powerful goddess of the ancient religion was manipulated and degraded to the figure of the human mother of God. Nonetheless Mary, conceived as a virgin, could not replace the functions of the divine "pagan" mother concerning *fertility*, which was then assigned to the character of Mary's mother, St. Anne.

However, because of oral traditions and incomplete knowledge of the official teachings,[73] even priests had not been saved from including apocryphal texts into their own world of faith. To this fact was added the church's wall paintings, serving to overcome illiteracy, but at the same time also helping the free flow of the repressed contents of the unconscious.[74] *Ipolyi,* a

---

[70] Cf. Madas, Edit: *Szöveggyűjtemény a régi magyar irodalom történetéhez. Középkor* [Reader to the history of old Hungarian literature. The Middle Ages], Tankönyvkiadó, Budapest, 1992, 321–322

[71] The private teacher of the prince Imre, son of Stephen

[72] Ortutay, Gyula (ed.): *Magyar Néprajzi Lexikon I–V.* [Hungarian Ethnographic Encyclopaedia, 5 volumes], 1977–1982, vol. I. (1977) 313; Tánczos 2000, 69–70. Cf. Franz, Marie-Louise von: *Női mesealakok* [Hungarian translation of "The Feminine in Fairy Tales"], Európa, Budapest, 1992, 38–39; Daly, Mary: *Beyond God the Father – Toward a Philosophy of Women's Liberation,* Boston, Beacon Press, 1973, 83–84

[73] Even after the synod at Torda (Transylvania – 1558) Lutheran priests were constantly urged to acquire at the very least, a Bible as basic requirement for their pastoral work. In: Lammel, Annamária – Nagy, Ilona (eds.): *Parasztbiblia – Magyar népi biblikus történetek* [Peasantbible Hungarian biblical folk stories], Osiris, Budapest, ²1995, 295–315

[74] Cf.: Tóth, Melinda: *Árpád-kori falfestészet* [Wall-painting in the Arpadian age], Budapest, 1974 (Művészettörténeti Füzetek 9)

Hungarian Catholic bishop in the 19th century drew clear attention in his research to the fact that the ancient national beliefs could not disappear immediately and could not be replaced suddenly by a new, alien system of religion from a foreign land, translated from another language by foreigners. Such a new system is definitely incomprehensible to a community founded upon traditional images of a special cultural, linguistic, economic, political environment of previous centuries.[75]

## The concrete marks of inculturation

The fact of consciously directed inculturation is easily understood with the help of the following table.[76] It shows the biggest feast days of the *Happy Woman* of "Hungarian Christianity" influenced by folk religion, parallel with those of *Mary* of the Western church, decreed in the course of history by male clerics educated in Rome.

The Hungarian naming of the feast days show evidently a close natural relationship with the fertile Mother Earth. While naming Mary of the Christian tradition *"Little" Happy Woman*, the folk knew unambiguously about the greater divine woman of the ancient religion, the *"Great" Happy Woman*[77] of fertility, who was later interpreted as the figure of St. Anne, the mother of Mary. The official church only embraced her legends from the 5th century AD.

The list of these feast days shows an excellent consonance with the images of the Hungarian folk religion discussed further on, that are also partly reconciled with the rhythm of the circle of officially declared Catholic feasts. Simultaneously to the *female genealogy* of the Hungarian oral religious tradition, the *trinitarian* form manifested in the annual circle of feasts also introduces and maintains here the characters of St. *Anne*, Anne's daughter *Mary* and Mary's son *Jesus*. The feast of the Great Happy Woman (even if in Christianity she is characterised by the figure of Anne, we keep in mind her original divine significance) is situated into the divine middle,[78] in between

---

[75] Cf. Ipolyi, 1929, 58

[76] The data are taken from (1) Hungarian feast days: Pongrátz, Ester: *Igaz Isteni Szeretetnek Harmattyából Nevelkedett, Drága Kövekkel ki-rakott Arany Korona* [Golden crone brought up by the dew of the true divine love, trimmed with precious stones], with characters of the Royal University, Buda, 1808, 289; (2) Feast days of Mary in the universal Catholic Church: Kleinheyer, Bruno: *Marienfeiern im Kirchenjahr*, in: Beinert, Wolfgang – Petri, Heinrich (eds.): Handbuch der Marienkunde, Verlag Friedrich Pustet, Regensburg, 1984, 413–439

[77] Kálmány 1971, 321

[78] About being situated into the middle see a detailed explanation further on.

the series of feast days attributed to the birth of Jesus (Purificatio Mariae, Annuntiatio Mariae) and to the birth of Mary (Nativitas Mariae, Praesentatio Mariae, Immaculata Concepcio Mariae).

| | Local Catholic Church (Hungary) | Universal Catholic Church (Vatican) |
|---|---|---|
| 2 February | Candle-consecrating Happy Woman | Purificatio Mariae |
| 25 March | Fruit-budding Happy Woman | Annuntiatio Mariae |
| 2 July | Reaping Happy Woman | Visitatio Mariae (Universal Church: 30. Mai) |
| 15 August | Great Happy Woman | Assumptio Mariae (Orthodox Church: Dormitio M.) |
| 8 September | Little Happy Woman | Nativitas Mariae |
| 21 November | Presentation of the Happy Woman | Praesentatio Mariae (Before 1200 A. D. Feast of St. Anne) |
| 8 December | Conception of the Great Happy Woman | Immaculata Conceptio Mariae |

The parallel between the actively involved maternal respects of the biographies of Anne and Mary (conception, birth, purification) points to the parallel between the passive filial conditions of both Mary and Jesus (being conceived, being born, being presented in the church), while strengthening the *common*, combining characteristics of both the male and female individuals. The only notable big difference between the female and male child, is that the birth of a daughter calls forth a double[79] period of impure state for the mother, while a son makes her mother only half impure[80] as compared with daughters. This distinction shows the obvious inferior state of women of the patriarchal organised society influenced radically also the ecclesiastical mentality.

Although 25th December is not mentioned amongst the feast days of Mary, Christmas day is yet the representation of a special unity of both male (Jesus) and female (Mary) characters (however overshadowing the father figure ). The Sunday of Christ the King, feast of a sharp-featured male figure[81] on the last Sunday of the ecclesiastical year, and the female

---

[79] 7+(2x33)=73 days between 8 September and 21 November
[80] 7+33=40 days between 25 December and 2 February
[81] Cf. writings of Richard Rohr on manhood

beginning of the new year, the feast of the Virgin Mary (from 1964) on 1st January (in old Hungarian calendars January is dedicated to the Happy Woman), embrace the waiting time of Advent (=arrival) that finally brings the two characters together. As we shall see, this unity is manifested most evidently in the possible transposal of female and male features expressed beautifully in the images of the Hungarian oral religious tradition through the characters of Jesus and Mary, or the so-called Happy Woman. Let us now turn our attention to these *images of the subconscious.*[82]

## THE SOURCES AS "VERBAL ICONOGRAPHY"

A few decades ago, after a long pause in interest following World War II, a very intensive effort to assemble the slowly disappearing[83] ancient rural tradition began. One collection after the other was published for the book market. I will compare only a few basic selections that can offer us a comprehensive knowledge of the religious aspects of Hungarian rural communities. In my research I focus mainly on *archaic Hungarian folk prayers*[84] performed in a singsong voice, on *narrative texts combined with biblical stories*[85] and on *documents, interviews* relating to the personal biographies of two female seers, prophets of their own era in their own environment (1. Klára Csépe of Hasznos, 2. Mária Katona of Somos).

---

[82] Acknowledging with the Jungian psychologist Maria Kassel the subconscious as the place of divine revelation. Cf.: Kassel, Maria: *Traum, Symbol, Religion – Tiefenpsychologie und feministische Analyse*, Herder. Freiburg, 1991, 133–149

[83] However Eliade points out *the indestructible power and the repeated return* of archaic images. See: Eliade, Mircea: *Das Heilige und das Profane. Vom Wessen der Religiösen*, Rowohlt, Hamburg, 1957

[84] Erdélyi 1999, but further collectors of archaic Hungarian prayers like Sándor Bálint, who was the "spring" of the Hungarian religious ethnography (*Népünk imádságai*, Regnum Egyháztörténeti évkönyv II, Budapest, 1937, 19–47), Imre Harangozó (*Krisztusz háze arangyosz. Archaikus imák, ráolvasások, kántálók a gyimesi és moldvai magyarok hagyományából*, Ipolyi Arnold Népfőiskola, Újkígyós, 1998), Zoltán Polner (*Isten zsámolyánál. Népi vallásos költészet*, Bába és Társai, Szeged, 2000), Vilmos Tánczos (*Gyöngyökkel gyökereztél. Gyimesi és moldvai archaikus imádságok*, Pro-Print, Csíkszereda, 1995) etc. are also to be noted.

[85] Lammel – Nagy 1995; Bosnyák, Sándor: *Magyar biblia* [Hungarian Bible], Európai Folklór Intézet - L'Harmattan, Budapest, 2001; but further collections are also to be noticed (Zoltán Polner: *Csillagok tornácán. Táltosok, boszorkányok, hetvenkedők*, Bába és Társai, Szeged, 2001).

For a country with very limited written documents extant due to its tormented national history, *verbalism* makes the texts highly valid sources of the tradition. Compared with other countries where documents have been preserved better, the direct continuity between written texts and the *oral tradition* is obvious. But in our case we can speak only about "indirect continuity" which means that it is our oral tradition that refers to our past in an authentic way, and for lack of other evident sources many motifs must be reconstructed only through this "verbal iconography".[86] Some scholars date these type of texts to the late middle ages[87], while others, who had more national materials at their disposal, date their origins to the period before literature developed in the vernacular language.[88] The "pagan" elements of the texts and practices, however, suggest a much earlier, pre-Christian origin.

As we shall see from the images of God represented in the religious folk tradition we are able to conclude the everyday life of the faith community, the dominant family structure, the relation between man and woman, the gender roles, and the division of labour within the family. At the same time, the oral tradition reflects the influence of ecclesiastical and social expectations, even if in a negative way, resulting in negative attitudes toward the contemporary power politics. The texts relating to religion demonstrate clear gender-based characteristics. It depends, what kind of ideologies had to be supported by the gender groups within the community, or, exactly on the contrary, withdrawn into "inner emigration" within the burdensome domination of the commonly defined rules of the community.

All these obvious or hidden expressions of convictions can be explored in the pictorial descriptions of oral tradition. The derogatory female images in biblical stories, which were interpreted and enforced from a typical point of view of rural story-telling men, inform us unambiguously about their own self-preservation and hidden fears against women. The prayers and stories of peasant women, on the other hand, do not concentrate on men, but rather avoid the male elements, and, contradicting the

[86] Erdélyi, Zsuzsanna: *Az archaikus népi imádságzáradékok történeti kérdései* [The historical questions of the clause of archaic folk prayers], in: Erdélyi, Zsuzsanna (ed.): Boldogasszony ága – Tanulmányok a népi vallásosság köréből [The bough of the Happy Woman – Studies on the folk belief], SzIT, Budapest, 1992, 52–54

[87] Bálint, Sándor: *Népünk imádságai* [Prayers of our people], in: Regnum, Budapest, 1937, 19–47

[88] Cf. Toschi, Paolo: *La poesia religiosa del popolo italiano*, Firenze, 1922

everyday experiences of male oppression, they visualise absolute female power. At the same time, behind these words the desire for earlier equality can be noted.


ARCHAIC HUNGARIAN FOLK PRAYERS


The 321 prayers found in the volume of *Erdélyi* are only a very narrow segment of her work.[89] Nonetheless this selection includes texts from all areas of Hungarian native speaking communities.[90] We find concrete references to typical national mythological, or historical characteristics like "the seeds of Árpád"[91], "the white horse"[92], "St. Stephen king",[93] and most often "the Happy Woman".[94]

These prayers have been preserved by rural, uneducated people, but at the same time *Pócs* points to the danger of the very artificial differentiation between "rural" and "elite", and instead she emphasises specific common elements of the culture and the collective ritual forms.[95] It is, however, a fact that these traditions were retained to a greater degree by closed rural communities than by elite groups exposed to more external influ-

---

[89] As stated to me by Erdélyi (born in 1921) on 1st September 2000 she chose the most typical texts from her collection of more than 10,000 prayers. [90] Also from areas beyond the national boundaries: Transylvania, Moldva, Vojvodina...

[91] See prayer nr. 222. Cf. prayer nr. 271: "the seeds of Adam"

[92] See prayer nr. 257: Mary is meeting a white horse

[93] See prayer nr. 254

[94] *"Happy"* as synonym of *"blessed"*, *"rich"*, *"beautiful"* (cf. Daczó, Árpád: *Népünk hitvilága* [The world of our folk's belief], Kolozsvár/Cluj, 1992), but in its initial meaning – *révül:* "falling into trance" comes from the word *rév.* means "farry" or "haven": "farry" that leads to "haven" › *heaven* – shows shamanic features (cf. Erdélyi 1999, 99 and Falvay 2001, 120); and cf. the concept of "altered states of consciousness" (ASC), mentioned by Bourguignon, Erika (ed.): *Religion, Altered States of Consciousness and Social Change*, Ohio University Press, Columbus, 1973, 3–38

[95] Pócs, Éva: *Transz és látomás Európa népi kultúráiban* [Trance and vision in the folk culture of Europe] in: Pócs, Éva (ed.): Eksztázis, álom, látomás – Vallásetnológiai fogalmak tudományközi megközelítésben [Extasy, dream, vision – An interdisciplinary approach of religious-ethnological concepts], Balassi, Budapest, 1998, 16–17. But see also: Bálint, Sándor: *A magyar vallásos népélet kutatása* [The examination of the Hungarian popular belief], in: Dankó, Imre – Küllős, Imola (eds.): Vallási néprajz III. – Módszerek és történeti adatok [Religious ethnography 3. – Methods and historical data], Budapest, ELTE Folklore Tanszék, 1987, 8–65. Bálint maintains that the concept "folk" meaning all the lay people and even the priest when he gets connected with the cult as a private person.

ences through communication with the "outside world". Therefore I use "folk" in the sense of the preserver stratum of the collective cultural tradition. It is also worth mentioning that although we find *both* women and men among those saying these prayers, there is nonetheless often a difference in content and attitude between texts coming from a male or a female (whose numbers are in any case much higher in this context). This is a point, to which I shall refer repeatedly in the future.

These texts have never been regarded officially as "prayers", but are at best considered treasures of religious folklore[96]. There are several reasons for forbidding this mixture of magic and mystery. We shall explore them explicitly after a quick overview of their contents. Many of the texts are a construction of three clearly separable parts, namely *the initial picture, the main central part* and *the clause.*

The initial image suggests a *formulae of vision,*[97] e.g.:
*"I go out of my door,*
*I look up to the high heaven,*
*there I see [...] "*[98]

Many, more complicated variations can also be found in this section; the image can begin, for instance, with earlier events of the daily rhythm like "getting up" or even "going to bed"[99] motifs, which are usually followed by a divinely "revealed"[100] reality. When *King* draws attention to the special characteristics of the visions, he stresses the importance of the anti-rational and anti-hierarchical impulses[101] found in these images.

---

[96] Cf. Tomisa, Ilona: *A Magyar Növendékpapság Néprajzi Munkaközössége* [The ethnographical co-operation of the Hungarian Seminarists], in: Dankó – Küllős 1987, 66–79[97] Cf. Erdélyi, Zsuzsanna: *A látomásformulák szerepe az archaikus népi imádságokban* [The role of the formulae of vision in archaic Hungarian folk prayers], in: Pócs 1998, 405–433

[98] See e.g. prayer nr. 92, 107 etc.

[99] *"I go to my bed, to my bodily-spiritual coffin, in the clothes of angels, in the holy presence of Jesus Christ; go round, cross; take care of me, angel; so that we can rest in the name of Jesus, Mary; Saint John with wounded neck, cover the whole region of the house, so that no hole can be found there; in the morning as I am getting up I look to the East* [note: in Hungarian "East" = "kelet" means also "sunrise"], *I see the door of heaven opened [...] "*, in: e.g. prayer nr. 85

[100] Cf. veil › remove the veil: reveal › revelation

[101] cf. Erdélyi met a wide range of emotional expressions given during the collecting process of praying these prayers (sniveling, crying, inarticulate whining), in: Erdélyi 1999, 37

Marginalised people[102], who, in order to evade the monopolised world of theologians and opposing officialdom, had to resort to religious illegality, turn into heroes of their own world with the help of their own imaginations.[103]

Erdélyi describes *the central part* as the epic-lyric-dramatic representation of the Passion.[104] The delineation of the Passion looks back upon a long historical and art historical past. However I am focusing on the very *strong female dominance* expressed in the figure of Mary or, as the case may be, of the Happy Woman. I shall examine these images in detail in the following pages.

*The clause* or the concluding formula seems to be the section most problematic for the institutional church.[105] This short closing form with its ancient, magical worldview, is not a uniquely Hungarian formula. It can also be found in other national traditions and in other languages such as Italian, French, Spanish, Rumanian, German, Irish, English, Danish, Icelandic, Russian,[106] Polish, Serbian, Croatian, Slovenian, Slovakian etc.[107] Even the Hungarian version has a wide range of variations. Let us turn to a few examples:

*"Whoever says this little prayer in the morning and in the evening, the door of the dear beautiful heaven will be opened to him/her."*[108]

or:

---

[102] children, women, uneducated poor people, cf. Beinert 1997. Nevertheless, *Gábor Magyar*, Hungarian medical doctor, looks at the phenomenon from another perspective. In his opinion that part of the sacred appears on earth which is essentially missing. The reason of the strong devotion to Mary or to Her synonymous female figure is the lack of female presence in the religious practice. In: Székely, Orsolya: *Gondolatok a vallásos világkép női princípiumáról* [Thinking about the female principle of the religious world view], Duna TV – Ikon Stúdió 2003, documentary, 55'

[103] King, Herbert: *Die Bedeutung der Marienerscheinungen im kirchlichen Leben der Neuzeit*, in: Ziegenaus, A. (ed.): Marienerscheinungen, Ihre Echtheit und Bedeutung im Leben der Kirche, Mariologische Studien X, Pustet, Regensburg, 1995, 119–120

[104] Cf. Erdélyi 1999, 35

[105] Nonetheless I see an inseparable coherence between the powerful female images of the central part and the question of the religious authenticity of the clause.

[106] Cf. Orosz 1996, 36

[107] See a useful list of referring literature to this topic in: Erdélyi 1992, 58–63, 138–142

[108] Prayer nr. 68. Notice that in the Hungarian language there is no grammatical gender difference, and it is valid also in the case of a pronoun. However as we shall see later there *are* typical explicit gender differences in the language, but only with the regard to the content.

[central part:
"There I see a golden tree, gold without, merciful within,
under that there is a golden basin,[109]
there are three drops of our Virgin Mother's milk, three drops of the
Lord Jesus' blood in it,]
*whoever washes oneself in it in the morning, in the evening,
will be remitted one's seven mortal sins.* "[110]

or:

[Mary says:]
*"Go, my Holy Son to the black earth, to the sinful sons of Adam,
proclaim my two or three words:
who can say it* [the whole prayer], *let become a virgin, like me, the virgin,
who cannot say it, let him/her not be able to pass the gate of the heaven.* "[111]

From these short quotations we can demonstrate of following typical characteristics:

They offer a rhythm of time and remind us of magic art that is animated by the belief in the special creative, magical power of each word.[112]

There are nevertheless women (and men) in history who instinctively know that being faithful to the heritage of ancestors and ancestries means however personal engagement and involvement rather than turning into mechanical routine. Even if we often meet a kind of reciting style in folk religion, those involved in the ritual, as contrasted with the official, often burnt out, cynic clerics at the altar, manifest strong personal conviction, inspiration and devotion to the whirling power of mantra-like repeated words.

---

[109] It can be the symbol of Gral, cf. in: Erdélyi 1999, 243

[110] Prayer nr. 52

[111] Prayer nr. 229

[112] Cf. Erdélyi 1999, 40; Lovász, Irén: *Az imádkozásról – Nyelvészeti-pragmatikai és a kulturális antropológiai megközelítés* [About praying – Linguistic-pragmatical and cultural anthropological approach], 3, in: Barna, Gábor (ed.): "Nyisd meg, Uram, szent ajtódat..." – Köszöntő kötet Erdélyi Zsuzsanna 80. születésnapjára ["Open your holy door, my Lord..." – Congratulatory volume for the 80th birthday of Zsuzsanna Erdélyi], SzIT, Budapest, 2001, 3–27; Keszeg, Vilmos: *Jóslások a Mezőségen. Etnomantikai elemzés.* [Predictions in the Mezőség. Ethnomantic analysis], Bon-Ami, Sepsiszentgyörgy, 1997, 120: *"The prayer is the christianising form of word-magic."*

They are not a request or a call, nor even adoration, but rather a disclosure of facts that had been established by a divine person (most often Mary or the Happy Woman). However as *Lovász* points out, the form of imperative is not even necessary here because it is implicitly given in the acknowledgement of the divine will. "Validity gained in Heaven ensures that these prayers are really effective and powerful. Since the Sacred Word, God's Word, is the guarantee, the success of the speech act is also guaranteed [...]"[113] Although Lovász does not accentuate the female power of these particular words at all.

When Erdélyi discusses the ecclesiastical prohibition of the texts[114] she claims that the prayers are/were forbidden because of their close relationship to "pagan" magical rituals. *Alszeghy*, the Jesuit theologian, confirms this view. He tries to be sympathetic to the ecclesiastical approach while attempting to draw a clear distinction between these "magic" texts and the indulgences accepted or even encouraged by the church. According to him, the old penitential practice concentrated on the real inner conversion while these texts offer *only* the forgiveness of sins.[115] Erdélyi however points to the *similarities* of the two practices coming from different backgrounds.[116]

Another possible reason for the prohibition is articulated by the prayers of the rural people: The prayers offer an opportunity to *avoid* the ecclesi-

---

[113] See Lovász, Irén: *Oral Christianity in Hungary: Interpreting Interpretations*, in: Davis, Jon – Wollaston, Isabel (eds.): *The Sociology of Sacred Texts*, Sheffield Academic Press, Sheffield, 1993, 72–82, here 81. Cf. Fettich 1971

[114] Although they could occur even during the mass, in silent minutes of the service – without the priest's knowledge. Cf. Lovász 2001, 17

[115] See Erdélyi's correspondence with Zoltán Alszeghy SJ, in: Erdélyi 1992, 127–136

[116] I would like to refer here to an obvious contemporary proof that confirms this presumed similarity. See: Baum, William Wakefield – Magistris, Luigi De: *Decree of the Sacred Penitentiary on the Conditions for Gaining the Jubilee Indulgence*, Rome, 29 November 1998. "the rule that a plenary indulgence can be gained only once a day remains in force during the entire Jubilee year. [...] These two culminating moments (cf. sacraments of penance and of the eucharist) must be accompanied [...] by prayer for the intentions of the Roman Pontiff, and also by acts of charity and penance, following the indications given below. [...] With regard to the required conditions, the faithful can gain the Jubilee indulgence: 1. In Rom [...], 2. In the Holy Land [...], 3. In other ecclesiastical territories [...], 4. In any place [...]. The faithful will certainly wish to repeat these visits throughout the Holy Year, since on each occasion they can gain the plenary indulgence, although obviously not more that once a day. (5) [...] through actions which express in a particular [...] way the penitential spirit [...] This would include abstaining for at least one whole day from unnecessary consumption (e. g., from smoking or alcohol...) [...]."

astical hierarchy by keeping away from the confession and the "father-confessor" himself.[117] However in the eyes of rural communities there is no conflict with the confession, Nor do they preclude the possible co-efficient adoption of both of these practices.[118]

## BIBLICAL STORIES BUILT INTO THE HUNGARIAN FOLK NARRATIVES

The biblical stories interpreted by narratives of the Hungarian folk religion demonstrate clearly the social-individual screening of Hungarian peasantry, through which the scenes of the Bible are put in a new light of the rural aspect. The collectors of narrative texts integrated with biblical stories named the synthesis of their work subjectively. Both the so-called *Peasant Bible*[119] and the so-called *Hungarian Bible*[120] show the *connection with*, but also the *difference from* the officially accepted canonised texts of the Bible. The popular versions of the biblical stories have been explored all over Hungary, but an even more alive epic tradition has been found and collected in the last decades outside of the Hungarian borders, in the Hungarian speaking areas of neighbouring countries (Slovakia, Ukraine, Rumania, Yugoslavia, Austria). These variations come from both male and female peasant storytellers, most often above the age of 60, but in several more archaising, traditionalist areas they are also known among the youth.

Because of the central location of Hungary between East and West, both the western and the eastern religious-cultural world view had an effect on developing Hungarian religious practice. This literary form of this type of inculturation is again not exceptional. The stories are strongly influenced by "heretical" trends of thought appearing in the 12–13th century in the southern part of Hungary. The dualistic creation myths obviously derive from Bogumil legends coming from Bulgaria and from the entire of the Balkans. Nevertheless Franciscans fighting against the surrounding "heretical" movements preached the Gospel in ways similar to their enemies, while using images comparable to those of the heretics.

---

[117] *"Many knew this prayer but then gave it up [...] the priests forbade it [...] It was not accepted because how can it happen then that seven mortal sins are forgiven without confession?"* – claimed by a woman on the 16th November 1971 in Himód/Győr-Sopron, in: Erdélyi 1999, 67

[118] Cf. Lovász 2001, 18

[119] Lammel – Nagy (eds.) 1995

[120] Bosnyák 2001

The peasantry integrated these images into its own culture and gave shape to them through its own perspective, anyway. We find a wide range of variant stories and even of one given story, depending on the cultural area where they were collected. These myths, fables, and yarns interpret biblical stories often in a very provocative way, as we shall see. The rural community usually enriched the narratives with local motifs and left out all those elements that did not serve its own closed world's understanding of the ordered principles. In this manner these narratives do offer a scale of values and provide answers for such important questions as to why some are rich and others poor, why women experience pain in child bearing, or why the woman should be obedient to her husband, etc. The narration of these stories occurred in the family circle, outside of the liturgy, but was nonetheless often bound to particular ecclesiastical feasts like Christmas or Easter. However figures, time and space, just as in the above-mentioned folk prayers, all become *linearly* relative in this context and only through the exceptional world of symbols can we explore the particularly created *circular* order.[121]

The sagas, just like the biblical holy texts, can be united into a kind of series, and tell the story of humankind from the origin till the end of the world. Their frame is also similar to those narratives of the Bible, but the essential meaning of their content often differ. In these tales instead of scribes and clerks the whole human nation manifests itself. These legends are the results of the intertwining universal oral tradition of the ancient Egyptian, Persian, Skythian, European etc. understanding of human living-space. The *new* coming generations identified themselves only with those *old* ideas that resounded their inner living world.[122] Consequently the stories were sanctified rather by the people than by clerical corps, although Christian elements have definitely effected the voice of the Hungarian people in the last thousand years. Even if the sagas of the oral tradition were put down in writing only recently, they seem to be more archaic than the biblical texts in many respects.[123]

---

[121] See also: Lammel – Nagy (eds.) 1995, 295–315

[122] See more about the usual social process of legitimising (re-interpreting and accepting) old ideas by younger generations, in: Tomka, Ferenc: *Intézmény és karizma az egyházban* [Institution and charisma in the church], Országos Lelkipásztori Intézet, Budapest, 1991, 18–69

[123] Cf. Bosnyák 2001, 5

ADDITIONAL DOCUMENTS

Images of both the archaic folk prayers and the biblical narratives give a wide overview of the treatment of women and, generally speaking, of gender roles in the religious folklore, but specific individual female characteristics can be revealed in more detail only by biographical references. Although religious images confirm individual rituals, the personal religious practice normally, if the dialogue between the traditional shape and the individual is given free rein, has repercussion on popular religious worldviews. As we shall see, newer prayers and other holy texts describing a more recent reality are gradually added to the already exercised rituals of the old tradition. In this way the continuity within tradition and among traditional elements is ensured and well protected.

This is why we also need to consider more closely some individual examples of the Hungarian popular religion. Biographies of Klára Csépe and Mária Katona will therefore be examined and compared through published writings, manuscripts, documentary films, interviews etc. In these materials we shall explore already investigated ritual elements of the Hungarian popular belief.

I had many difficulties while discovering all the sources I needed for a better understanding of special human behaviour. Certain documents were simply surrounded by impenetrable mysteriousness. Slowly I have realised that officially published dates were often disclosed and interpreted in an extremely one-sided way. It seems that both clerical and socialist authors of the era were not allowed by higher official leaders (or they themselves did not allow) to reveal numerous facts in public. This mysteriousness associated with complete rejection is still present in the official church, but also in the ethnography, medicine, or the media, even if there are, naturally, reassuring exceptions. We might presume that the practical projection of the "incomprehensible antics"[124] can be approached more easily, with less ideological responsibility by ethnographers and medical doctors, who examine religious phenomena purely from the standpoints of religious ethnography and psychiatry, without obligatory personal religious involvement. However it does not seem to be so simple.

I myself find the personal engagement of the researcher particularly essential and identifiable in any type of scientific work. While reading through all the studies and descriptions about the two peasant women I was

---

[124] As the religious practice of uneducated people is often regarded.

interested in, a wide scale of interpretations of moral and empathy had been obviously manifested in the relating scientific works.[125] Whilst drawing the portrait of the two female spiritual leaders by a synthesis of numerous studies, I shall show, even unintentionally, the manipulatory power of any kind of approach to the theme.

---

[125] It could be a well examinable explicit subject of another study.

# The imagery of femaleness in the
## oral tradition of Hungarian rural communities

Living in the tension of the wide scale of gender characteristics, behind fragile role identities deemed previously stable, shows a permanent hidden yearning for integrated *wholeness* of both female and male individuals.[126]

I always admired the harmonious formulae and the multi-coloured variety of folk art, until after a performance I talked to an elderly lady who was a member of a famous dancing group in Transylvania. From the stage the whole group smiled during its powerful moves, but after the appearance, when I asked her personally about the dance, she let me into her sad life that was accompanied by everyday male violence. In that very instant a radical change began in my attitude towards all kinds of artistic expressions. Now I am more interested in the everyday reality of the many anonymous people's artists themselves rather than only in their artistic forms.

Similarly whenever I look at Hungarian folkdance I am able to recognise some particular habitual roles of men and women in history. Men have a wide variety of improvisations in their dance while the option for a style is much narrower for female dancers. Often women look at men – dancing in the middle – only from the background while men watch themselves being looked at and adored by *women on the edge*. Male dancers play the leading role in the dance; their movement seems to have greater importance in the performance than that of the bodily and spiritual involvement of women. This patriarchal structured hierarchy is evident in group dances. Nevertheless part of the music brings people together into pairs where men, as moving central points, give dynamic impulses to their female counterparts who are actually determined to go round "their male centre". Music can initiate a solo dance for

---

[126] Cf. Howell, Signe – Melhuus, Marit: *The study of kinship; the study of person; a study of gender?*, in: del Valle, Teresa (ed.): Gendered Anthropology, Routledge, London, 1993, 38–53

men (but never for a woman) when one or more male dancers separate from the group and come together in the middle of the dance floor to show their expertise and their responsible creativity with regard to their own bodies. They are dancing together but without touching, this expresses a great autonomy within the male dancing community. At the same time the female task is to withdraw into the background, from here women are to fix their eyes on their male companions. But sometimes they are also allowed to do some very simple movements – usually very few steps – in a circle, closed with handshakes into their own separate but never single-handed world.

The outcasts of this male-dominant society happened to be gathered in their own female communities where they were able to share their dreams and wounds. The female workshops of handicrafts offered a good atmosphere for women to leave their ancient female spiritual knowledge to the coming generations of daughters. The heritage of typical female jobs as weaving and needlework suggests a greater *equality and mutuality* of women and men in the many miraculous symbols of hand weaving made by Hungarian women.

In the background of the sacred sphere of life, Hungarian female yearnings are expressed in even more characteristic features, in the thousands of ancient folk prayers. These prayers are characterised by enormous evidence of the ancient matrifocal tribal belief in the so-called Happy Woman (Boldogasszony), who creates, heals, leads to eternal life, and later in Christianity identified with Mary the merciful mother of God – in contradiction to the dreadful Judge, the paternal God. *She* is the earth who has given birth to the sky. The manipulating identification of the Goddess with Mary, directed by Christian missionaries, led to interesting combinations of the two female images, although the powerful female representations always remained *forbidden* and *claimed as pagan* in the Catholic church – not accidentally.

The Glorious God the Father and his Holy Son presented, intentionally and consciously overbore the images of an actively involved powerful woman represented in the texts, by patriarchal interpretations of Christianity. Nonetheless, the belief in female strength survived the androcentric centuries of repression, and, even men's soul was yearning for their *anima*,[127] the Magna Mater, who is the representation of the *active*, powerful female defending cosmic circulation.[128] It is essentially different from that of the *pas-*

---

[127] Numerous male members of the Catholic church are, not accidentally, also devoted to the cult of the divine Happy Woman.

[128] Cf. Keszeg's interpretation about the dualistic view of the circle's symbolism, namely, the

*sive* "going round a male centre" directed by the male partner in the dance and/or in everyday life.[129] The Magna Mater can be found even today in the character of uneducated Wise Women who are experts in adopting and applying the forgotten forces of nature.

It is obvious however that even the identity of these respected wise women had to go through the socio-cultural extremity of understanding womanhood, from roles of the fearful or humiliatable witch empowered with evil forces to the divine, untouchable female figure put on a pedestal.

## THE DIVINE WOMAN:
## BLESSING OR CURSING FEMALE POWER?

### THE CREATIVE "HAPPY WOMAN"

Many variations of images representing femaleness in a positive way exist in the Hungarian religious oral tradition. These are interwoven into prayers, frame the daily rhythm and offer the experience of *female integrity* to all women – and *men* – involved in their own cult.[130] Even today Feasts of the Happy Woman are signposts and comparing points for elderly Hungarians, but also for the younger generations in more traditional areas. The everyday life of people in Hungarian speaking areas was naturally and totally combined with this female figure until the Second World War.

The continuous re-animation of her influence was however somehow directed by state and ecclesiastical authorities in a hidden way. The *"land of Mary"* was rather a political slogan that utilised the popular belief of the lower classes devoted to the Happy Woman, on behalf of higher social and ecclesiastical

---

defense of the objects within the circle from the outside chaotic world. In: Keszeg, Vilmos: *A kör szemantikája és szerkezete* [The semantics and structure of the circle], in: Művelődés L. 4., 1997, 34–37

[129] Cf. The powerful shamanic dance involving *actively* the *whole* personality of the healing female shaman.

[130] Jung and the Jungians point to the importance of both the *anima* and the *animus*. If one of them dominates the society and the psyche more intensely, it makes the system(s) incomplete and therefore distorted and ill. See: e. g. Kassel 1991; Kassel, Maria: *Biblische Urbilder*, Herder, Freiburg, 1992; Johnson, Robert A.: *The Fisher King and the Handless Maiden: Understanding the Wounded Feeling Function in Masculine and Feminine Psychology*, HarperSanFrancisco, NY, 1993; and: Bly, Robert – Woodmann, Marion: *The Maiden King: The Reunion of Masculine and Feminine*, Henry Holt, NY, 1998

circles. It is certainly not a unique phenomenon in the course of history. During the formation and evolution of the so-called civilised world the vivid, long established traditional cultures were soon institutionalised and victimised on the altar of social-political ideologies, without any periodical exception.

Instead of the highly cultivated artificial religious ideas, here I intend to focus on the positive roots of heritage describing femaleness from *"below"*. Although, as it has been pointed out earlier, it represents the unconscious spontaneity and the intuition of the instinctive level of any strata rather than the habitual rules fixed on lower social states. However these two aspects are often combined in scientific studies, because the complexity of examined texts gives no room for pure separation between intuition and social ranging. Nevertheless, even if I set out from vigorous female images of the subconscious, I see easily the obvious touch of various ideologies influencing negatively the self-valuation and the understanding of womanhood at the same time.


*Female trinity*

Various European representations of three women

The motif of *three women* is a well-known symbol of womanhood in the cults of Europe. Hans Christoph Schöll's work was one of the most revolutionary approaches to this kind of female representation in his age, while breaking through the usual common christianised interpretations of the image. Contemporary researchers of the era described the phenomenon exclusively from Christian aspects and reduced the description of the female figures to fertility, pregnancy and birth. In opposition to them Schöll dates the image from the epoch of pre-Christianity. In this way the three female characters can be identified with the pagan *Moon, Sun and Earth* Mother *as part* of the tradition of the Great Goddess. The cosmic circle expressed in the celestial bodies of the earth, the sun and the moon basically simultaneously refer to the *whole world*, but in its abstract sense, also to the continuously renewing life. This world described by the Celtic word *BET* is in close connection with another Celtic notion *BIVO* (= "lively", "vivid"), with the Latin *vivere* (= "live"), with the Greek *bio* (= "life"), and with the Old Irish *BITH* (gen.: *beth-o*) meaning *"always existing"*, *"eternal"*.[131]

---

[131] Schöll, Hans Christoph: *Die Drei Ewigen. Eine Untersuchung über den germanischen Bauernglauben,* Jena, 1936, 42

Further parallels are also to be noted: The Scandinavian *Norns*, just like the Greek *Moires* or the Saxon *Weird* (= fate) *Sisters* (the Fates) symbolised the past, the present and the future – the wholeness of life.[132] These female characters ruled over all male gods. They lived by the magic roots of the world tree, where the fate of all creatures was decided. The three women have often been associated with the three lunar phases: with the full, the waning and the waxing moon.[133]

The three *Graces* are always returning female figures of the Greek and Roman arts, but similar representations can be seen in Indian Temples. The Trinitarian depiction of being divine, beautiful and heart-warming leads into the Oneness of the Goddess. The word *grace* origins from the Greek notion *charis* that is the gift of creativity, friendship and love presented by the Goddess.[134] In the New Testament the female character of graciousness is forgotten, charis gets into close relationship with paternal *charitas*, which means love and mercifulness at the same time, and will overcome both faith and hope.[135]

Exactly the opposite can be said about the three *Furies* whom are called *"the daughters of the Earth and Shadow"* by Sophocles.[136] The shadow symbolises all those fears, which are hidden in the unconscious female psyche. In a psychological sense the three destroying female figures are projections of caring mothers being afraid of the delicate health of their infants.[137]

*Kutter* points out further numerous representations of the cult of three maiden explored in German speaking areas of Europe like South-Tirol, Bayern, Austria, Klerant, Meransen, Brixen, Worms, Leutstetten etc.[138]

## Three women around the Hungarian Happy Woman

In the Hungarian oral tradition the central female divine figure, the Happy

---

[132] Campbell, Joseph: *The Masks of God. Creative Mythology*, Viking, New York, 1970, 121
[133] Branston, Brian: *Gods of the North*. Thames &Hudson. 1955, 208–209
[134] Cf. Walker, G. Barbara: *Die geheimen Symbole der Frauen. Lexikon der weiblichen Spiritualität*, Hugendubel, München, 1997, 342
[135] 1 Cor 13
[136] Graves, Robert: *The Greek Myths*, 2 Vol., Penguin Books, New York, 1955, Vol. 1, 122
[137] Walker, 1997, 335–336
[138] Cf. Kutter, Erni: *Der Kult der drei Jungfrauen. Eine Kraftquelle weiblicher Spiritualität neu entdeckt*, Kösel, München, 1997

Woman is often surrounded by three women. In several verses we detect these protagonist powerful caring women while accompanying the divine effective activity of the Goddess.

*"[...] The Happy Woman is in front of me,*
*Above my head there are three Maries [...] "*[139]
*"[...] There are three Maries keeping an eye on him*[140].
*The fourth is waiting for my soul [...] "*[141]

In this way the three female characters practically confirm the almighty state of the Goddess. The *Happy Woman* obviously plays a special role in concentrated moments presented in the prayers. Her world is the other world; she behaves like a gazing, all-knowing goddess.

The rural communities devoted to the Happy Woman understandably interpret her figure in quite an arbitrary way. The following magical strophe illustrates the complexity of the ancient symbolic way of thinking of our ancestries, and its detailed analysis can offer us the taste of an almost vanished and forgotten world of powerful magic.

*"Beside the field there are three virgin girls,*
*one carries golden fire,*
*the other carries golden water,*
*the third one carries the golden broom.*
*Let the Happy Virgin Mary sweep the soul of this girl or boy. "*[142]

The four elements (earth [~ field], fire, water and air [~ symbolised by the broom]) having *magic* function in various pagan cults are in our case helping means of the Happy Virgin Mary to purify the soul.[143]

In alchemy *gold* is symbolised by the sign of the Sun as an energetic centre. Its chemical material is stabile; therefore it is in close connection with

---

[139] Prayer nr. 19
[140] Cf. on Jesus lying in a coffin
[141] Prayer nr. 277
[142] Prayer nr. 12. Cf.: Pócs, Éva: *Szem meglátott, szív megvert. Magyar ráolvasások* [Eye had seen, heart had cursed. Hungarian incantations], Helikon, Budapest, 1986, 181. Incantation from South-West Hungary, Osztopán/Somogy.
[143] As Weiler puts it, *"Ma-gie = Matriarchale Ener-gie".* See: Weiler, Gerda: *Der enteignete Mythos. Eine feministische Revision der Archetypenlehre C.G. Jungs und Erich Neumanns,* Campus, Frankfurt am Main, 1991, 72

immortality. This is why in Egypt and in oriental cults the dead body was closed into a golden coffin, as the symbol of hope in life everlasting, and this is why in Hinduism gold is seen as *"the Light in mineral form"*.[144] In Hungarian folk religion it is a regularly returning concomitant of the Happy Woman or of Mary for expressing her divine power. The gold combined with the four basic elements emphasises their distinguished significance and positive effect in the creating or healing process.

Many cults regard the *earth* as mother goddess and the very origin of the mythological beginning. Centuries ago Herodot pointed out that all the well-known notions concerning the earth were feminine.[145] According to Apache legends the earth gave birth to all creatures at the beginning of the world precisely the same way as mothers give birth to their children today.[146] The maternal function can also be explored in the Gypsy cult, which preserves its belief in the mystery of life that comes from the earth.[147]

The presumed connection between the earth and human birth can best be described by a new born laid on the earth immediately after his or her birth to be blessed by earthly maternal forces. This earthly defence accompanying the human being along a life time can evidently be seen in the example of any place (cave, cellar) under the earth helping the human being to keep off the evil forces, in particular witchcraft. In this supposed situation two female forces clash.[148] Nevertheless witchcraft is seen by a male storyteller representing the Hungarian folk religion as knowledge assigned to certain women by Jesus Himself.[149]

---

[144] Cirlot, Juan Eduardo: *A Dictionary of Symbols*. Philosophical Library, New York, 1962, 58, 114

[145] Herodot: *Historien*, Kröner, Stuttgart, 1971, 226

[146] Cf. Campbell, Joseph: *The Masks of God. Primitive Mythology*, Viking, New York, 1959, 240

[147] Derlon, Pierre: *Die Gärten der Einweihung. Und andere Geheimnisse der Zigeuner*, Hugendubel, München, 1991, 135

[148] Hoffmann-Krayer, Eduard – Bächtold-Stäubli, Hanns: *Handwörterbuch des Deutschen Aberglaubens*, 10 Volumes, Vol. 2, Walter de Gruyter & Co., Berlin und Leipzig, 1929/1930, 898–899

[149] *"When Jesus was crucified, his genitals were not properly covered. Some women went there to cover them from the eyes of the people. Jesus asked them what He could do for them. They asked for power that no other women had. Jesus replied: 'If you want you can get it, but then you will never see the kingdom of my Father.' I heard from my father, may he rest in peace, that this is the story of how witches received their knowledge."* See: Bosnyák 2001, 91. Jesus rewards with mysterious female craft the chaste women acting in accordance with the law of their society. The male narrator brings witchcraft peculiarly into connection with sexuality, which has been a taboo in almost all cults. Regarding body and nakedness as sinful reality to be hidden, was a particularly false interpretation in the course of history of the

According to Jung the *mate*rnal aspect of the earth has been turned to a materialistic type of understanding of *mate*rial that has lost its original spiritual meaning, since it has been separated from its source, the living earth mother.[150] Nevertheless the virgins of our Hungarian version staying beside the field seem to be still in organic relation with this maternal female power.

The *fire* attributed to the first virgin expresses the power of both the abilities of life-giving and destroying, healing and damaging. On the one hand, in the form of the *hearth*, fire has practically always played a central spiritual role in the human home, as the *heart* of the family circle. It had both a profane and a sacred function in the house, by giving warmth, offering the opportunity to make nurturing food and at the same time as the symbol of divine love. It was the responsibility of the female members of the family to keep an eye on it, while the men had their own business out of the house.[151]

An ill or deformed child symbolically thrown into the oven refers to the belief in the purifying power of fire and smoke[152] accompanying it.[153] This superstition is nevertheless in close connection with the image of Purgatory, the purifying fire, but, on the other hand, also with that of symbolising hell, where all bad things are burned up and annihilated. In this way both *fiery* love and hatred have their common roots, as signs of the vivid relation or its lack with the divine. Not accidentally in medieval Christianity both the light of the heavenly[154] and the darkness of the underground[155] sphere were represented by the same fire symbol.[156] In our context fire attributed with gold, the symbol of power, hope and eternal life, definitely appear as positive, purifying means of a healing process.

The golden *watery* character of the second virgin is an affirmatively curing message. The expression "water of life" is based on the teaching of sev-

---

Judeo-Christian cultural heritage. Cf. Hoppál, Mihály: *A meztelenség mint az erósz tagadása* [Nakedness as the denial of eros], in: Hoppál, Mihály – Szepes, Erika (eds.): A szerelem kertjében. Erotikus jelképek a művészetben [In the garden of love. Erotic symbols in the art], Budapest, 1987, 223–239. Both sexuality and witchcraft often appear in different cults as mysterious, magical, powerful, therefore frightening symbols of the "other world".

[150] Jung, Carl Gustav: *Man and His Symbol*, Doubleday, New York, 1964, 95

[151] Hoffmann-Krayer – Bächtold-Stäubli, Vol. 2, 1929/1930, 1394–1395

[152] Cf. The smoke plays a purifying role in different religious rituals, as e.g. fuming with incense the altar and the faithful both in the Orthodox and Catholic rites.

[153] Cf. e.g. Pócs, 1986, fig. 3.

[154] Cf. The Easter candle lit from the fire of Holy Saturday symbolising resurrection and renewed life; the fire as the symbol of the Holy Spirit and of spiritual divine inspiration.

[155] Cf. Fire of hell.

[156] Hoffmann-Krayer – Bächtold-Stäubli, Vol. 2, 1929/1930, 1392, 1400–1402

eral creation stories, according to which water is the beginning, the *arché*[157] of the world. Rivers of Paradise are symbols of flourishing oasises, physically experienced phenomenon of the nature that are borrowed, lifted up and set against "desert-feelings", that is, the lack of God's presence by later spiritual writers of religious literature. The spring or well meant safe life for the human beings and animals of all nomadic tribes and communities of land. This is probably why sources play a special role in certain local traditional beliefs surrounded by the cult of the Goddess, as it is manifested for instance in the case of Celtic religion. Numerous local Celtic communities called the Goddess of Sources *Coventina*, who was represented in typical female Trinitarian forms, and whose naming is in close connection with the English notion *"coven"* describing witches' Sabbath.[158] With the help of biographical data of two Hungarian women of the 20th century we shall see the exceptional significance of healing water springs attributed to the wish and power of the Happy Woman in Hungarian faith communities.

Life originating from water is beautifully described by the Hungarian notion of the so-called *"embryonic water"*,[159] the life-giving water for the foetus, that is basically the amniotic fluid. Baptism in water, as a symbol of rebirth, leads back to a strong Hindu conviction, namely, that being immersed in water keeps evil spirits away from the person better than any recited mantra or prayer.[160] This defending function can also be explored in European traditions of superstition. Being washed in water or pouring water on persons and objects, provides the best shelter from demons appearing often as dirty spirits or, at least, as friends of dirt.[161]

The symbolic meaning of the *broom* of the third virgin went through a long and deep transformation in the course of history. Witches of the Middle Ages were called *"broom-amazons"*.[162] The broom has been associated with female magic as an instrument of every female magician since the Roman age. Midwives, who swept the whole house after delivering a baby, and in a symbolic way also the bad feelings between mother and infant, were regarded as one type of these sacral magicians. The broom functioned as a female

[157] Cf. Also the teaching of Thales about the water as arché, in: Campbell, Joseph: *The Masks of God. Occidental Mythology*, Viking, New York, 1964, 181

[158] Cf. Green, Miranda: *The Gods of the Celts*, Barnes & Noble, Totowa, 1986, 80, 153, 165

[159] in Hungarian: *"magzatvíz"*, see also below

[160] Cf. Avalon, Arthur: *Shakti and Shakta*, Dover, New York, 1978, 208–209

[161] Hoffmann-Krayer – Bächtold-Stäubli, Vol. 9, 1938/1941, 107–115

[162] Cf. Dürr, Hans Peter: *Traumzeit über die Grenzen zwischen Wildnis und Zivilisation*, Suhrkamp, Frankfurt am Main, 1985, 174

priestly symbol at wedding rituals. During gypsy wedding ceremonies jumping over the broom of the assisting midwife is still a living part of the ritual.[163] In the medieval world of superstitions women under sentence of heresy were most often regarded as witches and were represented by a broom. In this way its original life-giving message also expressed in the Hungarian folk religion has been left behind, and is turned to be the general symbol of danger and ravage in European Christian cults.[164]

Our short text quoted above shows that these four powerful elements play an organic part in female rituals, they appear as attributions of the Happy Woman or of the Happy Virgin Mary, and serve as helping means of the healing act. Nevertheless the image of this curing good witch[165] went through the process of the *"Verhexung der Göttin"*,[166] which basically means the harassment and murdering of all Wise Women (*femina saga*)[167], who made themselves masters of natural healing (*magia licita*)[168]. This monstrous period of history mirrors the male fear of the unknown, therefore inconceivable female power.[169] This is why attempts to interpret it fell into contradiction, while according to medieval writings witches represented both divine and evil at the same time, or rather the divine turned into evil.[170]

---

[163] Cf. Trigg, Elwood B.: *Gypsy Demons and Divinities*, Citadel Press, Secaucus, 1973, 86–87

[164] Cf. Lys, Claudia de: *The Giant Book of Superstitions*, Citadel Press, Secaucus, 1979, 467

[165] Cf. Die gute Hexe, in: Achterberg, Jeanne: *Die Frau als Heilerin. Die schöpferische Rolle der heilkundigen Frau in Geschichte und Gegenwart*, Scherz, Bern, 1990, 128–131

[166] Cf. Scherf, Dagmar: *Der Teufel und das Weib. Eine kulturgeschichtliche Spurensuche*, Fischer Taschenbuch V., Frankfurt am Main, 1990, 230–236; Grynaeus, Tamás: *Sozialpsychologische Aspekte der ungarischen Hexenprozesse und des Hexenglaubens*, in: Acta Ethnographica Acad. Sci. Hung., Budapest, 1991–1992, 37 (1–4) 479–488

[167] Cf. Achterberg 1990, 128

[168] Cf. Achterberg 1990, 133. Let us see a proper example for this so-called natural healing: Prayer nr. 5. supplement (see also below as description of 'the cooking-wise woman'):
"When Jesus was on the earth,
The Virgin Mary cast water on her Holy Son,
from boughs,
from thistles,
from flowers.
It did the little Jesus good.
In the same way let my water casting be efficacious to you, Ilona. "

[169] Cf. Achterberg 1990, 137–141

[170] Cf. Scherf 1990, 232

*Female genealogy*

According to the official Catholic teaching Mary is the fully human mother of the Divine Son, Jesus. Her paradox role (birth-giving virgin) is nevertheless released in Hungarian popular tradition, while her Christian human representation is permeated intentionally (both through the official "above" and the popular "below", even if motivated by different ideologies) by the divine character of the above-mentioned female fertility figure, the Happy Woman. Nonetheless her divine power is transferred to *Mary* as an effect of Christian-ecclesiastical inculturation.[171] In the Hungarian folk religion Mary enters upon this divine role and now *she* is the one, who inherits and transmits the female heritage of the "Magna Mater".[172]

While the inculturating process from the official ecclesiastical upper level is based on the degrading ideology of replacing natural fertility with untouchable and unattainable super-natural virginity, popular efforts on a lower level are to imbue Mary's ambivalent *asexual* but *human* character with the *powerful-fertile divine* figure of the Happy Woman. This helped to preserve and salvage the main pagan female character of the ancient Hungarian tribal-nomadic religion. Both those situated above and below are motivated by their complexes originating from the inhumane circumstances of both the oppressed folk and the exalted rulers. The ones above go about in fear of their almost divine ecclesiastical-state authorities. The ones below however have to survive the daily torment of their humiliated life. Therefore the direction of the ambitions from "above" putting down the female divine character of the Happy Woman, and replacing Her with the Divine Son supporting patriarchal authority, is in contradistinction with the direction of the ambitions from "below" lifting up the female human figure of Mary, and praising her highly as Goddess tantamount to the Happy Woman. These two ambitions meet in the complex stature of the Happy Virgin Mary, that is, the mixture of the characters of the Happy Woman and Mary.

## The Earth has given birth to the Sky

Let us now look at the complexity of the female divine character appearing in the persons of the Happy Woman, of the Virgin Mary, or most often of the

---

[171] See above: The advice of bishop Gellért
[172] Cf. Falvay 2001, 97–101

Happy (~ Blessed, in Latin: *"Beata"*) Virgin Mary. The images embrace the universal threefold classification of the phases of female life, all described above by agricultural terms. The fertility periods of flower-growth-harvest demonstrate the close female connection with the earth.[173] The life-giving aspects of growing are described in this case unambiguously as female principles.

> *"White rose, Mary,*
> *is in pearl bud,*
> *is rooted in golden.*
> The Earth has given birth to the Sky,
> *the sky has given birth to St. Anne,*
> *St. Anne has given birth to Mary,*
> *Mary has given birth to her Holy Son,*
> *the Redeemer of the world.[174]*
> *In the four corners of our house*
> *four beautiful angels are looking after me.*
> *Oh, angels, take care of me.*
> *Crosses, turn round.*
> *Let me take a rest in the bed of the Happy Woman[175],*
> *in the arms of Abraham[176] [...] "[177]*

or:

> *"The earth has given birth to Anne,*
> *Anne has given birth to Mary,*

---

[173] As it is clearly expressed in Prayer nr. 227: *"(We offer this prayer) to Mary, the flower of three lives, to the Virgin Mary who became the daughter of our heavenly Holy Father, holy mother of the Son-God, fiancée of the Holy Spirit."*, See also the mythological parallels of the threefold categorisation in: Falvay 2001, 123

[174] In prayer nr. 73 continued with the following motif: *"Christ has given birth to us."* – as a reference to the life Jesus offered by the well to the Samaritan woman (Jn 4: 8–15). This life however springs originally from the Earth.
In prayer nr. 157: *"Saint Anne has given birth to his Holy Son [...]"*, cf. *"Naomi has a son"* (in the context of reality Naomi has a grand son) in: Ruth 4: 13–17; in prayer nr. 169: *"Anne has given birth to Mary, the redeemer of the world."* Reference to the shared co-redemptive function of Mary and Jesus. Erdélyi clearly acknowledges the co-redemptive function of Mary beside Jesus, best represented in ancient texts of the Christianised folk religion, in: Székely, Orsolya: *Hittörténeti archívum – búcsújáróhelyek* [Archives of the history of divinity – places of pilgrimage], Duna TV – Ikon Stúdió 2002, documentary, 40'

[175] "Bed of the Happy Woman": bed for giving birth

[176] Often "the arms of Mary" or "the arms of the Happy Woman"

[177] Prayer nr. 300, italics mine

*Mary has given birth to the Redeemer of the world.*
*Whoever gives birth to a greater one,*
*Can only do harm to us.* "[178]

This *female* genesis and *genealogy* bears witness to a rich ancient symbolism. In the above quoted paragraph, the young, virgin female phase is symbolised in the figure of Mary by the *white rose*. She appears, however, in other texts often in *red dawn, the location* of the rising sun or light.[179] The *black*[180] earth, is basically and originally the good earth mother,[181] the Great Woman,[182] although it can be interpreted also in a negative sense.[183]

Often we find another, more dominant version of the image that suggests rather a male associated character of the origin of the world: *"the sky has given birth to the earth"*. *Falvay*'s interpretation of the powers above and below is surprising however. As he points out, according to the saga of the Egyptian *Nut* and *Geb* the *sky* is originally a female symbol.[184] But it is also connected with the myth of a fight taking place between *Tiamat*, the ancient chaos and ancestress, and her son, *Marduk*, the patriarchal sun-god, who finally overcomes his mother and transforms the upper part of the maternal body into *sky* and the lower part of it into *nether world*.[185] According to the myth the female body consequently involves *the whole circulation of nature*.

---

[178] Prayer nr. 26. supplement

[179] The motif of the red dawn is actually often followed by the birth itself (E. g. *"Beautiful Red Dawn, the lord is born from you, the sun is risen from you [...] "*). Cf. Sun and light as Christian symbols of Jesus go back to ancient motifs that are not necessarily male symbols. See more: Falvay 2001, 80–84

[180] See the parallels of these three colours (white, red, black) elsewhere, in: Pahnke, Donate: *Ethik und Geschlecht. Menschenbild und Religion in Patriarchat und Feminismus*, Diagonal, Marburg, 1991, 221–228: Das Symbolsystem der Göttinreligion

[181] Earth: Urd, Erda, Ertha, Hretha, Eortha, Nerthus, Erze, Urth, Artha, Edda, Heortha, Gaia, Terra, Rhea, Ops, Hel, Hera, Demeter and many other synonyms are to describe the earth as universal mother goddess. Cf. Walker, 1997, 454

[182] The figure of the Great Mother is often differentiated from the Happy Woman, that shows Christian influence: the Virgin Mary identified with the Happy Woman is certainly not the best symbol of fertility. In these cases the *Great Woman* can be identified with Anne, whose fertile human conception is less questionable, although dominant religious male tendencies of Christian tradition tried to asexualise her figure, too, in the course of history of Christian civilisation.

[183] See further on: *"black earth"*~ the sinful earth.

[184] Wild, Henri: *"Geb* is first of all earth-god. His name is not yet explained." in: *Lexikon der Ägyptologie*, vol. 2, Otto Harrassowitz, Wiesbaden, 1980, keyword: *Geb*. Cf. Falvay 2001, 231–232

[185] See: Gimbutas, Marija: *The Language of the Goddess*, Harper & Row, San Francisco, 1989, 338–343

In Falvay's opinion, since the *man* is born and dies *only* to be reborn just like the seed sown into the soil,[186] there can also be drawn a male, but rather passive *circulation* of birth-death-rebirth. At the same time the woman herself is actively involved in *constant* birth/*creation,* therefore survives, permanently prepared to transmit life and food[187] just like the earth. In Hungarian the concepts of *"life"* (*él*et) and *"food"* (*él*elem) both come from the verb *"live": él.* The "seed" as the promise of new life is also often called "life" by Hungarian farmers, which refers to the life of the seed that can grow only in the good mother earth.

<br>

### The holy mouth of the Happy Woman

Not only is the origin of the world attributed to womanhood in the Hungarian popular religion, but further divine features are also associated with her. In the prayers it is usually the Happy Woman[188] who symbolises this female power. Elements of the Old Testament return here in a quite different, female context. דבר יהוה is the creating and ever present instructing *"Word of Yahweh"* in the Old Testament. In the Hungarian religious tradition this rather masculine character is however replaced by the creating, healing divine word given to or originating from the mouth of the Happy Woman.

> *"Proclaim the words coming from the* holy mouth of the Happy Woman."[189]

or: *"Happy Woman, give orders to the diseases with your holy words [...]* "[190]

It is she, or her synonym, Mary, who *creates:*

> *"Oh, my mother, Mary,*
> *before you created me,*
> *you have already known me,*
> *my body, my soul, my cross.* "[191]

---

[186] Cf. Further mythological references to resurrection
[187] See: Falvay 2001, 21, 63
[188] Sometimes also Jesus
[189] Prayer nr. 184. italics mine
[190] Prayer nr. 1
[191] Prayer nr. 268. Cf. Ps 139. italics mine

She is the one who *heals*:

*"The happy holy Mary took her Blessed Holy Son,*
*the Lord Jesus Christ to the garden of Eden.*
*Having fallen into sleep under the shadow of a beautiful palm*
*He looked up to its top,*
*one of its beautiful flowers fell into His eyes,*
*His mood had changed,*
*His Holy heart had withered.*
*The happy holy Mary asked Him:*
*What happened to you, my Beloved Son, bright Jesus?*
*What happened to me, oh, my blessed holy mother?*
*Oh, my blessed Holy Son,*
*come with me to the water of Jordan,*
*I wash you there,*[192]
I blow you with my holy breath coming from my mouth.[193]
*As the eyes of the Lord Jesus had been purified*[194]
*Let this eye be purified in the same way [...] "*[195]

Although in the Old Testament רוח is derived from Yahweh the male God called often Adonai Tzebaoth, the biblical life-giving, actually feminine *rûah*[196] gets back her originally independent female meaning and is associated here with the Hungarian Goddess. Notice that the Jewish tradition distinguishes נפש (unique human soul) from רוח, the divine spirit or breath. In Hungarian, according to the Ural-Altaic belief in transmigration of souls, one and the same concept *"lélek"* refers to *both* meanings.[197] The above quoted texts witness the religious conviction that the spirit (rûah) of the Goddess (Happy Woman) acts in the world and in the human being.

---

[192] Cf. the ancient healing method with water mentioned also in the New testament (e. g. Jn 5: 1–9), but see also the healing method with spittle, the fluid of the mouth (e.g. Mk 8:22–25 or 7:32–35)

[193] Cf. The same verse can be found in Orthodox Russian religious songs, cf. Orosz 1996, 13

[194] It shows connection between illness and sin, cf. the ancient understanding and interpretation of any defect of the body or of the soul.

[195] Prayer nr. 11, italics mine. Cf. the supplement of prayer nr. 11:
*"Our mother, Virgin Mary, I do see nothing with my eyes.*
*Do not worry, my son, do not worry, my daughter,*
*I wipe them with my holy hand,*
*I renew them with my Holy Spirit [...]"*

[196] e. g.: Gen 2:7

[197] Cf. Lükő 2001, 42–43, 183

The palm branch is a returning motif of the prayers attributed to the Happy Woman and Mary, and grows most often from the sea, a watery female symbol. It is dominantly identified with the male penis,[198] which can refer to conception in the context of water. Probably a more suitable interpretation is focused on its magical power activated in the course of female witchcraft,[199] although the Christian symbolism uses this image as the sign of Jesus' arrival to Jerusalem, the city of His suffering and resurrection.[200] Though it remains a symbol of birth and new life, it is built into a new context of religious ideas.

*Female privileges: birth and nurture*

The Hungarian Moon Woman

Since the 3rd century BC notes of Chinese historiographers represent detailed historical data about the so-called *Hiungnus*, namely, the Asian Huns coming from the areas of China and Central-Mongolia. In these Chinese writings, beside numerous war reports, we get a wide range of valuable information about the world of the Hun tribal belief, in which the moon played an especially powerful role. Its changing reality was not only in close relation with the female fertility period and with the whole female existence, but it also fully influenced several – apparently exclusively male – political acts stressed later on as unique historical events of the era by the male Chinese historians. The reigning prince, the *sanjü* bowed every morning before the sun and every evening before the moon. Wars only began when there was a full moon, and it had to be finished in accordance with the waning moon. The time of offerings to the ancestries, to the earth, to the sky or to the spirits also depended on the states of the moon.[201]

This particular significance of the moon as a guide of life events can be explored in the image of "Babba Mária", a special, localisable name for the Happy Woman. According to religious contents of the dominant popular belief existing among Hungarians in certain areas of Transylvania/Rumania, She is

---

[198] Cf. *Book of the Dead* (revised edition: Wallis Budge), Bell, New York, 1960, 518
[199] Cf. Hoffmann-Krayer – Bächtold-Stäubli, Vol 6, 1934/1935, 1372–1373
[200] *"The next day the great body of pilgrims who had come to the festival, hearing that Jesus was on the way to Jerusalem, took palm branches and went out to meet him, shouting: 'Hosanna! Blessings to Him who comes in the name of the Lord!'"* Jn 12:12–13
[201] Cf. Erdélyi – Sugár 1982, 93–94

the Moon herself.[202] In her religious context she appears most often as independent goddess, but sometimes she seems to be identical with the "Beautiful Virgin Mary". The divine power of "Babba", which notion literally means "Beautiful" in her Transylvanian surroundings, the all-knowing and omnipotent Transylvanian female figure seems to overcome the God of Christianity:

> *"I have asked the Beautiful Virgin Mary and the blessed Babba Mária and the good God to deliver her* [cf. the daughter of the narrator]. [...] *But we ask Babba Mária first, before the good God".*[203]

Daczó and others identify her with the Mesopotamian Bau, Bawa or Baba, the ancient Mother Goddess of all the living.[204] This ancient pagan character is blooming repeatedly in the figure of Mary, the mother of the Christian God:

> *"In my childhood my mother always told me that She is in the moon: 'Look, it is the Virgin Mary there, the Virgin Mary looks at us.' And I looked at her long-lastingly and often said to myself: 'Look, how right my mother is. She comes down this way, and She seems to have long hair."*[205]

The moon is endued with irresistible healing power in numerous faith-cures of different types of furuncles. The praying person touches the pock-marks and looks up to the moon by saying:

> *"What I see, let that increase,*
> *What I take hold of, let that decrease."*[206]
> *"Let the moon be renewed,*
> *What I wash, let that disappear."*[207]

The Moon Woman[208] is continuously in synchronous pulsation with all her female fellows. As we have seen earlier, fertility and healing power are

---

[202] Cf. Daczó 2002, 65
[203] Cf. Daczó 2002, 62–63
[204] Cf. Daczó 2002, 40
[205] Bosnyák 2001, 99
[206] Pócs 1986, 108
[207] Pócs 1986, 108
[208] Cf. Her presence in other contemporary cultures, like in Lituania, in: Kiškūnaitė, Laimė: *About a Moonwoman – Giving birth* Part II. Klubas "Gimtis", Vilnius, 1997, video, 42'

almost synonyms manifested in the same female figure.

### The divine female birth-giving gate

In Hungarian folk prayers *Mary's gate* is represented as a typical feminine symbol of both fertility and spiritual birth.[209] The following formulations of it can be read accompanied most often with the motif of Jesus' birth:

> *"Red dawn is breaking,*
> *Mary is resting in it,*[210]
> *the Lord is born from Her,*
> *The hell is broken by Him*[211]
> *[...] If I made a confession,*
> *I could enter the gate of Mary.*"[212]
> *"The gate of Mary is opening,*
> *the Son of God is born [...]*"[213]
> *"If I made a confession every day,*
> *I would be opened in the gate of Mary,*
> *I would be at the birth of Jesus.*"[214]

There is a notable parallel between the terms *breaking red dawn* and *vir-*

---

[209] Cf.: *"This gate shall be kept shut; it must not be opened. No-one may enter by it, for the Lord, the God of Israel has entered by it."* Ez 44:2 and see: "Gaudete", in: *Jistebnice Cantional 1420*, Oxford University Press:
"Gaudete, gaudete,
Christus est natus
Ex Maria virgine,
Gaudete.
[...] Ezechielis porta
Clausa pertransitur;
Unde lux est orta,
Salus invenitur."
(Let us rejoice, Christ is born of the Virgin Mary, Rejoice! [...]The closed gate of Ezekiel has been penetrated, from the origin of light [= the East] salvation has come.)

[210] Sometimes: *"Mary is resting in me"*

[211] Or: *"by her"*? The gender of the word is not shown clearly in the context.

[212] E.g. in: prayer nr. 54

[213] In: prayer nr. 57

[214] In: prayer nr. 67: The praying purified person is bearing Jesus together with Mary. italics mine

*gin, unbroken soil.* It was a male duty to break the soil and to sow the seeds into it.[215] Consequently Mary's rest in the red dawn refers to her ripening age and at the same time to the moment of conception. The gate of the sanctuary looking to the *East*[216] turns into *the gate* of Mary, through which only purified souls can pass after *"the Lord, God of Israel"*.

Furthermore, the very location of both the physical and spiritual birth of a new life, the female *vulva* is often represented in the ancient Babylonian and Syrian/Anatolian art. This is in the form of a *triangle*[217], sometimes on the head of a bull, the horns of which refer to the female ovaries.[218] The *ovary* is depicted as the tips of an *omega*, at both sides ending in the form of a *spiral*[219]. All these symbols are signs of divine power and refer to the divine origin of female fertility and *life-giving ability*. Both the triangle and the omega are used as symbols of the male *God* in Christianity,[220] but the spiral, which has vanished as the symbol of the ovary, calls *female circulation* to our mind.[221] The original female symbols are transformed into a symbol of a *male* life-giving God through patriarchal interpretations.

Even Erdélyi emphasises the *virginity* of *Mary* whose biological-physical

---

[215] Cf.: "virgin/unbroken soil" as a female symbol, and "ploughing-sowing" as male symbols, in: Lükő 2001, 119–128; Falvay 2001, 37. But notice that *"unbroken, breaking"* can also be associated with violence, which refers rather to the dependence and defencelessness of the woman.
Cf. Falvay 2001, 127–131: Falvay shows the spiritual dimension within the natural bodily endowment itself. He does not separate the two. He refers also to Hungarian folk games that were usually played by adolescent girls. For example: A gate is made by the arms of two girls while all the other girls sing:
*"Come in, come in, green bough, green leaf,*
*the golden gate is open, just come in. "*
Similar representation can be found in the form of a terracotta from Cyprus (Chytroi) of the 7–6th century BC, which presents three women dancing round a bough or tree (cf. phallic symbol, but also the symbol of female fertility), hand in hand, in a closed circle (cf. vagina). Cf. Danthine, Hélène: *Le palmier-dattier et les arbres sacrées dans l'iconographie de l'asie occidentale ancienne*, 2 vol. (Texts and Plates), Geuthner, Paris, 1937, fig. 1097

[216] Cf. "red dawn"

[217] Cf. e.g. Akurgal, E. – Hirmer, M.: *Die Kunst der Hethiter*, Munnich, 1961, Table 35; Negbi, Ora: *Canaanite Gods in Metal. An archaeological study of ancient Syro-Palestinian figurines*, Tel Aviv, 1976, fig. 119, nr. 1701; Özgüç, Nýmet: *The Anatolian Group of Cylinder Seal Impressions from Kültepe*, Ankara, 1965

[218] Cf. Gimbutas 1989, 307, fig. 486. According to Falvay the triangle drawn onto the head of a bull originates from the Sumerian culture, cf. Falvay 2001, 104

[219] Cf. Frankfort, H.: *A Note on the Lady of Birth*, Journal of Near Eastern Studies 3, 1944, 198–200, fig. 1

[220] Meier-Seethaler, Carola: *Von der göttlichen Löwin zum Wahrzeichen männlicher Macht. Ursprung und Wandel großer Symbole*, Kreuz, Zürich, 1993, 139–183

[221] Meier-Seethaler 1993, 190, 212

*"gate"* is closed after the birth of the *"King of Kings"*. It has been commanded by *Yahweh* to keep the gate *shut.*[222] Nonetheless in the interpretation of the aforementioned prayers, the gate can *still* be entered *in a spiritual way*. During the process of purification, the person experiences a kind of *rebirth*. In this sense Mary's gate is the bridge between the two worlds of earth and heaven. Only purified people can get through it.

### The feeding, life-giving holy tree

Similarly, from an androcentric point of view the birth provided by the *divine* mother appears to be of greater value than that provided by a *bodily* mother. We shall soon point out the split between the highly mystified image of *Mary* – who becomes almost bodiless in church history – and all the *other*, "average" *women*. It leads back to the artificial distinction of *nature* and *grace* – body and soul – that was created by false patriarchal interpretations.

*Gudorf* draws attention to the central contents of the Christian ritual feasts that actually originate from *natural* physical experiences (*birth, nourishing, consolation*) of women. These everyday experiences became *inferior* and *derivative*[223] to those of the normative Catholic sacraments (*baptism, Eucharist, absolution*), which were then exercised in a highly spiritualised way only by *men*.[224]

Nevertheless the figure of the combined life-giving, feeding woman is well known, not only in the Hungarian folk religion. Even in the mythology of highly cultivated cultures like ancient Egypt can be explored obvious representations of respected female nourishing, as it is mirrored in the image of a holy tree called the *Sycamore (Ficus sycomorus)*, a wild, African type of fig-tree, similar to the mulberry tree. Its fruits are not as sweet and tasty as the real fig tree, but its wood has the capacity to resist rotting, therefore it was an important *component of building* in ancient times. And because it bears fruit multiple times a year, it also became the *nourishing tree of the poor*.[225] According to a text found in one of the pyr-

---

[222] Cf. Erdélyi 1999, 410–411

[223] Cf.: *Inter Insigniores*, in: Origins 6:33, February 3, 1977, par. 27

[224] Gudorf, Christine: *The Power to Create: Sacraments and Men's Need to Birth*, in: Horizons 14, 1987, 296–309

[225] See: Zohary, Michael: *Pflanzen der Bibel*, Calver Verlag, Stuttgart, 1983. Cf. *"The king made silver as common in Jerusalem as stones, and cedar as plentiful as sycamore-fig in the Shephelah."* [1 Kings 10:27]; *"The bricks are fallen, but we will build in hewn stone; the sycamores are hacked down, but we will use cedars instead."* [Is 9:10]

amids, it stands by the eastern *gate of heaven*[226], from which *Re*[227] emerges every morning. The tree is, in other words, in the *eastern heaven*[228] and all the gods sit in its foliage. In this way it becomes the *"heavenly tree"*, connected with the goddess Hathor who was called, especially in Memphis, the *"lady of Sycamore"*, but it also appears in the form of the *heavenly goddess, Nut.*[229]

*"Also the Virgin Mary, our mother sits over there,*
*in the garden of Eden, on the bough of the golden twig."*[230]

The bough can refer both to female fertility and to the female overcoming of male authority.

The wild fig tree is most often represented on the decorations of pharaohs' tombs in a partly human form offering food and water from its foliage to the dead person.[231] The most unusual representation of the *feeding tree* has been found in the burial vault of Thutmosis III. (18th dynasty, 1540–1295 BC), where the tree *gives the breast to the king from its leafy boughs.*[232] Giving birth and breastfeeding are attached in the image of the feeding Sycamore standing by the birth giving eastern gate of heaven. (Table II. / Fig. 10.)

In the Hungarian religious tradition Jesus' birth binds the image of *Mary's gate* giving birth to her Son in red dawn (in the location of the rising sun, namely, in the East). It also binds the image of the life-giving *tree* or *bough* symbolising female genealogy, but often with its male crown on the top.[233]

Even if Mary, the queen of heaven, or the church itself (the "maternal holy church"[234]) appears in a similar way on medieval paintings,[235] this *motherly* feature of nourishment, in the Middle Ages, is mainly associated with

---

[226] Cf. "the gate of Mary"

[227] Cf. *Re* as sun-symbol > Jesus as sun-symbol

[228] Cf. East or *"red dawn"* as the place of sunrise, and in our texts as reference to the fertility of Mary and to the birth of Jesus.

[229] Cf. Posener, Georges – Sauneron, Serge – Yoyotte, Jean (eds.): *Knaurs Lexikon der ägyptischen Kultur*, Droemersche Verlagsanstalt Th. Knaur Nachf., Munnich, 1960, 167

[230] Cf. Prayer nr. 278, supplement

[231] Cf. Danthine, 1937, fig. 955, 956; Piankoff, Alexandre – Rambova, Natacha: *Mythological Papyri*, 2 vol., (Egyptian Religious Texts and representations III), NY, 1957, nr. 9

[232] Cf. Posener – Sauneron – Yoyotte 1960, 167

[233] See both prayer nr. 72 (below) and prayer nr. 300 (above): *"Mary gave birth to her Holy Son"*

[234] anyaszentegyház

[235] Cf. e.g. Falvay 2001, 179. The faithful are nourished by milk coming from breasts hidden under the cloak of the crowned woman, symbolising the church.

the *male* Jesus on the cross whose blood flows either into a cup held by angels, or directly into the mouths of the faithful.[236] This shows again, in contradiction to our texts, the male monopolisation and the perpetuated denial of the female body. The life-giving tree turns into the image of the Redeemer hanging on the cross. In this way the blood of the suffering Son is synonymous with the maternal feeding milk and blood, and symbolises the nourishment of both body and soul.[237]

The divine mother of the watery centre

In numerous prayers the Divine Kingdom is associated with Mary rather than with Jesus, in which Mary appears as *the mother of power*.[238] Because of total lack of paternal presence, *she* is the one who is sitting on golden throne like a queen that mirrors most probably feudal social relations:

> *"The Happy Beautiful Virgin Mary starts out with her Blessed Holy Son,*
> *enters her holy church,*
> *sits in her* golden[239] *arm-chair,*
> *her Son tells her:*
> *set free, my happy holy mother,*
> *my hands from my swaddling-bands [...] "*.[240]

She is usually in the *central point* of the scene.[241] This centre is often represented in the allegory of an island *in the middle of the sea*, which calls to mind the ancient waters of the very beginning that appear as specific ele-

---

[236] Cf. Soskice, Janet Martin: *Blood and Defilement*, in: ET: Journal of the European Society for Catholic Theology, Tübingen, booklet 2, 1994. See also: Bynum, Caroline Walker: *Jesus as Mother. Studies in the Spirituality of the High Middle Ages*, University of California Press, Berkeley, 1982.

[237] See its detailed interpretation below.

[238] Cf. Prayer nr. 13

[239] See the interpretation of gold above.

[240] Prayer nr. 7, italics mine

[241] *"In a house there are four corners, four angels in each,*
*the Virgin Mary in the middle, who takes care of her Son. "*, in: Prayer nr. 51;
*"Over there I see a consecrated holy chapel,*
*in that a consecrated holy chair,*
*Mary, our grandmother* (cf. great mother) *is sitting on it,*
*Saint John, the Baptist went to her, and asked:*

ments of different creation stories.[242] The symbol of the sea presages the sea of Mary or Jesus' tears as it is expressed in many passages.[243] Verses like "a palm in the *sea* gave birth to its bough",[244] "you are also the source of the *sea* of mercifulness",[245] "our lady, the Beautiful Virgin Mary sits outside, on the black earth, in the middle of the Red *Sea* "[246] recall a study about the "Hungarian God" from the 19th century.[247]

By following the centuries old Hungarian scientific research of tradition, *Kállay*, a Hungarian scholar of the 19th century extends the examination of the presumed continuity between Asian and Hungarian descriptions of the divine. While exploring *"trangi"*, an old Hungarian name of God, he takes into particular consideration several interesting aspects of the *Prodromus idiomatis scythico mogorico chuno avarici*, dated from 1770. This notion must be an ancient one, because it seems to have no etymological connection with *"Isten"*, the usual Hungarian expression for the divine. It involves the etym. *"is"* ~ *"ős"*, which means *"ancestor"* or *"ancestress"*. *"Trangi"* is related more closely to the concept *"tenger"*, denoting "sea" in Hungarian. Actually the Tartar notion *"trangi"* referred also to the sea.

The golden throne is not only the symbol of the ruling, divine status of Mary, but it refers also to the golden yellow colour of *honey*, which is the *food* of gods, and in this way it is the symbol of heavenly bliss.[248]

*"There is honey in your womb, let the whole world have a share in its wax* (or: *"let the whole world share in it ")*. "[249]

---

*What are you reading, Mary, our grandmother?*
*Oh, of course, I read, because I have enough to read.*
*Go out to Sinai, there you will see [...] ",* in: Prayer nr. 131

[242] Cf. Bosnyák, Sándor: *A világ teremtése a moldvai magyarok mondáiban* [The creation of the world in the legends of Hungarians comes from Moldva], in: Dankó – Küllős 1987, 348–354. Here Bosnyák is referring to Ural-Altaic (Vogul, Votjak, Cheremiss, Mordvine, Türkish, Bulgarian) creation stories. In another recent collection Bosnyák points out additional parallels of Babylonian, Mongolian and Greek legends in the Hungarian myths of genesis. In: Bosnyák 2001, 5–6

[243] Mary or Jesus is sitting in tears or in blood up to their elbows. The motif can be found e. g. in prayer 44, see above.

[244] Prayer nr. 72, italics mine

[245] Prayer nr. 306, italics mine

[246] Pócs 1986, 188, italics mine

[247] Cf. Kállay, Ferencz: *A pogány magyarok vallása* [Religion of pagan Hungarians], Lauffer and Stolp, Pest, 1861, reprinted by Püski, Budapest, 1999, 9–19

[248] Cf. Falvay 2001, 131

[249] Prayer nr. 273. supplement. Italics mine. Cf. in Hungarian: *"womb"* is *"méh"*, which also

*The divine nourishing honey* is the symbol of heavenly joy. The suckling infant is often attributed to this heavenly "sweet" joy. This is probably why honey and milk come into close connection in the following section:

*"Do you know where the bee comes from? When the Lord Jesus was born, the Virgin Mother had an enormous amount of milk, and it flowed out of both her breasts. For the little Jesus it was too much to suck. And well, she said: 'Woe, what comes next?' And in that moment the milk-drops coming out of her breasts turned into bees flying away."*[250]

"Being full of happiness" in Hungarian literally means *"swimming in happiness"*, which goes back to the divine embryonic state in the amniotic fluid, within the protection of the maternal womb or to the ancient waters, above which the blessing spirit (the female רוח) of God floats. The following quotation confirms this female origin:

*"You are the holy mother of the Great Merciful One,*
*you have carried the Great Mercifulness*
*through nine months in your virgin womb,*
*and what is more, you are also the* source *of the sea of mercifulness."*[251]

The amniotic fluid is identified with the infinite divine mercifulness. Representations of the female source of water appear on old Syrian and Akkad cylinder seals, where water flowing from jug(s) held by the goddess is offered to the combatant or king.[252] In this way we finally return to the symbol of the Goddess of the infinite sea.

---

means: *"honey bee"*. This coincidence refers to the ancient mythological figure of Artemis, who appears as queen-bee on a Sumerian representation. See: Falvay 2001, 45; but also: Barna, Ferdinánd: *ősvallásunk főistenei* [The principal gods of our ancient religion], MTA, Budapest, 1881, 70: The womb is described here in a quoted ballad as a dark beehive (*méh*kas). Quoted also by Falvay 2001, 45–46

[250] Bosnyák 2001, 47

[251] Prayer nr. 306. Italics mine. Cf.: *Gen 1:1.*: "In the beginning": בראשית > *"beginning"* (or "the first, the best part"): ראשית > from *"head"*, *"top"*: ראש; *Jn 1:1.*: "the beginning": ἀρχή: *beginning, starting-point, origin, source,.* Here Mary is the source of the sea (of mercifulness ~ of God, of Jesus, of the Word).

[252] Cf. El-Safadi, H. *Die Entstehung der syrischen Glyptik und ihre Entwicklung in der Zeit von Zimrilim bis Amitaquamma*, UF 6. 1975, 313–352, fig. 61; Boehmer, R. M.: *Die Entwicklung der Glyptik während der Akkad-Zeit*, Untersuchungen zur Assyriologie und Vorderasiatischen Archäologie 4, Berlin, 1965, fig. 542. Both representations can be seen in the Louvre.

## The immortal and sensible Divine Good Shepherd

I would like to refer here to a marvellous example of an argument that transpired between Mary and Jesus in a prayer in which three "souls" arrive at the gates of heaven. Jesus, Mary and Peter are waiting for them. The first one is pure, the second one is not as pure, and the third entirely guilty. A threefold classification of the world is given: Jesus decides the destiny of the three visitors as follows: the first one can enter heaven, the second one has to go to purgatory and the third one is sent to hell. Peter is assigned the task of interpreting Jesus' judgement to those involved. Mary appears and acts here in the image of the caring *Good Shepherd* of the New Testament. At this grievous moment Mary interferes in the *men's* world and intervenes on behalf of the one Jesus sent to hell, in a typical feminine way. She argues on the basis of emotions:

> *"Do not take this sinner to the bottom of hell,*
> *because when You were crucified*
> *I almost died [...]"* – says Mary to her Son.

Jesus is, however, inflexible. He adheres to the strict moral truth and He calls upon Peter again to do his duty. Mary continues her argument:

> *"Oh, my Son, my beloved Holy Son,*
> *do not take this sinner to hell,*
> *because when You were removed from the cross*
> *and were put into my holy virgin lap*[253]
> *I almost died."*

Because Jesus remains unmoved she pleads with him a third time:

> *"Oh, my Son, my beloved Son,*
> *when You were put into the tomb,*
> *I almost died."*

Here she is not asking Jesus not to send the sinner to hell, rather she only reminds Him with repeated emphasis of her heartfelt deep suffering, of the

---

[253] Notice: *"lap"* in Hungarian is: *"öl"*; in verbal use means also "kills"; but *"ölel"* means "gives a hug" which is in a more abstract level: "giving life". In this way a person with *lap* is the master of life and death. Midwives could tell us more about it.

sorrow for the loss of the most beloved One.[254] And the power of her words brings life to the sinner:

*"Oh, my mother, my beloved mother,*
*if this sinner is so dear to you,*
*take him/her into your holy arms,*
*take him/her into My Holy Kingdom,*
*let every kind of songs sound,*
*because there is greater joy over one sinner who repents*
*than over ninety-nine righteous people[255]. "[256]*

This discussion paints an authentic picture of the average European "Christian" family that has existed throughout the centuries in which the man, in the best case, was ready to make concessions to the women of his household who were obedient to him. Mary appears here as the *merciful caretaker* in contradistinction to the *dreadful Judge.*[257]

She is the one who leads to eternal life,[258] it is *her* name to be praised,[259] and she is the immortal one who dies for us.[260] She is the only one who hears the complaint:

*"A little bird flew up from the iron forest,*
*she built an iron nest,*
*laid an iron egg,*
*hatched an iron nestling,*
*walked along green grass, under leaves,*
*she did not find food anywhere for the little one,*
*she started to wail,*
no one listened to her, only the Happy Virgin Mary [...]"[261]

---

[254] It seems as though Jesus had nothing to do with his own passion, as if the figure of the risen Christ (here He is rather a dreadful judge) would have forgotten the experiences of the suffering Jesus. It reflects the ecclesiastical interpretation of the Lord of life and death rather than the original message of the gospels.

[255] Cf. Lk 15:7

[256] Prayer nr. 206

[257] Cf. also *"Through your entreaty commute the fair judgement of the dreadful Judge to compassion"* [ > com-passion > suffering together > having empathy towards the other], in: Prayer nr. 306. See furthermore stories of the OT where both these features appear in God's attitude to his/her folk.

[258] *"Mary, lead me to eternal life!"*, in: Prayer nr. 278

[259] *"The name of Mary is praised"*, in: Prayer nr. 53

[260] *"Oh, Mary, my mother, immortal, die for me."* in: Prayer nr. 111

[261] Prayer nr. 260, italics mine

The poor, worried peasant mother expresses her anxiety through a comparison, in which Mary's character is the positive message of hope in the midst of everyday struggle for survival.

The exceptional ability to hear, and the particular abilities in general, refer always to divine characteristics in symbolism,[262] but also to deep empathy that used to be associated with maternal love.

> *"Wake up, wake up Beautiful Virgin Mary,*
> *your Son has been caught,*
> *His side has been stabbed with a lance,*
> *a crown of thorns has been placed on His head,*
> *one drop of His blood has dropped down,*
> *the angels picked it up,*
> *took it up and put it before our Lord Christ,*
> *our Lord Christ is there in tears up to the elbows,*
> *in blood up to the knees,*
> *the Happy Woman, while taking a rest,*
> *looks through her window,*
> *there she sees a beautiful church,*[263]
> golden without, merciful within.
> *Who says this prayer in the evening [...] "*[264]

*"The motherly heart is a window. When you look into it you see God. "*[265] The Hungarian Jesuit, Nemeshegyi points out an essential difference between dominantly male images of God in the Bible and interpretations of the divine in the Eastern religions characterised by female, most often maternal features. The religious effect of the Far East is mirrored obviously in the maternal representation of Mary in Christianity.[266]

---

[262] Cf. Hoppál, Mihály – Jankovics, Marcell – Nagy, András – Szemadám, György (eds.): *Jelképtár* [Collection of symbols], Helikon, Budapest, 1990, 27, 152

[263] Notice that by the Hungarian speaking natives of Moldavia "church" means the place of the ritual, the community of the ritual, and the ritual itself at the same time. In: Tánczos 2000, 75

[264] Prayer nr. 44

[265] Nemeshegyi, Péter: *A Szép Szűz Mária Japánban* [The Beautiful Virgin Mary in Japan], in: Szolgálat, Eisenstadt (1975) Nr. 24, 73–80, here 75

[266] Cf. Nemeshegyi 1975, 73–80

## THE DESTRUCTIVE "BEAUTIFUL WOMAN"

Strangely the power of *beauty* describing the goodness of the Happy Woman, who is the Babba (~ the *Beautiful*), and identified with the "*Beautiful* Virgin Mary" is often associated rather with the dangerous and harmful "Beautiful Woman", whose activity is surrounded and supported by further numerous "beautiful women". Her witchcraft is a rather negative, destroying power against everything that represents Life coming from the Happy Woman.

The beautiful women usually come together in the darkness of the night on the lawn; they dance and clap hands. Whoever is lured to their group, will be danced to death by them.[267] Their invisibility at midnight, at midday or from midnight until daybreak manifests ghostlike features. Some believed that they lived in caves and took care of treasures being under curse.

The bed of the Beautiful Woman, in opposition to the life-giving and protecting bed of the Happy Woman, is the birthing bed of the unfortunate, which can mean the birth of a dead or ill child, or the death of the mother. According to the Hungarian popular belief the Beautiful Woman can easily exchange the healthy infant for an unhealthy, ugly child[268] if the mother is not wide-awake enough. Her evil power connected with the bed can also be the cause of venereal diseases.

Drinking from the cup of the Beautiful Woman, in opposition to the cup of the Happy Woman for blessing toasts, causes headaches. All those, who are covered in rashes, surely fell previously into the dish of the Beautiful Woman. Her name, in contradistinction to the always-praised name of the Happy Woman, should not be mentioned at all, because She does them harm. Her spit is bewitching, and hounds the person to death.[269] In contradiction to the holy healing breath of the Happy Woman, Her wind is rather an all-destroying tornado and hurricane that arises from Her and Her fellows' gaiety and often called the "dance of the beautiful women". The mythological beings go to drink to the well of the beautiful women.[270]

These female mischievous fellows sometimes appear in the figure of three cursing, bewitching women[271] who are the negative equivalent of the three healing women assisting the Happy Woman.

---

[267] Bihari, Anna (ed.): *Magyar Hiedelemmonda Katalógus* [Catalogue of the Hungarian myths of belief] , MTA Néprajzi Kutatócsoport, Budapest 1980, 149

[268] "changed child", see e.g. in: Bihari 1980, 40

[269] Ortutay, Gyula (ed.): *Magyar Néprajzi Lexikon* [Hungarian ethnographical encyclopedia] I–V, Akadémiai Kiadó, Budapest, 1982, vol. 5, 5

[270] Cf. Gunda, Béla: *Szépasszonyok kútja* [The well of the beautiful women], in: Ethnographia, Magyar Néprajzi Társaság, Budapest, 1947, 281–282

[271] Pócs 1986, 173, 174, 175

# THE HUMAN WOMAN:
# BLESSED OR CURSED FEMALE STATE?

Female issues can be understood only by someone who is in community of fate. In the following selected sections Mary appears as a real, bodily present woman whose lot is cast with all her fellow females. Nonetheless Mary has a much more active role in these texts than would normally be expected from a woman, and therefore she is an encouraging example for all women.

## ANCIENT FEMALE CHARACTERISTICS

### *The cooking-wise woman*

Several passages indicate that, despite her divine characteristics, Mary, just like her Son and all those poor people who say this prayer, come from the lower class:

*"Your nurse is not a queen, from a servant I turned into your mother."* [272]

According to the peasant female narrator she is doing the same jobs, that are done by all her female fellows of the lower class. Being a servant means for a peasant woman to take care of others' own beside her tasks in her own family circle: to clean others' house, to look after others' children, to cook for others' family, to wash others' clothes, and even to attend to others' kitchen-garden.

Female difficulties of a peasant culture is well described by the Peasant Bible:

*"The Virgin Mother and hers were very poor. They only had food for the same day. One morning there was nothing left in the pantry. The Virgin Mother turned to Saint Joseph and told him that she had no idea what to cook for dinner today because nothing was left to cook. Just then a pigeon flew in through the window. Joseph said, 'You see, here is the ingredient'. They caught it, the Virgin Mother cooked it, and they had it for dinner. It happened so that no one will be sorrowful, because God always orders as much as we need."* [273]

---

[272] Prayer nr. 239
[273] In: Lammel – Nagy 1995, 162

Mary is the fellow sufferer of all – everyday peasant women and men involved in the story. The average family scene finishes here with a miracle, with a "happy end" to encourage the story-teller herself and her family that often has nothing to eat.[274] Male and female attitudes are described different- ly here. Mary appears as a worrying woman in contradistinction to Joseph who according to the story seems to be much more relaxed. Further on we shall explore this great distinction between the cocksure man and the unsure and anguished woman.[275]

Cooking is however an only too obvious female task, therefore in our con- text it also goes without saying anything more in detail about one of the most important everyday female acts throughout the centuries. Although in the past and even now in tribal cultural communities, it plays a special ritual role in the religious process. The continuous stirring in a certain rhythm, drawing many times the same circle as a symbol of wholeness with the accompani- ment of songs about the divine female power, has a magical influencing power on the food or drink that has been made.

*"When Jesus was on the earth,*
*The Virgin Mary cast water on her Holy Son,*
*from boughs,*
*from thistles,*
*from flowers.*
*It did the little Jesus good.*
*In the same way let my water casting be efficacious to you, Ilona. "*[276]

The female knowledge and taming of natural forces during the cooking act has been forgotten and turned into unpleasant automatism of the accelerated modern woman. Cooking as part of the healing process is replaced by artifi- cial, industrial products both in the form of food and medicine that makes the woman uncreative and cuts her off from her female roots.[277]

In several languages "cooking" is not only the action of the hands, but also of the *soul* and *mind*. Making plans is in close relation with the English con- cept "brew". At the same time it is described in Hungarian with the words

---

[274] Cf. *King* (1995) mentioned above: *"Marginalised people turn into heroes of their own world with the help of their own imaginations. "*
[275] See the description below of dreaming in a regressive-female and in a progressive-male way.
[276] Prayer 5. supplement
[277] Achterberg 1991, 143–161: Die Geburt der modernen Medizin – ohne Heilerinnen.

*"cooking"* (= "főz") or *"boiling out"* (= "kifőz"). All these expressions refer to the intensive spiritual-mental work that had to accompany every ancient female activity.

## The spinning-wise woman

According to the story teller, because she came from the lower class Mary had to work hard for a living:

*"The Blessed Virgin earned her daily bread by spinning.*[278] *She spun for other women, and the little Jesus carried the yarn made by the Blessed Virgin to them [...]"*[279]

According to Pueblo-Indians spinning was the first act of creation of the most ancient first Beginning, the Goddess called *Spinning* or *Thinking Woman*, who divided the earth into four pieces in this spinning way.[280] It was delineated as a circle (the earth) with a cruciform core (the two yarns running from East to West and from North to South):

The connection between spinning *("fonás")* and thinking *("gondolkodás")* is well known in different languages and their cultures. The English expression *"spin a yarn"* means *"tell a tall story"* or *"tell a lie"*. In Hungarian the thought has its yarn *("a gondolat fonala")* that can be followed (understood) or lost (not understood) by its listener. The back side of cloth ("fon-ák") is in etymological and semantic relation with anomaly ("fon-ákság"). Machination and intrigue have the same Hungarian expression ("fon-dorlat") and are in close connection with magic art and witchcraft. Both the Hungarian and English synonym for intrigue (*fon*-dorlat, *fon* = spin) is weaving (= szövés) intrigues ("cselszövés"). The two distinguishable, but related handicrafts are used figuratively here to describe complex processes of cogitation.

---

[278] Cf. The motif of spinning in fairytales like "Sleeping Beauty". Here the *old spinning woman* symbolises *witchcraft.*

[279] Lammel – Nagy 1995, 163–164

[280] Stone, Merlin: *Ancient Mirrors of Womanhood. Our Goddess and Heroine Heritage*, 2 Volumes, New Sibylline, New York, 1979, Vol 2, 92

Spinning also refers to *rotation*, which formula is found in many Hungarian (and also other nations) children's games played most often by girls. The rotation is the symbol of the whole circle of the year, of the circulation of nature, and therefore the symbol of femaleness.[281]

> *"Our lady, the Beautiful Virgin Mary sits outside,*
> *on the black earth,*
> *in the middle of the Red Sea,*
> her distaff is in her lap,
> *she* spins *on her distaff,*
> she rocks her blessed Holy Son in her lap."[282]

Both the distaff and the child in the female lap refer to fertility.

But it is also a sign of the overburdened woman, to whom all the work in the household was left and, at the same time, the upbringing of the children. This type of family model is valid not only in peasant communities, but also in the middle class, as is reflected in numerous medieval works of art.[283]

## The house as a symbol of womanhood

The spinning and cooking woman within the walls of the house is actually a typical theme of medieval fine arts.[284] These representations *of the woman being within the house* can simply be the confirmation of the fact, that *the*

---

[281] See below how this divine, powerful circle turned into the circle of inner support against external violent male force.

[282] Cf. Pócs 1986, 188. Quotation from a Hungarian manuscript from 1635, italics mine

[283] Cf. Heemskerck, Maarten van: *Portrait of a married couple*, 1529, Amsterdam, Rijksmuseum; Illustration to *"Nützliche Lehre und Predigt, wie sich zwei Menschen in dem Sakrament der heiligen Ehe halten sollen"*, xylograph made by Johann Bämler, 1476, Augsburg, in: Schramm, Albert: Der Bilderschmuck der Frühdrucke, 23 volumes, Leipzig, 1920–1940, vol. 3, 469. Württembergische Landesbibliothek, Stuttgart; Illustration to *"S. Bernardus Haushalten"* xylograph made by B. Buchpinder, 1488, Munnich. The following image of family life is reflected on both xylographs: the father is *counting*, the son is *reading*, mother and daughter are both *spinning*, while the mother also rocks the cradle with her leg (performs housework and childcare at the same time).

[284] Cf. spinning woman: *"February"* from *"Breviarium Grimani"* Fol. 2ᵛ, Venice, Bibliotheca Marciana lat. XI. 67, miniature made by Simon Bening, around 1514–1516; kneading woman: Getijdenboek (Golf) MS. ADD. 24098, f. 29ᵛ, around 1500, British Library, London

*house*, especially if it is round[285], is again a *female* symbol.[286] It is associated with the *maternal womb*,[287] and in a wider sense, with *defence*.

Nonetheless this originally positive meaning disappeared through the reinterpretation of family roles inside and outside the house through the course of centuries. Male and female jobs were gradually fixed in stable images, in which the house meant comparatively freedom for the man and imprisonment, or confinement[288] for the woman.[289] In this way the beginning formulation of the prayers "I am going *out of my house*" becomes a strong expression of female yearning for freedom, in which female power dominating and confirming, is found.[290]

## FEMALE PRIESTLY MINISTRY

Numerous religions are familiar with female priestly ministry, depending on the dominating gender roles of the surrounding society and culture. The fate of Christian female clergy had no exception. Although the attitude of Jesus radically changed the understanding of the gender functions, this new view of equality existed in early Christian communities however could not survive the long-term patriarchal social-religious pressure. The communal life in the first two centuries of Christianity concentrated within the walls of private family houses, where women as the heart of the household always played a special role. This position in the family helped them to be practically prepared for ecclesiastical tasks and offices. They often engaged themselves to patronage of certain communities that led them to responsible leading posts within the local and later also in the universal church.

---

[285] See more about round and quadrate houses in: Tánczos 2000, 99–101: The *round* shape refers to the nomadic tenters, and it symbolises the intimacy of the already realised defence (garden, fruit, egg, stomach); the quadrate form, on the contrary, refers to the settled Hungarians living in real houses, which is the symbol of defensive inner integrity (house, city, citadel). Cf. also Durand 1969

[286] Cf. Falvay 2001, 43

[287] Cf. house and gate ~ womb and vagina. Notice that in old Hungarian the expression *"(become) round"* is the synonym of *"come into being"*, *"arise"*. In: Tánczos 2000, 188

[288] See above the connection with confinement as birthing bed.

[289] Cf. Ehlert, Trude: *Die Rolle von "Hausherr" und "Hausfrau" in der spätmittelalterlichen volkssprachigen Ökonomik*, in: Ehlert, Trude (ed.): Haushalt und Familie in Mittelalter und früher Neuzeit, Jan Thorbecke Verlag, Sigmaringen, 1991, 153–166; Dienst, Heide: *Männerarbeit und Frauenarbeit im Mittelalter*, in: Beiträge zur historischen Sozialkunde, 1981, Heft 3, 88–90

[290] Cf. the usual beginning formulation: *I go out of my house* (~ out of my earthy life or of my prison), *I look up* (~ far away from my everyday life) *to heaven* (~ to the fulfilling world of unfulfilled dreams), *where I see the Happy Woman* (~ the female power from which I can derive comfort, and I can take courage to survive).

The institutionalising process of the 3$^{rd}$ century damaged the vitality of these house churches and the colourful variety of leading functions that existed in them. During these centralising efforts these energetic, vigorous Christian groups slowly turned into a political corporation superintended by one single bishop. In the following two centuries a heavy fight developed against female leaders of ecclesiastical offices. Polemic writings of this period are the first documentation of arguments against female priestly ministry, based on Jesus' male character. As we have seen previously this hostile attitude towards women resulted in a society divided into a male territory of polis (town) associated with pride and real power and a female territory of the oikos (house) accordingly associated with private sphere and female shame to be hidden.[291] Women were put back and imprisoned into their household to exercise female power, far away from public political-ecclesiastical offices regarded anew only as male privileges. The male (and later also female) representatives of this gender-based idealisation of both social and ecclesiastical functions formed only a minority group in the first three centuries, the institutionalising interests however then gave free rein to these destructive ideas.[292]

Even in these patriarchal circumstances there always existed and continued to develop a tradition that cherished the memory of female spirituality of the so-called house churches and entertained the female awareness of the right to equal ecclesiastical positions in a male dominated Church for the moment.

### Motherhood as sacrificial priesthood

Our examples of Mary the priest refer surely to the pagan roots of female magical power, but sacerdotal function attributed to Mary is not alien in Christian tradition either. "*[...] She always offers the Eucharistic sacrifice, just as, at one with Him, she offered the sacrifice on Calvary.*"[293] (Fig. 2.)

---

[291] Cf. below the female-regressive and the male-progressive way of dreaming.

[292] Torjesen, Karen Jo: *Als Frauen noch Priesterinnen waren*, Zweitausendeins, Frankfurt am Main, 1995, 14–17

[293] Ferdinand Chirino de Salazar SJ (1575–1646), quoted by Wijngaards, John: *The Priesthood of Mary*, in: The Tablet, vol. 253, 4 Dec/1999, 1639

Posony Cfudalat Képe    Boldog Aſſony Posonyban.

Fig. 2. "The Image of the Miracle of Pozsony - The Happy Woman in Pozsony"[294]

This sentence is in harmony with a Hungarian representation of the Pieta, print of Pozsony,[295] of the turn of the 17th–18th century: The dead body of Jesus held in his mother's arms is covered by a sacerdotal stole hanging down from Mary's shoulders.

In the prayers there is a clear *exchange between the roles of Jesus and Mary*. It is often she who sends the apostles or even Jesus to the world to proclaim the good news. It is Mary who says: *"Amen, amen, I tell you [...]"*.[296] It seems that the two characters are deeply dependent on one another. The texts show an almost symbiotic relationship between mother and Son.[297] Let

---

[294] Mary as priestess, see its representation in: Esterházy, Pál: *A Boldogságos Szűz képeinek eredete* [The origin of the images of the Blessed Virgin], Nagyszombat, 1696 (Országos Széchenyi Könyvtár, Budapest, RMK1/1496)

[295] Now: Bratislava/Slovakia

[296] Cf. Prayer nr. 294

[297] Cf. Prayer nr. 146: The exchange of roles completes the identity of the two characters:
*"Where does our Lord Jesus Christ pray?*
*In His beloved garden,*
*in His beloved chair,*
*in blood up to the knees in tears up to the elbows,*
*His hair is let down, a book is in His hand,*
*He is reading it with tears in His eyes,*
*St Peter and St Paul are passing by,*
*and asking Him: 'Why are you crying, my Virgin Mother, Mary?'"*, *italics mine*

us look at the reasons behind and the consequences of this strong social and emotional link between the two persons.

There exists a long tradition of maternal Marian priesthood. She exercised priestly functions by offering Jesus as a sacrifice both after His birth at the Presentation in the Temple,[298] and before His death on Calvary. This fact is illustrated by many ancient writers and it is called *"valid implicit, latent Tradition"* by *Wijngaards.*[299]

## Substantial blood and milk

The most evident bodily sign of the relationship between mother and child is *blood* through which the mother feeds her foetus during its embryonic state. The blood carries *life,* and at the same time, blood running out of the channel of the well organised blood-vessels leads to the chaos of the system, to bloodlessness, which results in the end of life, or *death.* However the *microcosm* of blood circulation intercommunicates with the *macrocosmic* circulation of nature, therefore no one drop falling down is lost. This continuous intercommunication is wonderfully depicted in numerous prayers of our selection.

> *"Our Lord Christ is born today,*
> *His* (or her?) *Holy blood dripped down,*
> *the angels picked it up,*
> *the apostles tied it,*
> *three virgins played with it [...]"*[300]

It would be evident to interpret the blood dripping as the blood of the child-bearing mother for whom the sight of her own blood is "routine, and the message it gives is usually fertility and birth", while for a man "the sight of his own blood must always be associated with trauma, violence",[301] and wounds, just as rituals of initiation, circumcision and castration. This is why Neumann[302] is crit-

---

[298] Cf. Lk 2:22–35
[299] Cf. the homepage of John Wijngaards: *www.womenpriests.org*
[300] Prayer nr. 42. The holy blood dripping down originates from the mother, but in the minute, that the navel string is cut, the circulation of the child is physically separated from that of the mother. But this does not mean separation at the emotional level of "circulation".
[301] Cf. Beattie, Tina: *Mary, the Virgin Priest?,* in: The Month 257, December 1996, 485–493
[302] Neumann, Erich: *Die Große Mutter,* Olten, 1974

icised by Weiler for identifying menstruation and birth with female blood offering, that seems rather the projection of the patriarchal psyche.[303]

According to the texts of several selected prayers, the power of this blood circulation is used together with the substantial milk of the mother for purifying (= healing).[304]

> *"There I see a golden tree, gold without, merciful within,*
> *under that there is a golden basin,*
> *there are three drops of our Virgin* Mother's milk,
> *three drops of the Lord* Jesus' blood *in it,*
> *whoever washes oneself in it in the morning, in the evening,*
> will be remitted *one's seven mortal sins.* "[305]

Beside blood relationship there existed and played an even more particular role in numerous cultures the so-called "milk relationship", especially in Egypt and Mongolia. Milk not only means the general essentials of life for nomadic people, but also the sign of the binding power of the maternal breast, if two infants, even if being out of blood relation, suckle from the same female breasts. Milk relationship could even hinder marriage if both members of the loving pair were suckling at the same breast in their childhood.[306]

---

[303] Weiler 1991, 78

[304] Prayer nr. 270, italics mine: *"[...]* Away with you, Witch, *with the help of thousand boughs, with the help of the case of the virgin young woman,* with the help of the milk of the Happy Woman *[...]* ". The milk of the Happy Woman seems to be the healing power keeping off evil female witchcraft. This interpretation already mirrors a later patriarchal society, in which between women of the devil and the divine Goddess a total contradistinction is made. Cf.: *"Away with you, Satan"* Mt 4:10, Mt 16:23, Mk 8:33

[305] Prayer nr. 52, italics mine Cf. prayer nr. 54:
*"There I see little birds,*
*not little birds, but angels with wings,*
*crown under their wings,*
*in the crown a true garden,*
*the Garden of Eden,*
*in the middle of it a golden bough,*
*on that golden bough a golden nail,*
*on the golden nail a golden towel,*
*three drops of the blood of Jesus Christ,*
*three drops of the milk of the Happy Woman,*
*anyone who washes oneself in it, and dries oneself with the golden towel[...]* "

[306] This practice was also known in Hungary and in Southern Slav areas. Cf. also Hoffmann-Krayer – Bächtold-Stäubli, Vol 6, 1934/1935, 289

The importance of this connection is best described by a Mongolian legend, in which a king does not kill a boy, because he ate cake made with the milk of the boy's mother, that means that he is in milk relationship with the lad.[307]

This symbiotic relationship is fulfilled in the common suffering of mother and son. The whole message of the prayers is supported by the dominant framework of the Passion. Not only is the suffering emphasised here, but the person *who* suffers, the suffering of both male and *female*, and the mutual standby. Both son and mother ask one another: "*Why are you sad, my son/mother?*"[308] It is not only Jesus on the cross who offers His soul to God, saying: "*Father, into thy hands I commit My spirit*",[309] according to the male evangelist Luke, but also the praying peasant Hungarian women who *offer their soul "to the Virgin Mother, Mary lamenting under the high cross"*.[310] And it is not only Jesus' blood and water dripping down from the cross onto Mary,[311] but also the blood of the Happy Woman.[312] According to *Soskice*,[313] the blood and water flowing onto Mary basically refers to the fluids mingling together at childbirth. This logic is easy to follow in those images, in which the two characters are totally blended: the blood of either Jesus *or* Mary is picked up by either the angels, Jesus, Mary, *or* the *Happy Woman*,[314] carried into heaven, and put into the presence of either God, Jesus *or* the *Happy Woman*.[315] The circulation (of blood or of nature) does not require permanent separation and hierarchy of male and female elements. "*The language of sacrifice is used in a context that opens the imagination not primarily to the dead*

---

[307] Hoffmann-Krayer – Bächtold-Stäubli, Vol 6, 1934/1935, 289

[308] Cf. prayers nr. 16. supplement, 17, 48, 112, 127, 130, 158, 159, 160 (also Luke asks Mary: "Why do you cry, my lady, my *friend?*"), 161, 162 (Luke asks Mary), 163, etc.

[309] Lk 23:46; cf. Ps 31:5: "*into thy keeping I commit my spirit*"

[310] Cf. Prayer nr. 145; Jn 19:25: "*Standing by the cross was His mother.*"

[311] Cf. prayer nr. 174: "*Oh, my Son, my Son, my beloved Holy Son, I gave you birth not in order to carry the cross! Oh, my mother, my mother, I suffered the pains of hell, I broke hell...my side was stabbed with a lance, and blood and water dripped down onto my mother from it [...] My mother, do not cry for me, because I have to die anyway.*" See also prayer nr. 303

[312] Cf. prayer nr. 295. supplement: "*The Happy Woman looked through her large window... my Son, my Son, let us give our* (royal plural) *prayer to the sinful son of Adam, let anyone who knows proclaim it: seven drops of* the blood of our Great Lady *dripped down, angels picked them up [...]*", italics mine

[313] Cf. Soskice, 1994

[314] Cf. prayer nr. 300: "*One drop of His blood dropped down, the Happy Woman went there, picked it up, carried it into the high heavens...*", italics mine

[315] Cf. prayers nr. 43 (the presence of Jesus), 51 (the presence of Mary and Jesus), 55 and 266 (the presence of God), 268 (*"put into the presence of our mother, the Happy Virgin Mary"*), etc.

*and bloodied man on the cross and the violence that surrounds him, but to the mother's love for her child, a maternal sacrifice of love and care* for the salvation of the world."[316]

## Female tears and male blood in one cup

Women's need for a redeeming answer to their own everyday torments is most beautifully expressed in the image of the one cup offered at the altar which include both the blood of Christ and the tears of Mary, the symbols of both male and female suffering.

> *"As the Virgin Mother was crying,*
> her tears fell into the blood of Jesus,
> *the angels picked them up,*
> *put them into a* golden cup,
> *placed it on* the high altar.
> *Then the Virgin Mother told them:*
> Amen, amen, I tell you [...]"*[317]

The redeeming God also appears with both male and female characteristics:

> *"Oh, I greet the Happy Virgin Mary*
> *with these three angelic greetings,*
> *with 366 angels,*
> *Jesus takes my right arm,*
> *Mary takes my left arm,*
> *Carry me to heaven [...]"*[318]

Nevertheless the male understanding of the power of blood led to a negative attitude towards natural female fecundity.[319] The powerful, life-giving symbol of blood, namely the chaotic female fertility of the maternal pagan

---

[316] Cf. Beattie 1996, italics mine

[317] Prayer nr. 294, italics mine. See also: prayer nr. 301. supplement: *"Anne gave birth to Mary, Mary gave birth to her Holy Son. Mary let her tear fall, the angels picked it up, poured it into the cup [...]"*, italics mine

[318] Prayer nr. 37

[319] Cf. Irigaray, Luce: *Sexes and Genealogies,* Columbia University Press, NY, 1993, 73–88: Women, the Sacred, Money

cults, was therefore gradually replaced by the limited male Judeo-Christian interpretation of sacrifice, that is, the respect of laws based on social rituals associated with purity and impurity.[320]

## Mary reading mass

Dominating and officially supported Christian theological theories influenced by Greek philosophical ideas proclaim that the historical Jesus is the embodied symbol of the masculine-like rationalism, the *Logos*. In this way the incarnated Word points to the man as normative and to the woman as derivative.[321] This type of Christology results in the justification of male superiority, since the Son of God Himself chose the more honourable masculine form of incarnation. This is the basic point of official Catholic argumentation against ordaining women, because only the "natural (masculine) image" of Christ can authentically present Him.[322] Women, though able to receive the divine grace, are not allowed to act *in persona Christi*. It confirms the artificially created images of the female physical embodiment, whose body appears in this context only as a prison confining[323] and isolating from female identification with the divine. According to this approach the Word incarnated in female form is simply unimaginable.[324]

Nevertheless the Hungarian popular religion just as the religious folk tradition of most cultures involves really impressing motives of *Mary reading mass*:

*"I get out of my bed,*
*like the Lord Jesus from the coffin,*
*I go out, in front of my house,*
*I see the opened door of heaven,*
*gold within, mercy without,*
*our lady, the Virgin* Mary reads mass,

[320] Cf. Kristeva, Iulia: *Powers of Horror – An Essay on Abjection*, Columbia University Press, NY, 1982, 90–132. According to Kristeva, Christ was the only one who in Himself reconciled the maternal flesh of the pagan world and the linguistic order of Israel, but Christianity failed to live up to it.

[321] Ruether, Rosemary Radford: *Sexism and God-Talk: Toward a Feminist Theology*, Beacon Press, Boston, 1983, 117

[322] *Inter Insigniores*, in: *Origins 6:33*, February 3, 1977, par. 27

[323] See above: confinement

[324] LaCugna, Catherine Mowry (ed.): *Freeing Theology – The Essentials of Theology in Feminist Perspective*, HarperCollins, N. Y., 1993, 119

*she kneels on her holy knee,*
*she leans on her elbow,*
*she reads her holy reading.*
*St John passes there:*
*Leave it, leave, our lady, Virgin Mary,*
*your holy kneeling,*
*your holy leaning,*
*your holy reading,*
*because the innocent Jesus has been captured.*
*See, I told you, St. John,*
*you will be aware of it,*
*I shall be sorrowful in it.*
*Go to the black earth,*
*proclaim my little prayer,*
*who says this every morning,*
will be with me in Paradise."[325]

The concluding formula is not only a promise, but also the motivation to preserve the strong female tradition. Nevertheless in Erdélyi's commentary the verse about Mary reading mass is interpreted as Mary *attending* mass.[326] But in other cases, in which the same expression "reading mass"[327] can be found in relation *to Jesus, Peter or Paul*, Erdélyi does *not* have similar interpretations, guided probably by the wide-spread, general conviction that from a Catholic point of view reading mass seems to be "naturally" a *male task*, in contradiction to Mary (or any other woman).

We also find however the representation of the unquestionable powerful sacerdotal figure of *Mary reading mass* in the Peasant Bible as follows.[328]

*"Behind the beyond, beyond the seven seas, beside the house of my brother grew a poplar tree. It had 366 boughs, 366 ravens sitting in them, 366*

---

[325] Prayer nr. 125, italics mine

[326] Erdélyi 1999, 430. She tries to support this theory with the following reference: Bartók, Béla: Kol. 84. When I interviewed Erdélyi in Budapest on the 2nd September 2000, she claimed that the formulation of *"Mary reads mass"* was probably simply a mistake of the praying woman. She thinks that the peasant woman wanted to say: *"Mary hears mass"*. Nevertheless, as we shall see, Mary appears much more active in further popular religious texts than it is suggested by Erdélyi. Cf. Lammel – Nagy 1995, 281-287

[327] In Hungarian: *"misét szolgáltat"*, cf. prayer nr. 4, 73, 98, 129, 263 (Jesus); 115, 116, 117, 118 (Peter and Paul)

[328] Cf. Lammel – Nagy 1995, 281–287

*donkeys sitting by its base. Whoever laughs at my fairytale, or makes a joke of it, let that person's eye be hollowed out by those 366 ravens, and let s/he be butted by those 366 donkeys."* – begins the story. It goes on with the motif of virgin conception: After getting up and sweeping her room, a very holy woman finds one single pea on the floor which she tries to avoid but it is always in her way. She then eats it, and immediately becomes pregnant. She broods over what to do so that her pregnancy will remain a secret. She goes to the mountains in order to be devoured by wild animals. As soon as she gets to the forest she gives birth to a girl with golden-blond hair. She wants to take the little one back to the town to be baptised, but the Virgin Mary appears, and offers herself to take the little one to be baptised, and to return again with her at the age of twelve. She takes the girl who is then baptised. On the third day the girl has already grown up as a thirteen-year-old. Mary directs her to sweep ten rooms, but never to peep into the eleventh one. The girl is able to resist the temptation on the first six days, but on the seventh day she peeps in. She can see Jesus, Peter and Mary together in the room, where Jesus is reading mass, Peter and Mary however listen to Him. Later, when Mary asks her if she had seen anything, she disclaims everything. The same happens on the following day, but when she peers in she sees Peter reading mass, while Jesus and Mary listen to him. Afterwards the girl denies everything again. On the third day she again sees the three persons in the eleventh room where, this time, *Mary is reading mass,* while Jesus and Peter listen to her. But, this time, the girl is brutally punished as a consequence of her denial. First she is sent to the top of a big tree in the middle of the meadow. After continuous denial she falls out of the tree, and becomes blind and deaf. The girl then tries to hide under a hayrack. The Royal Prince passes there during hunting. When he notices his hound disappearing into the hayrack with a peace of bread, he follows it, and sees a golden hand reaching out from the hayrack, which he catches and surprised finds a beautiful, but blind and deaf girl. He carries her home, and marries her. When the old king is asked to go to war, the young prince offers to go himself instead of his father. Anxiously he leaves his pregnant wife at home who then gives birth to two children with golden-blond hair. Here *Mary appears again.* She heals the young mother in order to show her the two beautiful children. But while the young woman keeps on denying Mary threatens to seize her children. It does not help, the woman persistently denies. Mary carries the children away, makes the woman blind and deaf again, and leaves behind a bloody knife. The old king informs his son about his young wife who *"killed and ate her children"*. After the prince's return from war twelve wise men are asked how to exterminate the young queen. One 366-year old man looks at her and, as he is fascinated by her beauty, he suggests throwing her immediately to preserve. All the beasts go to attack her, but the eldest one acknowledges her as queen of the wild animals. He suggests that all animals open their mouths and blow warm air onto the woman who is freezing. Here *Mary appears again for the third time.* She again heals the woman only in order to show her all the beasts with opened mouths towards her. *"Do you believe, that your life is now really perishable?"* The young woman, at this time (when she is not attacked but actually cared for by the beasts), believes it, and proclaims that she had seen Jesus, Peter and Mary all reading mass one after the other in that particular eleventh room. *"And then, on the third day I saw the Virgin Mary reading mass, while Jesus and Peter were listening to her."* *"You see, my goddaughter, you could have told me earlier what you had seen, because then you would not have suffered so much."* And Mary creates a diamond castle with twelve floors, on a cock's leg, with a golden chain bound to a golden star, and turned always to the sun. It is all given to the young woman who also gets back her two children. In the whole world only one man, the Royal Prince, can manage to get up to the perpetually turning diamond castle, who then surprisingly recognises his beloved wife and children there.

When I asked the opinion of a psychoanalyst from München/Germany about the text, he gave me the following answer:[329]

− It must be a very individual story because of the many special elements in it.

− It is abundant in extraordinary phenomena like the 366 days, the miraculous conception, the beautiful child with gold-blond hair, the diamond castle etc., that all refer to transcendence.

− The virgin's conception through eating a pea means, that the mother, instead of giving birth, wants to eat her child (cannibalism).

− The "trinity" of Mary, Jesus and Peter is interesting from a feminist point of view, because here Mary plays the main role, the two men are only just mentioned. Mary is possessed of divine omnipotence, God the Father is not mentioned at all.

− What is fascinating from the point of view of ecclesiastical debate on women's ordination, is that Mary reads mass, consequently fills the role of a priest.

---

[329] Rudolf Pfitzner in Innsbruck, on 16th November 2001

– The real mother of the girl is forgotten, although Mary promised the mother to give back her daughter at the age of twelve. It can be connected with the twelve year old Jesus, who expresses his affiliation through the denial of his parents, but especially of his father, Joseph. The beauty of the girl separates her from her "simple" mother. She belongs rather to a royal environment, in which the female elements dominate; king and prince appear only in passing.

– When the girl does not stand the test dictated by Mary, and denies what she had seen and heard earlier, she is made blind and deaf by the punishing Mary, who is not the charitable mother anymore.

– But the girl's unearthly beauty conquers both men and later the beasts, who then choose her to be their queen. It shows the very human destiny, which is to control our primitive impulses.

– After having managed that, the grown-up girl can confess all that she had seen and heard so that Mary restores her to a special, almost superhuman, divine position.

– The storyteller, who had to be a very simple soul, but who, at the same time, had an excellent sense of symbolism, was able to express and elaborate her own problems through this created story.

Finally my psychoanalyst friend added: *"As a man, I would be afraid of the storyteller, but especially of Mary!"*

It seems obvious to me however that neither the storyteller nor Mary is the one to be afraid of, but the institutionalised state and ecclesiastical authorities that devastated the belief in female power by fire and sword in the past. It is not Mary or the storyteller who punishes the girl in a horrific way, but the surrounding judging *society* itself.

This torment is well illustrated in another story[330], in which the virgin's conception[331] takes place as the result of smelling roses. The parents of the pregnant girl consult the way to kill her. Finally, after listening to all the suggestions of the local residents, they cut her arms off, bind up her eyes and leave

---

[330] Lammel – Nagy 1995, 231–233

[331] The virgin conception is actually not unfamiliar to the Hungarian mythological mind. Emese, the ancient mother of Álmos (means: *"sleepy"*, *"having dream"*), the Hungarian tribal head, father of Árpád, was conceived in her sleep by a falcon. Later on the story became the symbol of the birth of the House of Árpád. Cf. *Képes Krónika* (Illustrated Chronicle), Magyar Helikon, Budapest, 1959, 74. See: Table II. / Fig. 11. *Emese with twigs in her hands symbolising fertility, falkon in the background.* Detail of a golden jug, part of the gold treasure of Nagyszentmiklós, 7-8th century (unearthed in 1799), in: Garam, Éva: The Nagyszentmiklós Treasure, Helikon, Budapest, 2002, 17 (Cf. the figure of the "bough-goddess", "Zweiggöttin")

her in the forest. The hunting Jesus (sic!) and Peter find her with two children. Her arms are cured similarly to the story of a gypsy Christmas prayer [see below]. In that version Mary calls upon the arm-less gypsy girl to pick up the baby Jesus. Here it is Jesus Himself, who invites the mother of the two children to wash them in the river. The naked woman is healed, her original state is restored, for Jesus provides her and her children with clothes, and with "kitchen, room, a beautiful home", which here is a sign of endowing with power and authority.[332]

Let us now see how the *ritual eating* as *unifying souls* was turned into the symbol of annihilation of another person, namely, to cannibalism. Psychoanalysts also attributed the eroticism of a kiss to cannibalism. According to Lükő the kiss originally refers to the exchange or the unity of souls. If we realise that our ancestors had drunk the blood of one another as a toast, and if we recognise the blood as the symbol of the living soul[333], then evidently food and drink also both refer to the unity and exchange of souls. The expressions *"my heart"*, *"I eat your heart"* or *"Let me eat you, my beauty"*[334] are told to the beloved lover (or "sweet*heart*") or a little child, and in this way eating is the symbol of love reflecting the yearning for unity.[335]


### Motherhood as discipleship

According to the Bible it seems that Mary and her female fellows were docile disciples at Jesus' side. As we shall see, Mary's spiritual ripening develops finally into complete identification with her Son. In the imagination of a peasant woman these created images are rather compensations of the *oppressed* popular cult permeated with the strong *character of the Goddess.*

As John's Gospel witnesses it was a *woman* who first proclaimed the good news of *new life* to the disciples.[336] In our case it is often the Virgin Mary *who is sent* to *proclaim the good news* in every part of the world.

---

[332] In contradistinction with the original meaning of ritual nakedness, that is total possession of one's own power. Cf. Hoppál – Szepes, 1987, 223–239, 224. While nakedness described by Hoppál refers to the divinely created original state of paradise and to the person being in the prime of life, our version follows rather the interpretation of nakedness as *shame* and taboo, God's punishment, the result of the Fall, here the Fall of the girl.

[333] see below

[334] in Hungarian *"Egyelek meg, szépségem"*

[335] Cf. Lükő 2001, 154–157

[336] See e. g. *"Mary of Magdala went to the disciples with her news: 'I have seen the Lord!' she said, and gave them his message."* Jn 20:18

*"Go, my mother, my Beautiful Virgin Mary,*
*to the black earth,*
*proclaim it to your sons,*
*proclaim it to your daughters... "*[337]

Or *she* is the one *who sends* the disciples and her own Son to proclaim the good news:

To Luke:

*"Go to the black earth,*
*proclaim my prayer... "*[338]

To Peter and Paul:

*"Go to the wide world, proclaim:*
*whoever says this [...], the* gate *of the heaven will be open for him/her. "*[339]

To Jesus:

*"A palm in the sea, gave birth to its bough,*
*its bough gave birth to its leaf,*
*its leaf gave birth to its fruit,*
*its fruit gave birth to St Anne,*
*St Anne gave birth to Mary,*
*Mary gave birth to her Holy Son.*
*Go, my Holy Son, my beautiful Jesus to the black earth,*
*direct Adam and Eve to proclaim it. Amen. "*[340]

She *baptises* in the circle of the twelve apostles:

*"Mary is exclaiming aloud at midnight:*
*Do you sleep, poor people?*
*Do sleep, poor people!*

---

[337] Prayer nr. 180. Cf. Mk 16:15. Jesus said to the apostles: *"Go forth to every part of the world, and proclaim the Good News to the whole creation. "*
[338] Prayer nr. 82
[339] Prayer nr. 99, italics mine
[340] Prayer nr. 72, see also above

*I shall baptise*
*with my five fingers,*
*with my hundred saints,*
*with thousands of angels,*
*with twelve apostles [...]* "[341]

The growing series of numbers (five, hundred, and thousands) that culminates in the figures of the twelve apostles[342] shows a special apostolic power behind the act. The named hour of the day (midnight) also refers to a particular, mysterious moment.

This motif goes on in the following strophe where time, space and roles are completely mixed up.[343] The original story of Bethlehem is influenced by the later Christian practice in an absurd way. Mary seems to become a Christian mother – already from Jesus' babyhood, long before the crucifixion, resurrection and even His baptism in the Jordan. The circumcision of Jesus is basically replaced by His baptism.

*"There is a rose in the middle of the field,*
*not a rose, but the happy Beautiful Virgin Mary,*
*who is swaddling her little Son*[344],
*is putting Him into the crib,*
*is making the sign of the cross on Him,*
*in this way let us also cross ourselves.*[345]
*Ready.* "[346]

We are already familiar with images of the anointing women, presented in the gospels.[347] We find the same motif connected with *Mary:*

---

[341] Prayer nr. 41

[342] According to the logic of mathematics the number twelve should fall out of queue here. But the power of the twelve apostles is more than that of thousands of angels.

[343] Notice that the Ural-Altaic people had probably no sense of the concept of *linear* time and were not aware of history, but saw everything in its entirety embraced by a kind of natural circulation. In: Lükő 2001, 83; Tánczos 2000, 317

[344] I am not able to translate it properly but rather *"changing the nappy of her little Son"*.

[345] In another version: *"He was put into the crib, was put into swaddling-clothes, was immediately baptised/christened there, let us be baptised/christened also in this way[...]"*, in: prayer nr. 58. The text refers to baptism/christening in childhood. The words "to cross (oneself)" and "to baptise" are confused here. Cf. in Hungarian: the cross = *kereszt;* to cross (oneself) = *kereszt*et vet; to baptise/christen = *kereszt*el!

[346] Prayer nr. 270

[347] *"Mary of Magdala, Mary the mother of James, and Salome bought aromatic oils intending to go and anoint him [...]"* Mk 16:1 (cf. Lk 24:1)

*"Here she comes, the Happy Virgin Mary,*
she brings us ointment, she brings the Eucharist[348],
*which purifies our wicked soul from damnation, amen. "*[349]

## Motherhood as political engagement

Mary is a sensible woman and therefore also political. Her active emotional compassion is stressed here more than in the original texts of the gospel. In our case she is not beside her crucified Son but on her way to find Him. She visits the wife of Pilate at the moment of the crucifixion so that through this encounter of female worlds behind male-dominant hierarchies she will be able to save her on. But she seems to be already too late.

*"Our lady, Virgin Mary sets out on a long journey,*
*roads grow sorrowful,*
*standing trees bow the knee and the head,*
*birds of the sky shed bloody tears [...],*
*our lady, Virgin Mary goes to the [...] house of Pilate's wife [...],*
*who asks her: What are you looking for, our lady, Virgin Mary?*
*I have looked for my blessed Holy Son for forty days and forty nights,*
*from hill to hill, from valley to valley,*
*but I did not find Him.*
*Go, my lady, Virgin Mary,*
*step five deep steps,*
*shed three bloody tears,*
*look up to the Calvary hill, to the high cross,*
*you will see your blessed Holy Son crucified [...] "*

This re-visioning and re-writing of Matthew's gospel[350] shows a truly real-

---

[348] italics mine, cf. *"I call the Virgin both priest and altar, she, the 'table-bearer' who has given us the Christ, the heavenly bread for the forgiveness of sins. "* Epiphanius II, 8th century, quoted by Wijngaards 1999, 1638–1640

[349] Prayer nr. 67. Prayed by a woman who learnt this prayer from her grandfather to whom it was passed by a 93 year old *nun.* It is prayed every day in the family, even by the children and the grandchildren. Cf. Prayer nr. 297: "Here she comes, the Happy Virgin Mary, s*he brings us the cup, the ointment, the Eucharist,* with which we salve our body and soul, that we will feel then relieved.", italics mine

[350] See Mt 27:19, here: Prayer no. 273

istic maternal love and devotion to human life in the simplicity of the country-side – far away from the official church teaching but very close to the experiences of all women. It is now the mother's desert of mourning. It is now Mary who is "led away by the Spirit into the wilderness"[351] for forty days and nights.

## DISCRIMINATION OF FEMALE FUNCTION

### Shameful bloody menstruation

One of the most basic signs of female fertility is menstruation. Mary, just like other women, had the monthly period. A story told by a woman from the northern part of Hungary shows a clear anthropomorphism shaped by local cultural customs that are noteworthy. In the past the everyday costume of women from this certain Hungarian area involved, among other things, seven skirts. Their consolation for the pain during their monthly period is the example of Mary whose blood *"was shown even through her seventh skirt, when she sat down during her purification. Only this spot left on her seventh skirt is passed onto us. We differ from her in having less than that of our Virgin Mother. Although she had a lot of it, but never complained. And how we complain!"*[352]

A woman from Moldova sees her own menstruation from another perspective: After the Fall it was the man first, a carpenter (sic!), to whom God left the monthly period, but because he did not realise his *shame* (did not feel ashamed!), and therefore did not address it, bloody spots were left everywhere on the shavings where he worked. His wife then followed him turning down all the shavings, because she *felt ashamed* of it. *"God told the woman: 'If you know so well the shame, then let it fall to your lot.' This is why women have it, because they know how to hide it."*[353]

### Impure pregnancy and child-birth

The hidden dimension of the concept *"purification"* expresses a similar negative view of the natural female monthly period, as the notion of *"shame"*. A similar attitude grew in relation to pregnancy or to the woman in *confine-*

---

[351] Cf. Mt 4:1

[352] Cf. Lammel – Nagy 1995, 163

[353] Cf. Lammel – Nagy 1995, 65, the story was collected by Vilmos Diószegi in 1951. See also Bosnyák 2001, 19

*ment*, in which the woman *herself* becomes taboo. The goal of these rules presented in a negative way was to save the community from what society saw as harmful phenomena. Most likely the prohibitions concerning pregnancy originally served to protect the expectant mother. It is difficult to uncover the process of how the originally protective attitude turned to a view of female sinfulness.[354] It is clear however that many of the taboos were gender-specific and were attached to fertility. They were regarded as holy states of female existence and, at the same time, as dangerous female power. In this way the woman herself gradually became simply dangerous,[355] losing entirely the holiness of her female being.

This negative attitude is well illustrated by *Csonka-Takács*[356], and also by the wide scale meanings of the English term "confinement"[357]. The menstruation[358], pregnancy to a certain degree, birth, the woman in birthing bed and all those who are connected with the child-bearing woman[359] were impure and therefore had to be isolated. The water used for washing clothes soiled by blood during the monthly period had to be poured out in a secret place. The clothes of the child-bearing woman, her bed[360] and her placenta[361] must have been annihilated in a similar way, hidden especially from the eyes of man. In order to save the tree from withering and the crop from rotting, during the monthly period climbing a tree or hoeing were forbidden[362]. For a pregnant woman conserving fruits or vegetables, and for a woman in child bearing, cooking, and carrying water from the well were not allowed, in order to save the food from impurity and the water from becoming spoiled.

---

[354] Cf. Douglas, Mary: *Purity and Danger. An Analysis of Concepts of Pollution and Taboo*, London-Hanley, 1966

[355] Frazer, James: *Az Aranyág* (Hungarian translation of "The Golden Bough"), Gondolat, Budapest, 1965, 129

[356] Csonka-Takács, Eszter: *Női tisztátalansági tabuk a magyar néphitben* [The taboos of female impurity in Hungarian folk belief], in: Küllős, Imola: Hagyományos női szerepek – Nők a populáris kultúrában és a folklórban [Traditional female roles – Women in popular culture and in folklore], MNT – SZCSM NT, Budapest, 1999, 266–272

[357] ~ detention, imprisonment, involuntary isolation

[358] In Hungarian it is mentioned often only as an *"illness"*

[359] The new-born baby, those who assist with the birth, but also the things touched by the child-bearing woman

[360] Her clothes and bed were removed similarly to those of a *dead* person.

[361] It was buried in the ground.

[362] Cf. the lectures given by *Kiss* in 1940 (EA 7820/45) and by *Diószegi* in 1950 (EA 4085/166), both quoted by Csonka-Takács 1999

But we never find a similar negative attitude toward Mary, except as the consequence of accidental misunderstandings.[363] Her motherhood is really a saving, divine state. Even now in rural communities the woman in birthing bed is often called woman lying in "the bed of the Happy Woman", and the toast is drunk to the new-born from the "glass of the Happy Woman".

The following story of the Peasant Bible however shows childbirth rather from the perspective of a single female left alone with her responsibility. The narrative focuses on divine punishment of all women who give birth out of wedlock:

> Jesus and Peter wander from village to village. Once they see a woman giving birth with great pain. Peter asks Jesus to pass half of this pain of women to men... Then they arrive at another village, where a woman, out of marriage, gives birth in the midst of the local residents, but no one knows, who is the father of the child. A man starts to wail, making obvious his paternal identity to the crowd. Therefore Peter asks Jesus again *"to give back the whole pain to the women, otherwise everyone will get to know whose child it is. In this way at least nobody will know."*[364]

Jesus and Peter's arrangement seems to defend the father and to leave the mother alone in the midst of communal scandal. Even if the story was interpreted by a peasant woman, it reflects unambiguously a patriarchal ordered rural community with its inhumane attitude towards women as evidenced by the words of Peter and the miraculous act of Jesus. We can imagine the subsequent destiny of a woman having a child without a husband in the local community. The man, however, is exempted from the consequences of his sexual relationship with the woman, from any kind of personal parental, marital, child caring responsibilities by the community of the village.

### Childcare as result of male divine punishment

In several texts of archaic prayers, Mary is often presented as a tender, car-

---

[363] See below Mary as "whore": The degrading attitude speaks about women in general, rather than about Mary herself.
[364] Lammel – Nagy 1995, 194–195

ing mother, who gives her baby a bath (in the Jordan),[365] swaddles him,[366] breastfeeds him,[367] tucks him in,[368] smiles at him,[369] and puts him to sleep.[370]

But male storytellers of the Peasant Bible demonstrate caring for the child rather as a result of *female disobedience* (to male desire) followed by divine *punishment.*

Once the women went to Jesus. All carried a child in their arms. They asked Jesus to allow them not to carry the child anymore, but as it is also in the world of animals, after a few days let their new-born walk. "Jesus replied: 'All right, but then let you give birth to children like the animals. Let you meet[371] your husband as often as the animals.' The women answered: 'In that way rather not, my Lord, Jesus!'" This is why women carry their little children in their arms to this day.[372]

Frequent sexual relations were obviously not the suggestion of Jesus, but of the subconscious of the man telling the story. The female rejection of the offer shows fear not only of the pain of multiple births, but also of sexual intercourse, which had always involved the possibility of conception. For a

---

[365] Prayer nr. 4

[366] Prayer nr. 60, 61, 270, 272: In the frame of a vision: *"In this house there are four corners, angels in each, our Lord Christ in the middle, Mary in the window. She swaddles her Holy Son, two angels fly over there."*

[367] Prayer nr. 212: *"Mary, heavenly star, who breastfed our Lord...withdraw your hand for love of the glorious star, whose dear breasts were suckled against our poisons [...]"*. The body is cleared, and, in a figurative sense, also the mind is purified (*healed!*) from poison by divine maternal milk, namely: maternal love. It is in accordance with psychological theories about parental love.

[368] Prayer nr. 4

[369] Prayer nr. 109. supplement: *"While the Beautiful Virgin Mary passing there, she smiles on Him: Stand up, my little Jesus from the door of the church, because here comes Jesus, Jesus who saves our souls, Jesus who brings peace [...]"* Two different characters of Jesus appear in the text at the same time, to all appearances, without any connection between the two: Jesus as child and as Redeemer. See the following footnote, too.

[370] Cf. Prayer nr. 231, 236, 239; 314: Here the baby Jesus appears again at the same time as the resurrected Saviour, but in another context: *"In heaven there is a little rocking cradle, in which lies the lord of the world, Jesus. Beside him sits our lady, Mary; the lord of the world, Jesus asks her: Why do you cry, why do you cry, our lady, Mary? [...]"* The response of Mary ("our lady") shows a distance between her and the "lord of the world", but at the same time the little child speaks in a grown-up, or even caring way. We find a similar motif in a prayer sang by *Anna Jánó* in Lészped, recorded by *Zoltán Kallós* in 1963: (while rocking the cradle, Mary tells her baby Son:) *"Sleep, sleep, Lamb of God, because you came* [past tense] *to redeem the world."*

[371] In order to have sexual intercourse.

[372] Lammel – Nagy 1995, 193, collected by Berza Nagy in 1935

peasant woman it often meant nothing more, than rape and the consequences of male violence, namely, being abandoned in the midst of infinite house-work, while taking care of numerous children all alone.

In most stories Mary usually appears *alone with her Son*. Joseph (or the Father, the male head of the family) disappeared from the scene of the "Holy Family". Joseph usually plays a very passive role both in the archaic prayers and in the so-called Peasant Bible. Most often we do not find the father figure at all in these texts.[373] It is the business of the mother and the Son, but sometimes a third person is involved like Eve, Adam, Abraham, Gabriel the archangel, John the Baptist, the wife of Pilate, Peter, Paul, or Luke. The lack of the father on the scene manifests the roles in a peasant family throughout the centuries. The stories evidently project the reality, or rather, the destiny of peasant women of the epoch.

Even in the first half of the 20th century, upon marrying a Hungarian peasant woman entered a totally new environment, moving to the family of the husband, where males were usually closely related by blood and property, but women had no previous contact with one another. This made the female members of the family completely defenceless. The wife[374] had to be permanently afraid of her husband, as she was also herself considered as property belonging to the man.[375]

*"Woman, be quiet!*
*Don't bother me!*
*Because I am your husband,*
*yes, you take your orders from me."*

---

[373] Here I would like to stress however a beautiful exception, in which female gentleness is expressed in a male character: *"Let our lives be bound under the touch of the gentle hand of our heavenly Holy Father [...]"*. The prayer was revealed by Mary in a vision to a male servant with the following words: *"My son, you will be thrashed, like my Holy Son was flogged, because the evil-minded ones do not believe. But never leave this prayer off, because you will be delivered from bodily and mental troubles only with its help."* This promise offers a good spiritual Father replacing and overwhelming the material level of the violent, physically present (usually male) landowner. The pain is easier tolerable, if it is compared with the suffering of the Divine Son of a divine mother.

[374] "Wife" means in Hungarian: "being half". It is however the name of the wife only, that refers to a one-sided female subordination within the family. Cf. "nő" means "woman" or, as a verb, "is growing" in Hungarian. It can be interpreted in a negative way: the woman is an eternal child, who is always just in a growing state. This growing state however can also refer to the *openness,* and flexibility of the woman, here "being a child" does not mean "childish", but refers to a person with always renewing heart and expresses the permeability of the female character. Cf. Gudorf 1987

[375] Cf. "female animal"

*Morvay*'s quotation represents the cold relation between wife and husband. The man took precedence when it came to distributing the food, he walked ahead, he was actually allowed to do whatever he wanted. Among the female members of the family the youngest wife was in the most humiliating situation. Regularly she had to wash the feet of all the other male and female members of the family from the eldest to the youngest.[376] During the year all female work increased the estate of the husband's larger family, but left nothing for the women themselves, except the result of their spinning and weaving in the winter time. With that she usually had to raise a dowry for her daughters.

It is now understandable why a boy was a "blessing" and a girl was a "nuisance" for the mother. The man was usually away the whole day in the mountains, in the fields or simply in the pub. He expected his carousing to be supported financially by his wife. The child welfare was left to the mother, or more often to the eldest wife in the family. The value of a female orphan, an old maid, a barren wife or a widow was nothing for they did not produce *manpower*, but only "consumed" the common good.[377] The strongest relationship in the family developed obviously between mother left to herself and her children, but especially her sons. As we have seen earlier it was not always like this. The female genealogy and power had a much more significant role in the bygone days, which is preserved nowadays only in the memory of the oral tradition.

## THE EVIL WOMAN:
## TURNING FROM VITALITY INTO HARM

To get a full picture (1) of the almost unchanging social conditions of Hungarian peasant women in the course of the development of society and (2) of the symbolism of the folk religion describing femaleness through its threefold differentiation (categories of the divine, the human and the evil), we have to examine more closely the obviously negative, dark side of our tradition concerning womanhood.

The main diabolic female figure is certainly (a) *Eve*, the universal biblical symbol of the female human being. Nevertheless the Hungarian popular belief knows the harmful, evil-divine character of the so-called (b) *Beautiful Woman*, who acts against the life creating, blessing and sustaining Happy

---

[376] Cf. Jn 13:5–16
[377] Morvay 1981, 13–70

Woman. Considering the negatively represented womanhood (c) *Mary* plays both resisting (Mary the "new", perfect Eve opposed to the devilish "old" Eve) and supporting (Mary the whore: common lot with women in their evil fate) roles, depending on the context of the narration. Nevertheless in these stories the outcome is always the same: women, including or not the figure of Mary, remain evil, because of their origin from the devil. It is consequently not Mary who supports or resists women, but the narrator all by oneself.

In this section we shall explore typical degrading approaches to femaleness, most often narrated by men, as part of their justification for the patriarchal order built up through the centuries. As I already referred to above, the condescending attitude derived from subconscious male jealousy and an inferiority complex, due to the lack of certain natural female endowments. Therefore I maintain that these degrading images also speak about the power of women, even if in a negative manner, in expressed fear and denial of female power.

## WOMEN IDENTIFIED WITH EVE, MEN IDENTIFIED WITH ADAM

Before examining the images in details, the common usage of the biblical names of the ancestress and ancestor (Eve and Adam) in folk beliefs should be illustrated first:

*"This again is a true story: it is something that happened to me. I was coming home here by the graveyard ditch; it was getting dark, too. There was a footpath leading across the graveyard, and I used to walk that way. Suddenly I heard something like the crying of a child in the ditch in the graveyard. I went near and had a look... as I went into the ditch... I listened... well; this is where the crying was coming from! You could hear it crying beneath the ground! I struck a match so that I could see better – well, there was a small grave there, but it was overgrown with weeds. God only knows how old it could have been. Well, I baptised it – this is what they say: 'I baptise you to God! If you are a girl, let your name be Eve! If you are a boy, let your name be Adam!' – And, sure enough, I have not heard anything since then; but it is certain that it was the crying of a child. I heard from old people back in the old days that children who were born earlier and were not baptised cried every seven years."*[378]

---

[378] Collected by Hoppál, M. in Varsány/H, 23rd February 1973 from István Jekkel. shepherd, 70

In the respect of understanding the social influence of the following references this above mentioned unconditional acknowledgement of gender roles is an essentially significant fact, since it says a lot about the seriousness of messages for both sexes hidden in the texts. The story obviously goes beyond the biblical figures of Adam and Eve, when it uses their characters for describing all men and women who are also called "Eve" and "Adam". It means that both of these biblical characters are seen as present in every human being. If (male and female) dead children are named after the biblical (male and female) ancestry, there is no doubt about their supposed derivation, and the close interdependence between the gender roles of biblical folk stories and of the contemporary surrounding society. As the narrators mirror the built-up human society, precisely the same way as society mirrors the communal preconceptions of the narratives. Let us look at examples and expectations of what growing up female and male members of certain rural communities had to face.

## THE DEFECTIVE FEMALE CREATURE

Creation stories speak about the presumed origin of earthly life and of its order. They were however plainly invented by human beings, who tried to give answers to their questions by drawing an order of the world with the help of means of their own cultures. Later on these attempts built up a whole system of religious ideas, that served as defining the way of progress of the individuals and of the whole community. The attempts became strict, binding definition, and its original formation fell into oblivion.[379]

The following creation stories are presented by their narrators as ready narratives. The storytellers are convinced of the divine will hidden behind the message of the orally transmitted texts. Nevertheless other psychological-sociological aspects of these messages can also be revealed, even if their "messengers" do not look into them. Their task is only to introduce the qual-

---

years old; Cf. Hoppál, Mihály: *Hiedelemrendszerünkről* [About the system of our folk beliefs], in: Bali, János – Jávor, Kata: Merítés. Néprajzi tanulmányok Szilágyi Miklós tiszteletére [Immertion. Ethnographical studies in honour of Miklós Szilágyi], Budapest, 2001, 433–440, italics mine

[379] Cf. Watzlawick, Paul – Weakland, John H. – Fisch, Richard: *Change. Principles of Problem Formation and Resolution*, Norton, New York, 1974. The authors describe the process of definition-making and its often harmful influence on everyday life. Definitions as helping means to describe reality come most often to the front and covers up reality itself, that was supposed to be more conceivable by defining and categorising.

ity of our "derivation". Let us look at an example for the creation of woman coming from a male storyteller.

God discusses the creation of woman with an archangel. The archangel's first suggestion is to create the woman from a bone of the male skull, but God rejects it saying that then the woman would be the head of the family. The second proposal, to create the woman from the shin of the man, is also refused for then she would be the doormat of the man. Finally they decide to create her from the rib of the man. But when they take it and lay it on the grass, a dog runs away with it. The archangel can only catch his tail, which remains in his hand. Having no other choice the woman is created *"by God from the tail of a dog"*.[380]

According to the story the position of the woman seems to be less than that of an animal in the eyes of men. Their male attitude is justified by their male calculated order of creation, in which it is clearly explained that God, even if He[381] is trying to be fair, creates the woman from the tail of a dog, *just by accident.* Similarly to the creation story of the Old Testament the woman exists here only in the relation of the man. God (and the storyteller) has no doubt about the grounds of the male being. According to the storyteller he already exists as independent reality. God however seems to be wise by taking stock of the situation, when He suggests equality between the two sexes. The final circumstances as comment on the good plan turned out badly is only the flip of the story telling man by showing that the patriarchal order of his contemporary society is supported by an accident that is even above God Himself, because God has no power (does not want to live with His power?) to change the situation. If God is acknowledged as the All-Mighty Creator, it is uncertain how the dog could enter the scene without the knowledge of God. The storyteller does not put forward such questions.

Even if the woman is created by God according to the narrative, it means no respect for her, because she is on a lower biological level (tail of a dog) than the man or even the dog. The story teller seems to be aware of the hierarchical teaching of Genesis 1, in which according to God's will the whole vegetation of the earth, included animals are placed under the human being.

---

[380] Lammel – Nagy 1995, 25. "Tail": phallic symbol. Does the woman here derive from phallic power?

[381] In the context of these stories God seems to be certainly a male character.

On the basis of the final conclusion our Hungarian version abases woman-hood deeply under the level of animals with reference to the divine order of earthly life.

In other re-narrated biblical texts the creating process of woman is apparently even worse, because already at the beginning point of creating the two sexes there is a split between their creations, in which the woman has obviously nothing to do with God. She is created by the devil instead. It means that her whole existence is only in communication with diabolic forces rather than with divine ones. Although the material used by the creation of both sexes is the same mud, the subordination of the woman to the man (as animal to the human being) is affirmed in these variations not only from a biological aspect, but also from the moral point of view, while she is attributed to devilish, sinful, destroying power in contradistinction with the man originating from the perfectly good God.

The devil has to dive three times into the water for some mud to create the earth in co-operation with God, because God finds that deal always too little. When God is finally satisfied with the mass of mud, they pug the clay together, till it is well flattened to be put onto the surface of the waters. The mud grows earth, but empty without life. Therefore both God and the devil scratch off the mud left under their nails to form human beings. Both God and the devil blow their breath into their created figures: *"the former made by God is the man, the latter made by the devil is the woman."*[382]

*Accident* is visibly a popular confirming element of several explanations regarding the quality of womanhood. The following example represents the man (Peter) seemingly as helpful and compassionate with women in their troubles. He wants to do his best, even if everything *accidentally* turns out badly. The re-creation or re-birth has a by no means positive message for the woman.

Jesus and Peter were travelling together, when Peter saw the devil intending to rape a woman. Peter asked Jesus' permission to cut off the head of the devil. Jesus is sceptical about the outcome of the action, He is afraid that Peter will accidentally cut off the head of both the devil and the woman. Peter promises careful caution, until he cuts off the heads of both, as it has already been foretold by Jesus. Peter tries to remedy his mistake, but first he puts the woman's head back with her face to her bottom. His second attempt proved a bigger failure, when he put the head of the devil on the neck of the woman. *"You killed this woman – says Jesus. But why, my Master? – asks Peter naively. As you see,*

---

[382] Bosnyák 2001, 12

*you put the head of the devil onto the body of the woman, therefore she will
never be just with her husband, because there is* an evil spirit in her.[383] – *replies
the Lord"* But Jesus does not allow Peter to experiment with the female head
anymore, consequently the woman carries the evil head for ever and therefore
she is always against the man.[384]

It is worth making a brief aside to the typical male and female interpretations of the same creation story collected and written down by *Bosnyák*
among Hungarian speaking people in Rumania[385]. Here we read six variations
of the Genesis story. Three were told by men and three by women. Some
interesting distinguishable aspects of gender appear in the texts:

(a) In almost all versions, God and the devil create the world together. In
these cases the story told by a woman ends with the creation of the earth.

(b) While all three "male" versions continue with the creation of the
human being: Adam was created by God and Eve was created by the devil.[386]
Therefore immediately after her creation she cuckolds her husband, because
of the "evil spirit" activated instantly in her.[387]

(c) In "female" versions, on the scene of creating human being, only God
alone occurs as Creator. Adam and Eve are *both* created by God! In these legends the figure of the devil cannot be found at all.

Finally a sad, but very illustrative example of the existed patriarchal order
comes from a female narrator, who seems to have gone through a complete
patriarchal brainwashing.

*"When God created Eve, God asked Adam: 'How is it going with your
wife, Adam? Are you not bored?' 'No, my Father, but she smells earthy.'
The woman had an earthy smell. Therefore God took the rib of Adam, and
put into Eve. Since then she no longer smelt earthy."*[388]

Gaia the fruitful Goddess disappears. Her creating feature is not seen anymore. The earth gives no birth to the sky anymore.[389] The female genealogy

---

[383] Italics mine
[384] Cf. Bosnyák 2001, 73
[385] See above: Dankó – Küllős 1987, 348–354
[386] Cf. also: Pócs 1986, 184–185: *"When our Lord Christ walked on the earth, He found a* good
man, *and a* bad woman. *"* (Lészped/Moldva) Or: *"When Jesus walked on the earth, He
found husband of* good will, *and an* unpious *housewife."* (Apátfalva/Csanád), italics mine.
Pócs however does not indicate the gender of the praying person in her volume.
[387] Although it is not mentioned who is the second partner of Eve.
[388] Bosnyák 2001, 14, italics mine
[389] See above: Prayer nr. 300

based on the earth is strongly despised and humiliated here. Belonging to Mother Earth and owning Her heritage is a shameful position. Patriarchal interpretations represent Her and all her daughters as stinking, repulsive beings, whose nauseous, loathsome character can only be redeemed by a much higher quality, namely, by Adam's rib, the male essence. The female storyteller experiences herself as a malodorous reality, and looks at her husband as her "better part", with which her lower female existence is not even to be compared.

## WOMANHOOD DOMESTICATED BY MAN

There is also some useful information about the reason why these male type of creation stories arise at all. A male narrative tells us for instance why the female character is so irritating for a man.

When God created Eve for Adam not to be alone anymore, God took the wiliness of the cat, the faithfulness of the dog, the pliability of the snake, the tameness of the lamb, the cruelty of the tiger, mixed them up and created the woman. After a week Adam complains to God that his wife, Eve is being so annoying. God takes her from him, but then he complains that he is lonely. Finally God gives Eve back to Adam and says that both should endure the other with patience. *"This is how only Eve remained for Adam and how all women inherited Eve's qualities."*[390]

The animals repeatedly are not left out of the female personality. Eve's mentioned animal characteristics can confirm her lower instinctive[391] position to the man of calm thoughts being in private, confidential relationship with God. At the same time the mixture of these features (wiliness, faithfulness, pliability, mildness and wildness) can refer to the creative versatility and the dangerous inscrutability of the woman, that reasonably frightens her male partner.

Considering other examples this male fear seems to be well founded. Several male narrators acquaint us with the original set up between woman and man.

According to these narratives the woman was primarily the head of the family, until Jesus changed the order. While she was much stronger than her husband, she thrashed him regularly, until the man asked Jesus for help, who then changed the situation by saying that *"From now men are the lords instead of women"*.[392] In other versions the wanderers Jesus and Peter get

---

[390] Bosnyák 2001, 14

[391] Instincts are most often represented by different animals in the course of art history.

[392] Bosnyák 2001, 66

accommodation for a night from a timorous husband in a house, where they themselves become eyewitnesses of female brutality. Here the *husband* is called *whore*, the guests are beaten all night by the drunken wife arriving home from the pub. Finally Jesus takes the hat off the wife's head and puts it on the husband's head. Since that time the man wears the hat symbolising his priority in the family.[393]

These male narratives unambiguously speak for male authority established by Jesus, even if He acted against the original divine order of female superiority proclaimed by several storytellers. Typical male characteristics like *being away from home, drunkenness, swearing, brawl* and further examples of brutality are attributed here to women, and considerably judged by the narrator (and so much the more by Jesus Himself). The final change of gender roles ordered by Jesus transfers the might and authority to the man, while confirming his superior status and even his violence.

In similar female versions it is most often the man, who plays the violent role, and there is no existential final positive change for the woman in the concluding formulae of these texts. Peter makes only a final statement, whereas he was spanked enough, but he does not ask for Jesus' help to make amends to the woman for the constant female torments that are caused by the man. No existential change is mentioned in gender roles. Does the female narrator so fear her male listeners that she describes male violence as an accepted fact? The female story stops before it would end up with the jurisdiction of a divine authority. It seems that male brutality finds room in the order established by God – namely by the male society.

Nevertheless whenever a sign of female independence appears, from a male perspective it is seen as sinful and disobedient to both *man and God*. According to male storytellers, God or an "accident" established this order. When Eve is disobedient to Adam, he runs to God to complain, who, certainly, always supports him.

God helps Adam for example *to grow a beard which makes him look more frightful*[394] and more authoritarian towards the seemingly disobedient, but in reality only fair-player Eve, who is inclined to work in the garden with, rather than without her husband.[395]

In this way God implies that Adam is actually always right in contradistinction to his wife, Eve. His will is obviously supported by a male God.

---

[393] Bosnyák 2001, 58–59

[394] See also Bosnyák 2001, 17–18, italics mine

[395] Lammel – Nagy 1995, 30–33

There is no room here for female manifestation. The Happy Woman as the symbol of omnipotent female divine power seems to be atrophied. The clear message of these folk stories hints at all peasant women: the husband seems to replace the mediating role of Mary's female character, and it seems that the God of husbands has nothing to do with the Goddess of wives. He has no communication with Her, only with husbands, because He (he) is not interested in female opinions, not even in supporting fairness within the family circle.

The only means left of women symbolising their power for asserting themselves towards their husbands is their *glib tongue* that cannot be silenced even by Jesus' divine power. The female narrator is obviously trying to maintain a piece of female territory against male omnipotence, justified by Jesus' impotence. Even if in several female versions the woman represents the original owner of power, these variations never finally turn out for the total benefit of the man. There must be a female area of authority that cannot be overwhelmed by male almightiness.

After being beaten all night by the woman Peter complains. *"My Lord, take her muscle off, so that she will not be able to hit me anymore.' And Jesus replies: 'I can take her muscle off, but I am not able to take her mouth off.' This is why the woman quarrels with her husband.* "[396]

## THE GUILTY WOMAN AND THE SELF-CONFIDENT MAN

Male and female narrators see the foresight of both the frightened Adam and Eve driven out of Eden differently. This distinction is best expressed in the content of dreams attributed to Eve or to Adam. According to the female storyteller only Eve had a dream about the future after being chased out.

> *"She had seen that women suffered a lot of pain by giving birth, not like she before, who had no idea of what pain meant. Then the devil showed her a lot of torments, hatreds and wars her descendants had to go through. Finally she saw fire that burnt everything. A black horseman passed by with a jug of water. Many thirsty people, who drank from it, became engaged to Satan. Eve suffered very much from her dream, and when she woke up, she fell on her knees, and asked God to remit her sin, and to save people from the dread she dreamed about.* "[397]

---

[396] Bosnyák 2001, 82
[397] Bosnyák 2001, 27–28 (Mrs Lőrinc Antal, Istensegíts)

The female narrator does not draw a distinctive parallel between man and woman; she only expresses her own fears and anxieties that finally lead her to guilty feelings. She looks at herself as the *reason of all troubles*, she begs for God's pardon and practises penitence.

In the male version Eve shares with Adam the horrible future vision she had seen in her dream, while dissolving into tears. The man however consoles the woman by saying that he was also shown a dream

> *"By God, in which he was encouraged to make trappings, to start to plough and to sow, to build houses, to give birth to children, and not to worry about their fate, because God would take care of them, if we kept God's advice, did our job and were constructive."*[398]

The male narrator emphasises the divine source of Adam's dream in contradistinction to Eve's prompted by the devil. The male attitude to the new situation outside of Eden, out of the divine blessing seems to be much more flexible, inventive, quick-witted, "constructive", as the storyteller himself puts it. Adam's fear completely disappears at the end of the narrative; the optimistic man supported by God's positive message is full of vivid energy for a new beginning. Eve's dream is rather pessimist by paralysing and hindering the advance. Here she is manifested as a psychically impeded person to explore the new possibilities offered by the new situation.

These two different types of the awareness of life represent typical everyday gender attitudes also detectable in contemporary society, in which it was usual practice to blame the woman for things that she had actually nothing to do with. Women obviously learnt quickly that they came from sinful Eve, who could be tempted by the snake, and who herself tempted Adam to resist the divine law. The female being grew up with *guilty feelings*, because she was regarded from her childhood as a useless penalty in the eyes of her parents, but especially in the eyes of her father. She was later seen by her husband, by the larger family and by the surrounding cultural community only as the means of reproducing strong, vigorous boys, who represented the potency of their father. On the basis of all these the regressive female attitudes manifested in Eve's dream and the cocksure male light-heartedly looking ahead characterised by Adam it is quite understandable.

What has remained from the Happy Woman as *source of life*? *Eve*, and all her daughters, turned out to be rather the *source* of all *troubles* in the course of history.

---

[398] Bosnyák 2001, 28 (János Benke, Klézse)

The difference between poor and rich on the earth is certainly her fault. We read it as follows in the Peasant Bible:

When God visited Eve and Adam, they did not have enough nice clothes for all of their 100 children. And it was Eve who, while feeling ashamed for not being spruce enough, hid from God 50 of the little ones having no nice clothes, with the result of receiving no divine blessing of the Visitor for those hidden ones. This is why at present there are poor and rich on the earth – according to the *male* storyteller.[399]

## FEMALENESS ABSORBED IN THE ASEXUAL "NEW EVE"

The biblical description of God's creation[400] gradually took over the above delineated strong male view about women. Consequently Eve, "the mother of all who *live*"[401] becomes only a tempted and tempting woman. As Jesus replaces Adam and is called the "new Adam", the figure of Mary becomes synonymous with the "new Eve". This idea suggests a dualistic interpretation of salvation. Whereas Jesus saved only men (Adam[402]), women need another, female redeemer in the character of Mary.[403] In some respects Mary's figure is understood in an arbitrary, ambivalent way. On the one hand, Mary's character connected with the Happy Woman symbolising female fertility is seen as positive maternal support especially for women, and is in organic continuity with the first woman, Eve, the mother of all living beings. On the other hand, because of the dominating official ecclesiastical teachings effected by the Augustinian interpretation of sin associated with conception, there has been drawn a sharp contrast between the fertile, therefore sexual and sinful Eve, and her counter-part, the virgin, therefore asexual and innocent Mary.[404] This latter

---

[399] Lammel – Nagy 1995, 35

[400] *"In the image of God s/he created human being: male and female s/he created them."* (Gen 1:27)

[401] Gen 3:20, Cf. the connection between the original Hebrew concepts of Yahweh and Eve based on notions like being and life as cognate ideas: The name Yahweh originated from the word: הוה = to be or היה = to be here, in *Hiph*.: to call into life. Yahweh (יהוה) is who Is (cf. Ex, 3:14: אהיה אשר אהיה) but also who maintains life. Eve (חוה) is life (חי) itself. Cf.: חיה = to live

[402] See the original Hebrew meaning: אדם = Adam > coming from אדמה = soil that has nothing to do with the gender-specified male character.

[403] Johnson, Elizabeth: *Mary and the Female Face of God*, in: Theological Studies 50, no. 3, 1989, 500–526

[404] Torjesen 1995, 139–155: Die Ehre einer Frau ist ihre Scham

Marian character then became the prevailing example of proper womanhood.[405]

*"Oh, sons of Eve,*
*it is good to keep in mind,*
*to hear, to bow the knee and the head,*
*to stand in front of God.*
First *woman, Mary,*
*will give birth to her Holy Son,*
*to the innocent little Jesus [...] "*[406]

Mary is the first woman. This reinterpreted female figure almost invalidates the real femininity, or even the human character, of Eve[407] as well as of all other women before and after Mary.[408] Daughters are not mentioned here. Consequently the female genealogy has passed. It is very near to the portrayal of Mary as a pious *nun*[409] described by the Franciscan *Temesvári* in his *Stellarium,*[410] which is the most basic starting-point for the growing Hungarian mariological literature. Although the original aim of Temesvári was to present the character of Mary, through a dialogical form with her Son, as the most beautiful earthly being and the greatest *knowing* person. This latter feature is regarded here as a divine attribution and was originally attached to shaman-like skills. However nothing has been left to the descendants from this fertile female heritage. The only universally appreciated spiritual way to live is self-denial and asceticism, for both men and women of the era.[411]

---

[405] As Scherf puts it, this phenomenon is basically *"Die Verteufelung des Fruchtbarkeitskults"*, in: Scherf 1990, 236–247

[406] Prayer nr. 280, italics mine

[407] *"The woman hath made an excuse for the woman... The one through the wood brought in* sin: *the other through the wood brought in against it a* blessing. " italics mine; Gregory of Nyssa, quoted by Livius, Thomas: *The Blessed Virgin in the Fathers of the First Six Centuries*, Burns & Oates Ltd., London, 1893, 48

[408] See the split between the highly mystified Mary and other women as mentioned above.

[409] Cf. Synods at Constantinople in 553 and at Lateran in 649: *Aiparthenosz* (= "virgin for ever")

[410] Temesvári, Pelbárt: *Stellarium Coronae Beatae Mariae Virginis*, 1498. Cf. *Új Magyar Irodalmi Lexikon* 3. [The new Hungarian encyclopaedia of literature], Akadémiai K., Budapest, 1994, 2071

[411] Cf. Ennen, Edith: *Frauen im Mittelalter*, Verlag Beck, München, ⁴1991, 112–125.: "Die weibliche Frömmigkeitsbewegung"

The old dualistic view about God and world[412], the strong belief in the sinfulness of the body, and therefore the glorification of self-denial was highly confirmed in Christianity by Augustine's distinction between use *(usus)* and enjoyment *(fruitio)* – influenced deeply by his own disappointing personal experiences and then by the ideology of manicheism. *Only* God is to be fully loved and enjoyed; all other things and relationships are *to be used* as a means toward that end. Although from the 13<sup>th</sup> century theologians tried to have a more positive view toward the world and human nature, which set the context in late medieval discussions for growing positive valuation of human psychology, too.[413]

## FEMALE BEAUTY AND FERTILITY = WHORING?

In Erdélyi's collection there is a Christmas song with particular characteristics describing male attitudes towards women sung by a gypsy man.[414] It is basically an interpretation of the biblical story about the pregnant Mary looking for accommodation for the night. In this case Joseph has disappeared from Mary's side. Mary as a single pregnant woman asks the pickpocket gypsy man for a room, but she is sent away with the following words:

*"I cannot give you accommodation,*
*because you are a whore,*
*and you are not allowed to enter my house. "*

However the disabled and blind daughter of the man secretly invites Mary to the stable in a typical friendly gypsy fashion:

*"Sit down, Mary,*
*lie down peacefully,*

---

[412] Cf. the dualistic view of Augustine about man and woman: *"...he* (cf. Jesus) *should take* the human nature of man, *the* more honourable *of the two sexes... ",* quoted by Børresen, Kari Elisabeth: *Subordination and Equivalence – The Nature and Role of Woman in Augustine and Thomas Aquinas,* Kok Pharos Publishing House, Kampen, 1995 (first edition: 1968), 74, italics mine

[413] Cf. Courtenay, William J.: *Between Despair and Love – Some Late Medieval Modifications of Augustine's Teaching on Fruition and Psychic States,* in: Hagen, Kenneth (ed.): Augustine, the Harvest, and Theology (1300–1650) – Essays Dedicated to Heiko Augustinus Oberman in Honour of his Sixtieth Birthday, E.J. Brill, Leiden, 1990, 5–19, italics mine

[414] Prayer nr. 244

*take your little mirror,*
*and rouge yourself."*

When Mary gives birth to her Son, she asks the girl to pick the child up, but because she does not have arms she cannot do it. Finally she is cured, attired in silk dress and when Mary leaves the property, she asks her father why he refused Mary shelter. The answer:

*"Oh, if I knew that it was the Virgin Mary,*
*I would have given strong drink to her,*
*and many thousand silver forints*
*so that she won't be so poor."*

When Erdélyi asked about the very insulting word, the praying man answered without hesitation that all women are called *"you fetid whore* because all of them are beautiful. And *"a woman who wants to enter a stranger's house alone is really a whore. Does she want to hide somewhere while pregnant? A decent woman would never do such a thing."*[415] But Mary seems to be an exception. When the man recognises Mary herself as the visitor, he immediately becomes hospitable and very helpful.

The transformation of Mary in Bethlehem to the so-called whore in our quotation is the result of a long, culturally-socially determined redaction, inspired, of course, by old and contemporary gypsy interpretations, but also by the legend of St. Anastasia.[416] In this story the characters of the disabled daughter and of the rich father always appear, but in contrast with the gypsy variation not only is the girl rewarded, but the father is punished in some noteworthy fashion. Usually the rich father becomes poor, which is an answer to the antagonism between rich and poor, oppressor and oppressed.[417] It is however a good question as to why we do not find the punishment of the father in our gypsy

---

[415] See: Erdélyi 1999, 734–735. Cf. *"Insofar as the female body has been treated as polluted, shameful, and surrounded with taboos and rituals of exclusion, it has been* an object of abjection. *Reclaiming eros is thus at the same time reclaiming the goodness of female bodily experiences."*, in: Grey, Mary: *Introducing Feminist Images of God*, Sheffield Academic Press, Sheffield, 2001, 79, italics mine

[416] Cf.: Kríza, Ildikó: *Az Anasztázia-monda magyar vonatkozásai* [The Hungarian relations of the legend of Anastasia], in: Barna (ed.) 2001, 49–64. and also partly in: Kalligram, Bratislava, 1–2/2001, 82–89. Kríza actually does not mention this formulation given above at all.

[417] Cf. Lk 16:19–31. The story of the rich man and Lazarus.

version. It seems that the male gypsy storyteller absolves his male fellows from the bad consequences of the judging attitude against women. This self-absolution is a usual phenomenon within the traditional gypsy cult.[418]

*Kríza* sets down several versions of the legend from different ages and areas. The variations influenced by the Byzantine traditions stress the miraculous healing process while leaving the reasons for the disability unnamed. But in Northern European countries, they are described as the result of the punishment meted out by the dreadful father to the "disobedient" daughter for refusing incest or rejecting marriage for a more humane life in a cloister. In this context the figure of the caring, healing Mother and at the same time of the woman with divine power to punish is more evident. Through the story of Anastasia, Mary becomes the protector of all innocent women. Nevertheless it is often a son rather than a daughter who is healed, because boys are always worthier of being cared for than girls.[419]

Although we do not find the gypsy version of the whore in any other variations of the legends of Anastasia, we still know about a woman, a so called Mary from the 4th (or the 6th?) century who lived in Egypt and at the age of 12 became a *whore*. Years later, with the help of the Virgin Mary, she was led into the desert and after a 17-year fight with her own body she finally came to peace.[420] Mary from Nazareth of the first century, called a whore by a gypsy man in the 20th century would likely be deeply sympathetic towards the woman from 4th century Egypt.

According to another male storyteller[421]

Whoring origins from the ancient time of Noah, who had four daughters and three sons and paired them. Because of being left without male part-

---

[418] See Bosnyák 2001, 94: A good example for self-absolution is the explanation why gypsies are allowed to steal: Jesus should have been crucified with four nails, but *"because the gypsy man stole one of them, his body was finally hammered with three nails onto the cross. This is why gypsies are allowed to thieve. They can do whatever they want, it will never be seen as sin."*

[419] Cf. It is worth seeing the contemporary linguistic practice e. g. in the Hungarian speaking areas of Transylvania. When someone is asked about the number of the children in the family, the answer is for instance: *"We have three children and two daughters"*, that means three *boys* and two girls (who are not remarkable as children). Italics mine

[420] Cf. Sartory, Gertrude and Thomas: *Maria von Ägypten – Allmacht der Buße*, Herderbücherei 977, Freiburg-Basel-Wien, 1982; Mulack, Christa: *Maria – Die geheime Göttin im Christentum*, Kreuz, Stuttgart, 1985, 59–63: Die Jungfrau und die Hure

[421] Péter Habari, Klézse/Rumanian, in: Bosnyák 2001, 39.

ner, the fourth girl cried all the time. She did not know what to do, but Noah suggested to her to put on beautiful dresses and an ever- laughing face so that she will be able to live among her brothers and sisters. Then she prepared herself exceptionally nicely, in the consequence of which she was loved by one after the other. This is the origin of whoring.

The question of incest obviously does not arise here at all. The main reason for becoming a whore seems to be the lack of the male partner. According to the narrative whoring is a role given to women. The narrator however seems to have sympathy for the girl by describing her as a lost, sad woman, to whom in Noah's opinion (in the opinion of the storyteller) whoring is the only, even if not really satisfying solution. Noah as a father has the privilege to decide the fate of all his children. The legend is not interested in the life of the other children, and does not comment on the quality of their lives at all.

Being left alone seems to be the greatest tragedy and shame of human life. As we have seen the girl did not know what to do, while she was single. Whoring seems to help her to be integrated into the expectations of the society, in which maidenhood without sexual act has a lower respect than the state of a courtesan. None of these types of conduct are judged by the narrator, but the despair of the girl lost within her own family mirrors the strong social pressure existing in her community of common heritage.

Beauty and merry liveliness, even if they are illusory ones, are highly valid in most cults. The problem of subjection and materialisation of human relationships has no room in this context. It is not accidental that in the course of European history girls often escaped into the protecting walls of a cloister, from the utilitarian patriarchal society overwhelming even the body and the soul of particularly female individuals.[422]

I have found only one exception of attributing whoring to *manhood*, but even in this context the narrator was aware of the humiliating role stuck rather to womanhood. In this version the drunken wife kicks the front door while

---

[422] About the attitude to a whore see also: Lammel – Nagy 1995, 287–288: The wife of a miller, the wife of an innkeeper and a prostitute went to heaven to Peter. Peter sends both the wives of the miller and of the innkeeper to *hell* because they both "stole and cheated the poor people. When he asks the prostitute: *"What did you do in your earthly life?"* She answers: *"Well, I was a prostitute, whoever asked me, I complied."* Peter says: *"My bed is over there, go, lie down on it."* This story was told by an 88 year-old man. I wonder whether the offer made by Peter should be accepted as a reward or a gain, repeatedly we meet the woman here as sexual object of the man.

shouting at her husband, *"Open the door, you whore!"* She thrashes her husband and his guests (Jesus and Peter), until Jesus takes off her hat and puts it on the head of the husband while telling him, *"It is yours!"* Since that time the man wears the hat, which means that since then he is the one who is endued with power and authority to say "whore" to his wife and to all women.[423]

# INTEGRATING FEMALE INTERIOR HAPPINESS WITH EXTERIOR BEAUTY

## THE DUALISM OF THE DESTROYING BEAUTIFUL WOMAN AND THE BLESSING HAPPY WOMAN

Interpretations describing women as defective, dangerous creatures of the devil draw a clear split between the human-earthly Eve's female offspring and the perfect world of the Virgin Mary. In the Hungarian folk religion this dualistic view of femaleness is best represented in the divine figures of the Beautiful Woman and the Happy Woman. Nevertheless in this case the gap is not between human and divine features, but between two divine existences, who represent evil (Beautiful Woman) and good (Happy Woman). The image of the damaging[424] *"Beautiful Woman"* being in a continuous fight with the blessed *"Happy Woman"*, is well known in ethnography. Both are in close relationship with fertility, especially with the childbearing (life-giving) woman and with the child itself. Their co-emphasised presence at this important event is not accidental.

In a patriarchal society the woman, as we have seen earlier, was considered nothing more than a *producer* of manpower for the world, which was at the same time the measure of her own value. This strongly extensive view determined the relationship between mother and child for many centuries. In these circumstances the *twofold, ambivalent*, rather anguished attitudes towards her own pregnancy can be easily understood. The socially and sexually defenceless woman often conceived against her wish, and had to take the responsibility for its consequences, often totally abandoned.

---

[423] Bosnyák 2001, 58–59. See its interpretation above.

[424] *"Adam and Eve lived very well in Paradise. The devil grew envious of their life free from cares, therefore he stole the water of the Beautiful Woman, and poured it on Adam. Wherever it dropped, there arose tumours. Since then the tumour is called 'the water of the Beautiful Woman'."* In: Lammel – Nagy 1995, 37

It created a particularly difficult and serious situation for a young, unmarried woman in a closed rural community full of taboos, who found herself in the *diabolic circle* of male *abuse* and, at the same time, as the result of her attitude (either opposing the man's will and bearing her secret child or, by chance, killing the new-born), of *punishment and exclusion* dictated by male judges.[425] Although it is worth bearing in mind that men were also limited by previously existing, inherited family-models, male roles and attitudes were also dictated by centuries old social expectations.

According to the popular belief, women *killing* – often mentioned as *"eating"* – the new-born in their desperation, are *punished, but later restored by the Happy Woman.* After her death the mother has to carry the head of her child in her apron till she meets the *Happy Woman,* again who, as herself being a female, understands the woman and then *gives her absolution.* The child of a peasant woman hiding her pregnancy from the community, is sentenced to muteness for a while, which refers also to the "sinfulness" and previous silence of the mother about being with child.[426]

Nevertheless in other stories we see *the Happy Woman* offering her *help and defence* to the pregnant woman, and appearing *as godmother* for the child. If this offer is rejected, the child is damned by the goddess.[427] The ill, deformed new-born, however, is the sign of the damnation of *the Beautiful Woman,* as a result of replacing the real new-born of the mother by her own deformed child. As is pointed out by *Kálmány,* the Happy Woman guards, the Beautiful Woman steals the child.[428] Consequently it is rather the *Beautiful Woman* who damns, judges, punishes, and therefore her negative characteristics can be clearly distinguished from the positive attitude of the Happy Woman.

The inner life of a peasant woman was strained between these two female characters. The *"child"* who is "bone from her bone, flesh from her flesh"[429], "her body and her blood",[430] can also be the symbol of the inner female power

---

[425] Cf.: Szenti, Tibor: *A nők társadalmi és szexuális kiszolgáltatottsága a magyar feudalizmus utolsó másfélszáz évében a Dél-Alföldön* [The social and sexual defencelessness of women in the last 150 years of Hungarian feudalism in the South of the Hungarian Great Plain], in: Küllős 1999, 27–45

[426] Cf. the collection of Kálmány, in: Diószegi 1971, 337–338

[427] Cf. The Sleeping Beauty; Ipolyi 1929, 202

[428] Cf. Kálmány, in: Diószegi 1971, 343–351. See: Reference to the *"changed child"* who is usually cured by symbolic "cooking" or "baking", in: Pócs 1986, 240, 258

[429] Cf. Gen 2:23

[430] Cf. Lk 22:19–20; 1 Kor 11:24;
"*Did the woman say,*
*When she held him for the first time in the dark of a stable,*

and energy that was *carefully kept* by the Happy Woman, but was *always attacked* by the Beautiful Woman.[431] In the past it was not accidental that a woman, who was not married but had regular relationships with several men, was also called in Hungarian *beautiful woman* (szépasszony). Whereas the wife had to hide her beauty from the public behind closed doors, her value was measured after her *assiduousness and obedience* to her husband. According to idealising arguments both of these characteristics were regarded as the *inner beauty* of the woman, much more valuable than her *outer* features. A man, though never wanting to marry a *beautiful woman*, beside his marriage, still had relationships with several others. In this way both types of female characteristics were disdained and used only to fulfil male yearnings.

Moreover the split between inner (symbolised by the Happy Woman) and outer (symbolised by the Beautiful Woman) female qualities again refer to the dualistic view of body and soul. As if interior happiness (soul) and exterior beauty (body) could not get on well together.[432] The internal male fear of female power and female fear of continuous suiting, anguish and aggression is expressed in the image of the maleficent Beautiful Woman or the malignant witch in the form of a beautiful woman, who is actually a repeated character of numerous fairytales.[433] "She destroys those she loves, or, at any rate, they come to grief."[434] Her beauty and love is dangerous.

On the other hand, in our story about Mary the priest[435] the young woman

---

*After the pain and the bleeding and the crying,*
*'This is my body, this is my blood'?*
*Did the woman say,*
*When she held him for the last time in the dark rain on a hilltop,*
*After the pain and the bleeding and the dying,*
*'This is my body, this is my blood'?"*, poem of Frances Croake Frank (poetess of the 20th century). Quoted by Susan A. Ross: *God's Embodiment and Women*, 185–186, in: LaCugna (ed.) 1993, 185–209

[431] Cf. Pócs 1986, 170:
"*The Happy Virgin Mary sent her Holy Son into the water of Jordan. He brought water from the Jordan so that she washed the hands and feet of her Blessed Holy Son. The blue-eyed one had seen him,* bewitched *him, Mary hears it,* cures *him. The green-eyed one had seen him,* bewitched *him, Mary hears it,* cures *him. The yellow-eyed one had seen him, bewitched him, Mary hears it,* cures *him [...]* " (Pokolpatak/Moldva), italics mine

[432] Nevertheless the *inner* harmony reflected in the *body* language is not a new invention.

[433] Cf. e. g. Little Snow-White: the beautiful queen is at the same time the malicious witch.

[434] As it is said about the Sumerian goddess, Inanna. Cf. Jacobsen, Thorkild: *The Treasures of Darkness. A History of Mesopotamian Religion.* Yale University Press, New Haven, 1976, 143

[435] Cf. Lammel – Nagy 1995, 281–287

recompenses for the acknowledgement of *Her* sacerdotal competence, and, first of all, of *Her* divine powers. Her final rewarding deed obtains particular emphasis as the pinnacle of a long series of punishing acts. In this way her last noble gesture suggests the strongest motivation to proclaim, to preserve and to transmit the explored female – priestly – knowledge to the next generations.

The story is not about cannibalism of the mother, but of the whole discriminating society, in which a pregnant woman without a husband was simply excommunicated, cast out and forced to hide her child, to "eat her shame". The tempting Beautiful Woman, who is always *against* life, was definitely not a creature of female imagination but forced into women's soul by a male dominant society. For this reason the appearance of the shadow, *aggressive*, but earlier *terrified* side of maternal love is not surprising at all anymore.

BEAUTY AND HAPPINESS AS DIFFERENT ASPECTS OF THE SAME FEMALE BEING

Let us however turn our attention to these two female divine characters from another perspective. Are they not only different aspects of the same female being? If we define femaleness, in contradistinction to dualistic interpretations, as an *integrated* human quality, the two separated goddesses can be, and by Ipolyi[436] *are* actually in a constructive way, unified within one person. As I already referred to, happiness and beauty, in the widest sense of the words, do not exclude one another, but *both* have rich positive content. For both Hungarian female divine characters we find examples in ancient times.

The *Happy Woman*, as the symbol of creating motherhood, fertility and nourishment, can basically be identified with the so-called "*bough-goddess*"[437], "tree-goddess" or "vegetation goddess",[438] which means constant, stable shelter. The *life-supporting, life-renewing goddess from 1750 BC* first

---

[436] Ipolyi 1929, 202–203

[437] Schroer, Silvia: *Die Zweiggöttin in Palästina/Israel. Von der Mittelbronze II B-Zeit bis zu Jesus Sirach*, in: Küchler, M. – Uehlinger, Ch. (eds.): Jerusalem. Texte – Bilder – Steine, Novum Testamentum et Orbis Antiquus 6, Freiburg Schweiz u. Göttingen, 1987, 201–225. Cf. Keel, Othmar – Uehlinger, Christoph: *Göttinnen, Götter und Gottessymbole*, Herder, Freiburg, 1992, 30, 44, 61, 76f, 80, 144, 377f
See the old-Syrian representations of the bough goddess e.g. in: Winter, Urs: *Frau und Göttin. Exegetische und ikonographische Studien zum weiblichen Gottesbild im Alten Israel und in dessen Umwelt*, Vandenhoeck & Ruprecht, Göttingen, 1983, figs. 269–289

[438] See also above: the Sycamore

turned into the character of *Ashera*, the goddess of the pagan religion surrounding the Israelite faith in Yahweh, and then from personified *"goddess"*
to impersonal ability of *"fertility"*, with which *Yahweh* blesses both man and
woman. It expresses the uniqueness and superiority of Yahweh within the
surrounding pagan world of the multitude of gods and goddesses. The power
of the "bough-goddess"[439] symbolising female fertility has gone.[440]

Representations of Hungarian popular art however still show the loving
woman or the *bride*[441] with a *bough* in her hand offering it (her fertility) to the
beloved man.[442] The bough can turn into a snake coming out of the water,
which is again the symbol of vitality, the concentration of meanings like
renewal (sloughing), ovary (spiral), phallus, and tree of life.[443] Its parallels can
also be found in Hungarian popular art.[444] Consequently the snake was originally associated not with the images of temptation or the tempting woman, but
rather with vigour, which also involves positive female divine energy.

---

[439] Cf. prayer nr. 27:
 *"The sky had given birth to the earth,*
 *the earth had given birth to the tree,*
 *the tree had given birth to its bough,*
 *its bough had given birth to its bud,*
 *its bud had given birth to its flower,*
 *its flower had given birth to Saint Anne,*
 *Saint Anna had given birth to Mary,*
 *Mary had given birth to our Lord Christ, the Redeemer of the world."*
 Or: prayer nr. 28:
 *"I go out of my door,*
 *I look up to the high heaven.*
 *There I see a tree,*
 *the tree bears its bough,*
 *its bough bears its leaf,*
 *its leaf bears its bud,*
 *its bud bears its flower,*
 *its flower bears Anne,*
 *Anne bears Mary,*
 *Mary bears her Holy Son.*
 *Whoever says this little prayer in the evening, in the morning,*
 *will gain the kingdom of heaven."*
[440] Cf. Braulik 1991, 114–115, 125–128
[441] Cf. "bride": in Hungarian "menyasszony" which means: "the lady of heaven". In: Falvay
2001, 40–45
[442] Cf. Lükő 2001, 75, 126–144
[443] Cf. Gimbutas 1989, 121
[444] Cf. Falvay 2001, 115–118

The *Beautiful Woman* however is reflected more in the character of the mobile *"lion-goddess"*, Inanna-Ishtar, the erotic-aggressive Sumerian Goddess,[445] whose essential features though have nothing to do with protecting motherhood, but rather with *seducement* (courtesan), *domination* (lady) and *fight* (warrior).[446] The latter is not very far from the *combatant* woman being anxious for her child, who is, according to our texts, actually incarnated personally in the Happy Woman.

In a healthy female psyche the wide range of all these peculiarities can and *must* be found together. A healthy woman is capable of not only nourishing, but also fighting. According to recent re-interpretations of being female both the *static* and *dynamic* elements must be accomplished in the *her-story* of a female individual. The integration of the two[447] helps women to regain their self-appreciation and independence. It also helps to express their yearnings and fears, so that their love will not be a danger for their surroundings, so that they and their beauty will not be the enemies of their own selves anymore, but able to find pleasure in their own embodied femaleness.

The storyteller, indeed, expressed and elaborated her own problems through *her* created *story*, while breaking through the surrounding ecclesiastical bigotry and social prudery regarding womanhood only as a tempting element of the male existence. This can often be associated with male fear and violence kept back and hidden under the surface level of the society. In her-story female beauty is re-evaluated and is seen no more as an evil temptation, but as the mirror of her inner harmony with her ancient female roots.

---

[445] Whose character was later turned into the symbol of male power. Cf. Meier-Seethaler 1993, 46–75: Von der göttlichen Löwin zum Wahrzeichen männlicher Macht

[446] Cf. Balz-Cochois, Helgard: *Inanna. Wesenbild und Kult einer unmütterlichen Göttin*, Gütersloher Verlagshaus Gerd Mohn, Gütersloh, 1992, 87–90

[447] See its representation in: Leibovitch, J.: *Kent et Qadech*, Syria 38 (1961) 23–34, here 28: A woman standing on a *lion*, holding a *bough* in her right hand and a *snake* in her left hand (19–20th dynasty), from the collection of Winchester College

# Female spirituality embodied in
# Hungarian rural communities
# at the end of the second millennium AD

The wide scale textual manifestations of female experiences are the only informing mirror of everyday reality. Stories and prayers are not only told but also lived through by their narrators. Elements of a special sort of hermeneutic circle embracing the continuous tension between ancient inherited tradition and contemporary practice are simultaneously the reasons and results of a never ending process of repeating mutual influence of both the acquired customs and the everyday experienced events.

Living in the richness of spiritual heritage has an inestimable effect on any average person.[448] This individual progress can be well observed below in the two studied female biographies. Being in fundamental symbiosis with powerful images of the oral tradition offers an unbroken confirmation of subjectively interpreted, but communally accepted worldviews. The often unnoticeable continuity of female identity is represented here through the particular cases of two women whose lives were essentially permeated by metaphorical messages of their religious-cultural environment, both in a negative and in a positive way.

The previously examined female images can be more or less explored in the individual course of these female lives. The manner, in which the culturally stressed metaphorical suggestions were selected to be part of the identity or to be avoided, made the research especially interesting. It seems, that women, who are – from habit, but with unquestionable references to traditional heritage – often treated as "evil daughters of Eve" by surroundings, find their bumpy way out of the long established prejudicial classification.

---

[448] Cf. Jung, Károly: *Köznapok és legendák – Tanulmányok a népi kultúra köréből* [Weekdays and legends – Studies from the area of the popular culture], Forum, Novi Sad, 1992, 131–145, where Jung makes an attempt to point out the obvious influence of ancient images of the popular culture effecting unquestionably the art and world view of the modern age.

# THE DUALISTIC "EVE-MARY" FATE OF KLÁRA CSÉPE, SEER OF FALLÓSKÚT

*"I am Mrs. László Sánta, maiden name Klára Csépe, I was born in 1913 in Hasznos. Since my childhood I have loved the Virgin Mother very much, She was, is and will be all my hope. I would have liked to enter a religious convent, but because there were 10 children in our family, and because I was the eldest one, I had to look after the others. Even then I prayed my Holy Beads. When I turned 15, my parents gave me in marriage. I gave birth to our first child, a boy, when I was 17. 6 years later I gave birth to a girl. My husband joined his regiment several times. There have been a lot of trials in my life."* (Fig. 3.)

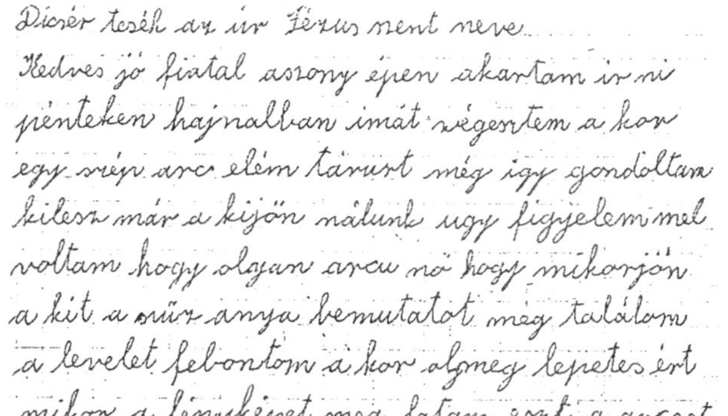
Dicsér tessék az úr Jézus szent neve.
Kedves jó fiatal asszony épen akartam írni
pénteken hajnalban imát végeztem a kor
egy szép arc elém tárult még igy gondoltam
kilesz már a kijön nálunk ugy figyelem mel
voltam hogy olyan arcu nő hogy mikorjön
a kit a szüz anya bemutatot még találom
a levelet felbontom a kor alyneg lepetes ért
mikor a fényképet meg latam ezt a arcsot
látam már hajnalban csak sirtam montam
édes jó szüz anya denagyon szereted ezt a
kis lant gyogyid megis. ak hajnalban az úr Jézus
is látam fehér ruhában miséret egy kehel volt
a kezében nem szoltak semit. Egészséget kivá-
nok a kis lanynak meg az egész családnak.
nagyon szépen köszönöm hogy a kápolnaban rende-
tete Isten fizesse meg a jóság juhak szüz anya olta-
l mában vegye Editket legyel jó a szüz anyához
Sok szor csokolom az egesz csalátot jó Isten
miclöb agyon sok örömet meg boldogsagot

Fig. 3. Handwriting of Klára Csépe

These are the first thoughts of Klára Csépe's diary,[449] in which she made notes unsystematically from the autumn of 1944 till the spring of 1982. She was truly sorely tired during this period, but at the same time she found her elevating spiritual task within her own local community that presented her with positive experiences of fulfilment.

I first came across her name years ago while reading a "rehabilitating" study of her simultaneously terrifying and plentiful ambivalent story.[450] The study made mention of her favourite prayer, the so-called "White Rose, Mary", that she learnt from her grandmother.[451]

*"White Rose, Mary,*
*You have found me, Christ,*
*You saved me with your blood.*
*God the Lord is on my door,*
*Mary is in my window,*
*Four guardian angels are in the four corners of my house.*
*Take care of me, take care of me, angel,*
*While Mary is resting.*
*Wake up, wake up, Mary,*
*Because your Holy Son was taken away,*
*He was crucified,*
*His Holy blood dripped down*
*The angels gathered it up and put it into the chalice.*
*In the middle of the sea there is a golden church,*
*In it there is a golden altar,*
*To which the Lord Jesus laid His Holy head*
*And revealed His five deep wounds.*
*Proclaim it on the black earth:*
*To all, who says this prayer in the morning and in the evening,*
*Will the door of heaven open.*
*Amen. "*[452]

---

[449] It has survived in manuscript.

[450] Jádi, Ferenc – Tüskés, Gábor: *A népi vallásosság pszichopatológiája. Egy hasznosi paraszt-asszony látomásai* [The psychopathology of the popular belief. The visions of a peasant woman from Hasznos], in: Tüskés, Gábor (ed.): "Mert ezt Isten hagyta...". Tanulmányok a népi vallásosság köréből ["Because it was devised by God...". Studies from the world of popular belief], Magvető, Budapest, 1986, 516–556

[451] Jádi – Tüskés 1986, 520–521

[452] Manga, János: *A hasznosi tömegpszichózis. A búcsújáróhelyek és a "hasznosi csoda" össze-függései* [The mass psychosis of Hasznos. The relations of the shrines and the "miracle of Hasznos"], Ethnographia, Nr. 3, 1962, 353–388, here 369

This prayer has numerous textual variations in the Hungarian speaking cultural communities. It is one of the most popular motifs of the Hungarian religious epic-lyric oral tradition. The developing leading spiritual role of Mrs. Sánta was surely in close connection with the ancient local synchretic religious-cultural heritage as this prayer witnesses. She obviously knew many other prayers built up similarly from magic textual elements, with the figures of Jesus and Mary permitted by pagan divine characteristics. The happenings at Fallóskút, the key place of her visions founding the legitimisation of the healing spring there manifest strong influence of the female figure of the pagan Happy Woman, the Hungarian Magna Mater. Since her whole mission was supported by dominating female religious ideas of her country properly focusing on Mary's character, the officially accepted Christian images play only a secondary mixed role in her belief.[453] In her life the importance of this female assistance becomes even more accented in the course of the trials produced by the different patriarchal parties concerned.

## The circumstances of the inquiry

Exploring the essential bond between the life of the Wise Woman Csépe and the investigated popular religious images led me to Hasznos, her birth- and dwelling-place, and to Fallóskút, a place of pilgrimage nearby. (Fig. 4.)

Fig. 4. The first, old chapel in the forest

[453] Jádi – Tüskés 1986, 521, cf. Jádi – Tüskés 1986, 546: The number of manifestations of different Christian characters are distributed in the visions as follows: *Mary 139*, Jesus 87, God the Father 25, Saint Joseph 18, Saint Anthony 13 times, other saints still less.

Here, in only a few days the inhabitants of surrounding villages built a chapel, by following the instructions of the healing woman in 1948. Both localities are situated in north-east Hungary, in the so-called Northern Mountain. In this area there are further numerous places of pilgrimage.[454] This fact partly refers to a rich historical heritage of the local pilgrim places, and partly to an awkward rivalling religious-cultural mentality of the region.

Even though the people in Hasznos talked about the former seer of the village affectionately, they obviously did not have too much confidence in me, because they answered my questions fairly briefly. It took me a lot of investigation until I was finally able to talk to András Sánta, the 70-year old son of Klára Csépe.[455] Even the old man did not let me into his home. He told me stories about his dead mother in front of his house, next door to his mother's cottage. I was not allowed to tape or to take any notes of his words, because he feared the possible consequences. (Table III. / Fig. 12.)[456]

He still remembered the frightening era of communism, in which his mother was at the mercy of both the state and the ecclesiastical authorities. Other members of Klára Csépe's family totally rejected the possibility of expressing their opinions about the events of the recent past.

I also visited the local "hermit"[457], the present guard of Fallóskút. For the first time I merely wanted to see how he represents the place and its story to the pilgrims, therefore I did not turn to him personally and directly, but withdrew myself to a pilgrim group of children and young people.[458] The man was

---

[454] e.g. Mátraverebély-Szentkút

[455] Interview with Mr. András Sánta on the 25th April 2001

[456] His own house is just next door

[457] Sándor Szél, brother Paszkál (born in 1942); he had a childhood of delicate health, he later worked as a tram driver in Budapest and sacrist in Máriabesnyő, in the monastery of the Capuchin friars, earlier married, but because of his brutality, his wife finally divorced him (Cf. Ipolyvölgyi Németh, Krizosztom: *Szívet keres a Szeretetláng a Kármelhegyi Boldogasszonnyal* [The Flame of Love looks for hearts with the Happy Woman of the Mount Carmel], booklet, Balassagyarmat, 1992, 45; see also the interview with Mr. and Mrs. Dér in Törökbálint on the 16th November 2002. He has been the guard of Fallóskút since 1991, when Árpád Kacsik, after a pilgrimage abroad invited him to stay there. Cf. Kerekes, József (ed.): *Egy zarándokhely kialakulása. Hasznos – Fallóskút* [The evolution of a pilgrim place. Hasznos – Fallóskút], Kerekes, Budapest, 2001, 60–61. Notice that it is the only available book about the place of pilgrimage in Fallóskút at the present time. However, for the most part the content of this edition is basically a selection of Klemm, Nándor (ed.): *Így történt. Fallóskút története* [The way it happened. The story of Fallóskút], private edition, 1999, although several pieces of information are left out and new pieces were adopted, like biographies of the parish priest and the so-called "hermit".

[458] This first "meeting" with the "hermit" took place in Fallóskút on the 16th July 2002.

astonishingly unfriendly towards us; he only talked about the financial relations of the chapel, and continuously reprimanded the pilgrims, especially
those present who were children. I soon realised that he would not give me
too much useful information. The pilgrims themselves were of a new generation; therefore they could also not help me in getting further in my research.
Some women seemed to be resistant to the official ecclesiastical develop-
ments, but they themselves did not shoulder any kind of compromising public statements.

Nevertheless I visited the "hermit" once more months later,[459] when the
local parish priest[460] guided me to him for the diary of Klára Csépe. The old
man sent me back to the priest, saying that the diary should be in the parish
of Mátraszentimre[461], but when I explained that the parish priest himself
directed me to him for the diary, he simply denied its existence. There I
received only an extremely short official ecclesiastical report of the happenings at Fallóskút dated from 19th August 1947.[462] Finally he reproved, as
usual, all the pilgrims, but in particular the women who, according to him,
were *"deeply devoted to the Virgin Mary instead of being humbly submitted
to their husbands"*.[463]

I was not satisfied with the material he offered, and that same day I followed the beaten track through the forest back to the parish priest. He seemed
to be mysterious, but finally he gave me a book,[464] the starting point of the next
step in my research. I could not easily find its editor; an old, retired Greek-
Catholic priest called Kisfalusi. Because he lives in a little village at the very
eastern border of Hungary and because of his old age, no one in his denomination could remember him personally. Finally one of my Greek-Catholic
friends found his address and telephone number in an ancient Directory of the
Greek-Catholic Church. I asked the priest[465] about the diary quoted in his
study, although obviously very insufficiently. He mentioned the name of a
couple called Dér as possible well informed people with a lot of information
about the story of Fallóskút, but he was not able to tell me the name of their

---

[459] Interview with the hermit on the 22nd October 2002
[460] Árpád Kacsik (born in 1944), parish priest of Mátraszentimre since 1982. Fallóskút belongs
to Mátraszentimre as its filia. Cf. Kerekes (ed.) 2001, 58–59.
[461] A small village, found through the woods about one hours' walk from the chapel at
Fallóskút.
[462] *Látomások a Mátrában* [Visions in the Mátra], Hasznos, 19th August 1947
[463] Cf. Interview with the hermit on the 22nd October 2002
[464] Kisfalusi János (ed.): *A fallóskúti (hasznosi) Mária-kápolna* [The chapel of Mary at
Fallóskút (Hasznos)], booklet, private edition, 1995
[465] 28th October 2002

dwelling place. He did not mention however the well known, detailed writings of Nándor Klemm on Fallóskút quoted by the book of Kerekes. Consequently he shared with me only a few useful bits of information about him, namely, that Klemm was a Roman Catholic priest in Budapest, but lived with his brother, whose address was also unknown to Kisfalusi. I noticed a massive lack of communication within the church among the hitherto basically exclusively *male clerics* elaborating the events at Fallóskút.

A complicated week later I finally found Mr. Klemm, who, in spite of his age, seemed to be fully fresh in mind and spirit. Besides his book he also presented me with an earlier, shorter version,[466] too. During our discussion he proved positively devoted to the whole problematic issue of Klára Csépe. As one of the key figures he revealed the ecclesiastical background of the situation at Fallóskút. From him I learned that the place with its miraculous phenomenon has always been a thorn in the side of both the official Catholic Church and the communist regime. In spite of this fact he himself tried to follow the fate of the seer and of her healing source with the little chapel next to the well.

Copies of the officially often sequestrated ecclesiastical, ethnographical, medical documents of the era saved by Klemm bear witness to numerous shocking church and state actions produced by the existence of an uneducated, simple female visionary hidden to the obscurity of a small village in the valley of the mountain Mátra. Klemm left all these secret, therefore perilous writings to the Dér couple, whom I found through Klemm. József and Anna Dér provided me with an enormous quantity of information. (Table III. / Fig. 13.) While investigating all these data it is a big question why this apparently insignificant peasant woman became such an important dangerous fact and difficulty to be humiliated continuously by the authorities.[467]

---

[466] Klemm, Nándor (ed.): *Fallóskút 50 éves* [Fallóskút is 50 years old], booklet, private edition, 1997

[467] During the last four decades three documentaries (Pásztory, János: *Hasznosi Mária* [Mary of Hasznos], MTV, Budapest 1966, cf. its communist critique in the article *"Gondolatok a képernyő előtt"* [Thoughts in front of the telescreen], in: Népszabadság, 1ˣ June 1966; Tóth, Péter Pál – Molnár V., József: *Aranyfűrész. Fallóskút 50 esztendeje* [Golden saw. Fallóskút for 50 years], Duna TV, Budapest 1998; Székely, Orsolya: *Fallóskút – Hasznos*, DunaTV, Budapest 2002) and several booklets partly elaborated the story. Gender based questions were however not proposed at all.

## BIOGRAPHICAL DATA

Klára Csépe was born in Hasznos on 26th January 1913. Her parents ran a farm of three hectares of cultivatable landed property. Klára was the first-born child, and according to her own personal narration, subsequent to her birth followed by eight barren years in the family, her parents offered her to God for monastic life. After a long period of intensive fasting and praying to St Anne, the mother of Mary, a further nine children were conceived and born, but only four of them survived.

The little Csépe was able to complete only the fifth form at school, because of the many commitments. According to the old inhabitants of her village she was always serious, quietly obedient. She started and finished her daily routine with prayer, and mostly preferred to stay at home, in the family circle. Even if she had to tend geese, her prayer book was her constant fellow in difficulties already from childhood. In wintertime she washed the family's clothes barefoot in the local cold stream, but she never complained. She was often missing from school because of illness. As a child she helped to build up the family house in an extremely hard way. Adults respected her reliability, but children of her age group usually made fun of her humbleness.[468]

She did not like to be involved in the social life of the local community and withdrew herself from her age group; she was often beaten by her mother. She was forcibly given in marriage in 1929 at the age of 16. Her husband, the local László Sánta was always a drunken, violent man, but she constantly tried to be patient with him. In 1930 Klára gave birth to a son called András, and in 1936 to a girl called Ilona. They worked hard for their living. Her husband was a carrier. This job kept him away from home sometimes for at least two weeks. In 1942 he joined the regiment, and during this time Klára had no news of him at all. Her visions began during this period, which resulted in numerous horrifying psychiatric treatments for her between 1949 and 1954 that temporarily gradually destroyed the frame of her mind.

Previously she had experienced the most intimate friendship full of vitality, with her Female Helper, the Happy Virgin Mary, who never hesitated to give useful instructions to her in the midst of patriarchal suppression. In 1948 she and her fellow believers from all over the country[469] built a little chapel

---

[468] Cf. Report made by József Zakkay, parish priest of Hasznos, 25th September 1947

[469] Interview with László Zakupszky, retired president of the local council, in: Notes of Klemm, Nándor, manuscript, 14th July 1980

in a forest of the Northern Mountain by the healing water indicated earlier to her in a vision by the Virgin Mary, without ecclesiastical permission. In the same year the Virgin Mother became the patroness of the place in the form of a life-sized statue symbolising real partnership between Herself and all the believers. This statue was ordered by the Virgin Mother Herself. It was made by István Szabó of Kisterenye, an area near to the pilgrim place. He did not know how to start his work. Klára asked him to pray for God's blessing. The sculpture was ready before the chapel had been painted; therefore it stood for a while in the house of the seer until 8th December 1948. Its transportation and later restorations were accompanied with numerous miraculous phenomena expressing its supernatural power. (Fig. 5.)[470]

Fig. 5. The life-sized statue of Mary in the company of Klára Csépe

In spite of the hostile atmosphere of medical doctors the simple people of her village visited Klára regularly in the psychiatric hospital and asked her, rather than the local parish priest, for spiritual support and practical advice.

---

[470] Cf. Klemm 1999, 24–26: According to the faithful many positive "accidental" events helped the realisation of the female divine will. Their reports witness a strong belief in the divine significance of every minute of their human life. They attach supernatural importance even to the most everyday happenings of their life. Even if surrounded by the modern secularised world, they live in constant divine presence where sacred and profane are totally interwoven, just as it was normal in the religious Hungarian past.

This human attitude gradually turned her negatively judged medical-social-ecclesiastical position into a positive role of the spiritual leader of the village. Nevertheless most members of the contemporary scientific society wanted to undermine the awakening ancient female self-consciousness at all costs. However, those who took courage from Klára's conviction in the ever present ancient female divine power, and found their way back to the roots of their identity, supported the almost damaged female soul until she regained strength to overcome her apparently powerful male enemies and to redefine her own leading role in the mirror of life-giving affirmative feed-back of her fellow-sufferers. Her mission met the spiritual claim of the many believers unsatisfied with the empty and even unfamiliar rituals offered by the official church.

Her influence developed increasingly in the area, in fact her fame spread gradually throughout the whole country and her message even reached beyond the national boundaries – in spite of any state and ecclesiastical struggle to stop her activity. Even though she tried to be loyal to the church, while allowing Horváth, a Catholic priest, to consecrate the little bell of the chapel in civilian clothes.[471] Circumspect caution was desperately needed in the "golden age" of both state and ecclesiastical spies. Beside the mass of supporters she faced also persistent bothering malice.

The *genius loci* gathered people into an intensively lively community. Together they looked after the place, and continuously offered their help whenever it was needed. The area around the small chapel was divided into very little parcels of flower garden cared for by the faithful, who actually lost their private properties in the course of the fashionably forced farmers' co-operatives of the Communist era. Chats accompanying gardening and other activities by the chapel meant a spiritual island of hope and freedom for the simple peasants that helped to relieve them of the everyday social-ecological-political burden. (Table IV. / Fig. 14.)

After the seer's death on the 9th December 1985 the chapel with the countless names of pilgrims and dates of their visit engraved in its brick-wall and the tiny flower gardens were destroyed.

The pilgrim place was suddenly taken over by ecclesiastical high authorities and the first Catholic mass was legally and officially celebrated on the 3rd October 1987 by Kacsik, the parish priest of Mátraszentimre. He became responsible for the place, where he built a bigger chapel, which will be soon enlarged to a cathedral with additional buildings. This new complex will apparently serve as a good financial source of ecclesiastical income.[472]

[471] Kisfalusi 1995, appendix
[472] Cf. Interview with the Dér couple, 16th November 2002

Fig. 6. The visionary Klára Csépe in her old age

FEMALE IDENTITY IN THE AMBIGUITY OF A PATRIARCHAL ORGANISED SOCIETY

Klára Csépe inherited the power of the Happy Woman from her grandmother, who taught her the most beautiful prayers dedicated to the ever present and supporting Mother, the Virgin Mary. This generations-old female spiritual background became a good breeding ground of a developing female leading role. The consistency and persistency of Csépe in the whole course of her life witnesses a strong-minded female character. The spiritual line followed by her could not be overcome by patriarchal authorities of the micro-society of the family or of the medical-political-ecclesiastical macro-society. The pilgrims of Fallóskút emerged mainly from the mass of women and children who, not accidentally, called Lady Klára *"happy woman"*.[473] This title repeatedly refers to the continuity between the divine Happy Woman and Her earthly representative, Klára, the so-called happy woman of Fallóskút. (Fig. 6.)

Except for a few supporting male believers, most men, being anxious about taking over of their power by a simple woman, played rather an oppressive role of the superman as it is certified below.

---

[473] Cf. Letter of János Manga (ethnographer) to Gyula Czapik, the archbishop of the diocese of Eger, Budapest, 2nd September 1947, 10

## Male dominated family life

After her marriage Klára arrived at the house of her husband's parents. Although her husband treated her roughly, most often with brute force, she always remained patient and hopeful, because she believed in the heavenly changing power of the Virgin Mary, who would surely and gradually turn their crazy life into harmony. In the nights her husband regularly chased her away from home, she often escaped to the pigsty or behind the bushes of the front garden. According to Klára Csépe once the Virgin Mary herself shielded the poor woman with Her wrap, so that the husband would not be able to notice and then to beat his wife.[474] Mary seemed to be the only trustworthy and understanding company for her. In another vision she saw "my Virgin Mother covered me with Her wrap. I feel *that I am always under Her wrap.*"[475]

She never had a bad word to say about her husband. Even her own mother never heard her complain. Anyone who scolded her husband was rejected, she proved always to be consistently optimistic.[476] Although from the very beginning, Mary's figure played a special role in regard to her relationship with her husband, the intensified intervention of the heavenly female character manifested first in 1947, where Mary pointed out Klára to find the spring-water in the forest, to become its guard and to be the spiritual leader of the faithful visiting the place later on.

When Csépe shared her first vision with her husband on 2nd July 1947, he refused the woman. In his opinion it could not be true, because he knew the region well and no source was to be found there. He warned her not to speak about her ridiculous dream, if she did not want to make a fool of herself. Klára was beaten by her husband because she "brought shame on him".[477] On account of the immense summer work on the fields, she had to postpone her visit to the "sacred place" pointed out by Mary. At the same time she asked the Virgin Mother to soften her wild husband, so that he would be open and helpful to find the source in the woods.

Finally on the 10th July 1947 they went to see the place. Her husband suggested to start travelling early in the morning, so that no one could see them in the village. Since only the man wore brogue, he broke the way for the barefooted woman[478] in the thicket. Before they departed he threatened his wife:

---

[474] Cf. Kerekes (ed.) 2001, 81
[475] Cf. Diary of Klára Csépe, Vision dates from 27th January 1974, italics mine
[476] Cf. Zakkay, Report, 25th September 1947
[477] Klemm 1999, 7
[478] The Virgin Mother also appears barefooted in Klára's visions. Cf. e.g. Diary of Klára Csépe.

"you won't return home, if what you have said is not true."[479] They found the source, but the husband asked the woman not to tell anyone, what they had seen, if they wanted to steer clear of mockery.

Klára agreed but a second vision revealed to her a big crowd of people surrounding the Virgin Mother, which encouraged her to spread the message of the healing spring-water. Mary confirmed the woman's vocation to be the representative of her celestial Mother on the 22nd July 1947 through an image, in which Mary handed a golden saw to Klára to cut the big snake coming out of the hazel bush and coiling up beside the feet of the Virgin. The heavenly mother said to Klára: "This has to be overcome by us, by you and me. [...] Do not be afraid. I shall be with you. I shall always help you."[480] The Virgin Mother commanded her to proclaim the mystical message because this is *the* true faith. Mary's face seemed to be the most beautiful phenomenon that Klára Csépe had ever seen. Finally they cut the snake together. The golden saw and the power of two women appeared as an omnipotent solution to all evil forces and human difficulties. This event helped Klára to break out of male violence and to explore her independent powerful female character influencing the life of many in the following decades.

From this time her husband played an almost negligible secondary part in the twist of happenings. Years later he shows up as a worrying husband who tries to save the very exhausted woman from the tiring job she shouldered. He often locks his wife in so that she can rest. He denies her presence at home among the endless inquirers and faithful that ask about the wise "happy woman". But in these cases Klára simply opens the window to answer the questions and to help the needy.[481] (Table IV. / Fig. 15.)

Lady Klára[482] becomes an independent woman in her local community during the years that makes her character widely respectful in the whole religious society of the Hungarian peasantry. Nevertheless this fact does not change her undermined role in her narrower family, even if her husband slowly turns into a humble devoted believer in the following decades. Klára does not strive for a leading position, but remains a simple, obedient wife to her husband.[483] The man even has the right to comment on his wife's words

---

Vision dated from 2nd July 1947: "I have seen the Virgin Mother [...]. She was barefooted.", see also Morvay 1981, 13–70, in: Chapter III.

[479] Klemm 1999, 8

[480] Klemm 1999, 9

[481] Klemm 1999, 49

[482] As she was and is still called among the faithful.

[483] Klemm 1999, 59

in situations when she gives interviews to scientific experts.[484] Although he finally accepts the leading role of his wife in the community, but studies do not mention any personal gentle characteristics of the male consort towards Klára. Accordingly the woman yearning for male tenderness built up the supernatural world of pure erotism culminating in the figure of Jesus.[485]

### Ethnographical research influenced by actual political ideologies

The objectivity of science is most descriptively refuted by the ethnographer Manga, who formulates different opinions about the story of Fallóskút, depending precisely on the actual ideological trend of the era. The gradual change in his thinking can be well explored in his writings of different ages.

In his *letter to the Archbishop Czapik, dated from 1947,* he more or less offers a statement of facts about the phenomenon at Fallóskút. He gives an account of a legend – existing intensively among the local people – about an old hermit who lived in the forest near Fallóskút before the First World War. This man standing always on the same rock in the woods taught about love, but also prophesied about the two world wars, about the Communist regime and about a young woman becoming the spiritual leader of the area later on. This story permeated the thoughts of every local resident of Hasznos, who tried to see the connection between the old prophet of the past and the young prophetess of the present. In his study sent to Czapik, Manga acknowledges Klára Csépe as a suggestive leading character, who enjoys a high reputation in her village and in its neighbourhood. He points out the big crowd of listeners surrounding the seer all the time, whom for this reason is almost impossible to approach and to meet personally. Without any negative comment Manga verifies the general belief in her miraculous power originating from Mary, who actually, according to Csépe's diary, often appeared to her *in light* or *in bush,* sometimes with a crown on Her head.

In less than 15 years Manga publishes a second article[486] on the theme, in which he interprets the phenomenon unambiguously negatively while using the expression "mass psychosis". He emphasises that the visions originate

---

[484] Manga 1962, 369

[485] Cf. Diary of Klára Csépe, Vision dated from 28th November 1965: *"He embraced me and His forehead touched mine."*

[486] Manga, János: *Hasznos. Egy vallási tömegpszichózis története a néprajzkutató szemével* [Hasznos. The story of a religious mass psychosis interpreted by the ethnographer], in: Világosság, Nr. 7, 1961, 44–48

from the lower class of the poor peasantry, who lived in the world of super-stitions caused by continuous uncertainty of life accompanied with various bodily handicaps and illnesses supported by primitive modes of production prior to the modern "liberating" communist era. He quotes Lenin:

*"The deepest root of religion is the social oppression of working people and their apparently total helplessness towards the blind forces of capital-ism, which causes for the simple workers in every hour of the day a thou-sand times more horrifying sufferings and a thousand times more mon-strous torture than any extraordinary event like war, earthquake etc. "*[487]

Manga concludes that the roots of religion grew stronger in the age of feudalism, when the landlord, the Turkish Empire and the church held the people equally to ransom. He forgets to outline the parallels of the Communist era referring to the co-operation among the Hungarian Communist leaders started on a shoestring, the Soviet occupants and the opportunist Hungarian church leaders against the descendants of the same peasantry mentioned by Manga, but stresses unilaterally the conflict between ecclesiastical leaders and simple believers, while covering up the enormous tension existing between peasants and the farmer's co-operatives that confiscated the private landed and other properties at all costs in the name of "the State".[488]

Indisputably the dominating political mentality full of paranoid elements makes any open ways of self-expression extremely difficult. Clerics and believers supporting Csépe's religious world and Csépe herself are considered as politically *reactionary*, disintegrating, hostile, a dangerous power within the society, therefore the whole issue should be eliminated.[489] Ecclesiastical leaders, being afraid of political pressure and consequently being ready atten-dants of the contemporary ideologies, became inauthentic blind tools of state authorities in the simple, but not stupid faithful's eyes kept open.

According to Manga the emotional life and thoughts of the peasantry, being in constant relationship with the soil, "are taken captive by the power

---

[487] Lenin quoted by Manga 1961, 45. Cf. The Hungarian translation of Konstantinow, F. V. (ed.): *A marxista filozófia alapjai* [The bases of Marxist philosophy], Budapest, 1961, 626. We already know that in the era of Hungarian fellow-Communists following the violating way and instructions of marxism-leninism the above mentioned ideological words unfortu-nately meant nothing good for the simple people.

[488] Cf. Manga 1961, 45–47

[489] Manga 1961, 47

of the *earth and nature*".[490] Faith and religion are seen by him as the most primitive and most conservative form of ideology. In Manga's world of thought the powerful existence of Mother Earth and the human emotions of the farmer bound to Her figure must obviously be overcome by the rational mind devoted to communism. He believes that the issue of Klára Csépe and of her fellow-sufferers must be examined in detail by the representatives of Marxist psychology.[491]

## Impotent communist public authority

In 1967 the local daily paper[492] informed the public about the events at Fallóskút with a series of articles entitled *"Is Lady Klára up to some mischief?"* The author surveys the place and introduces the "priestess" of the area as a puritan but artful woman who is "reluctant to grasp our political rule, our social ambition, which does not stand this kind of initiative any more. [...] The train of Mrs Sánta is decades late." She is represented as an adventurer and her pilgrim place is seen as the possible locality of a future profitable tourism better used by Communist authorities. According to one of her visions,[493] a snake has to be cut with a golden saw used by co-operating two women, the Virgin Mary and herself. In the later popular oral tradition the ugly crawler turns into red, which in this way becomes the symbol of communist idealism that has to be mastered by a powerful woman with the supportive figure of Mary in the background.[494]

The mass of old women being up to anything stood the humiliating political tests because the armed force remained helpless against the growing numbers of pilgrims during the decades of the Communist regime persecuting any form of faith. Although in 1966 one well-known Hungarian communist daily paper interpreted the place as a "profitable holy place, to where thousands of people go on a pilgrimage to give up their human dignity and to throw away everything that is dictated by the common human sense. They lift up their eyes rather to heaven and wait for hoped magic coming from beyond the earth."[495]

---

[490] Cf. Manga 1962, 354
[491] Cf. Manga 1962, 388
[492] Gulyás, Ernő: *Miben sántikál Klára asszony?* [Is Lady Klára up to some mischief?], in: Nógrád Megyei Napló, Balassagyarmat, 1966 (series)
[493] Diary of Klára Csépe, 22nd July 1947
[494] Cf. Interview with the Dér couple, 16th November 2002
[495] *A gebines kápolna*, in: Népszava, 26th May 1966

## Medical doctors of the era interpreting the phenomenon

Medical doctors, especially licensed psychiatrists, officially appointed experts of the soul and mind have an enormous power and responsibility towards their human fellows that is not always realised in practice.[496] In the case of Csépe a series of misuses of the professional power is manifested by doctors writing their official statements to higher political authorities about a completely defenceless woman standing in the way of different interests. It took a long time to rehabilitate her after the humiliating medical treatments, which lasted for years on end.

### Negative, malicious way of looking at the happenings

The first medical report about the pilgrim place is dated from 23rd October 1947. The district doctor confirms that he previously never treated anybody from the family of Klára Csépe. In his opinion "supernatural events do not happen" at the place. "Unfortunately the enlightening of the people is simply impossible, because the inhabitants of Hasznos behave threateningly with all those who do not believe the so-called wonder."[497]

Nevertheless Klára Csépe spent long months in numerous hospitals, where she was subjected to psychiatric treatments of the epoch. Places and dates of her psychiatric treatment were the following:[498]

*1. Gyöngyös, 15. 07. – 30. 12. 1949:* In 1949 she was pregnant with her third child, whom she gave birth to in the normal way during the first humiliating psychiatric treatment. She was put into a railed bed while pregnant with the four-month-old female embryo in Gyöngyös. Even though Mrs. Sánta was treated as a dangerous sick person behind closed doors in hospital, *Éva-Mária*, her little daughter received all the maternal care she needed from her mother.[499] The untroubled, healthy childbirth and birthing bed in the meantime is mentioned however only once in medical reports. She is threatened by authorities: if her delusions go beyond the bournes and become reac-

---

[496] Cf. Laing, Ronald David: *Wisdom, Madness and Folly. The Making of a Psychiatrist,* McGraw-Hill Book Company, New York, 1985

[497] Report by László Székely (parish priest of Pásztó, the nearest town to Hasznos, the birth and dwelling place of Klára Csépe) and Emil Jeszenszky (chaplain of Pásztó) with the medical doctor Miklós Tóth in Pásztó, 23rd October 1947

[498] Cf. Jádi – Tüskés 1986, 522–532

[499] Jádi – Tüskés 1986, 519–526

tionary ideas, she will be punished through the penal law. "Éva-Mária", the chosen name of her new born daughter is surely not accidental. Klára herself experienced ambivalently both being as sinful and dangerous as Eve in the eyes of the state and church authorities, and at the same time, a saving spiritual leader representing Mary's presence among her fellow sufferers. These seemingly irreconcilable female aspects of her life are mirrored in the naming. "The Virgin Mother told me: *'Eight days after the birth* of your child you will be let home. You will bring her up.'"[500] According to the Jewish law[501] the ritual of eight days symbolise both the male child's first religious initiation and the purification of the birth-giving mother regarded impure until the day of circumcision of her man-child. This custom still exists in the New Testament[502] and in several traditional cultures today. The Christian churches practised a sort of purifying rite being in close connection with the old law.[503] Klára probably also knew about this practice, but she built this symbol into her female world of faith in a different way. Her *female* child and her own *female* being both get the divine *female* promise of release from the caring Magna Mater. This female world of faith offers the opportunity to the previously negatively judged character of Eve and to all of her female fellows throughout the centuries to find the way back to their positive female roots. Medical doctors obviously left this ambition to restore female identity out of consideration. Although she answers the questions openly and with a clear mind, after all she is suggested to be put into a closed hospital ward in the capital, far away from the faithful still keeping in touch with her here in this nearer district hospital of Gyöngyös.

*2. Budapest, 17. 09 – 14. 10. 1952:* The diagnosis written by Dr. Varga about her contains the following:

*"She maintained that her being taken to hospital is only the action of her enemies. Great emotional unstability can be observed: once she cries, another time she simulates apostolic tranquillity, and even in the ward she prays, whenever she can. [...] Pathological and paranoid development based on primitive, uncommunicative personality, characterisable by hallucinations and delusions fulfilling desires effected by the environment and the situation."*[504]

---

[500] Cf. Diary of Klára Csépe, Vision dated from October 1947, italics mine

[501] Lev 12:1–8

[502] Lk 2:21

[503] Cf. Csonka-Takács 1999, 266–272, in: Chapter III

[504] Cf. Varga, Lajos: *Hasznos. Egy vallási tömegpszichózis története, ahogy az ideggyógyász látja* [Hasznos. The story of a religious mass psychosis as it is seen by the neurologist], in: Világosság, Nr. 7, 1961, 40–44, here 42

*3. Gyöngyös, 17. 09 – 14. 10. 1952:* At this time she is again put in the hospital by force. She is officially "in observation". After a while she is transported to the hospital of Gyula.

*4. Gyula, 14. 10. 1952 – 05. 04. 1954:* Even beside the visions and secondary paranoid thoughts no further pathological deviation is explored, she is treated twenty times by electric shock, and after its failure she is submitted to a sleeping cure. The treatment takes place as follows: Every time she says yes to Dr. Juba's question if God exists, she gets an electric shock. When another medical doctor employed by the hospital asks her to say that there is no God, she answers that God was, is and ever will be. She is convinced that she herself will be saved, similarly to the prophet Daniel who was put amongst lions, but God rescued him safely. During this time the Virgin Mary Herself makes known to Lady Klára that it is the archbishop of Eger, Gyula Czapik himself, who wants her to be kept in the psychiatric department of the hospital under horrifying conditions.[505] The treatment results in depression and total indifference towards the world for the "patient". The following head surgeon gets to know that she is interned in hospital *"because of religion"*.[506] She is soon transferred again to Budapest.

*5. Budapest, 05. 04 – 13. 04. 1954:* In this period the previously lively and spirited woman is described by medical doctors as a mannered, awkward ill person with penurious emotional world. Her delusions are gone. After all the earlier described horrifying treatments we can believe the bulletin of health.

In his study about the case of Klára Csépe, the neurologist Varga specifies several "extreme" systems of thought coming from the capitalist West like freudism or the writings of Ortega[507], which must be regarded as dangerous reactionary ideas jeopardising the social achievements of the communist Hungary as Csépe herself. He describes the groups of people being under the negative influence of *religion* that appear as mass hallucinations, fanatic delusions led by paranoid psychopaths, which can cause contagious *spiritual infection*. At the same time he explores other groups of people led by *positive* goals formulated by their leaders of the *socialist* construction and revolutions, which can make up for lost centuries in a few years or days. For him religion and religious thoughts are only manifestations of the ill, defective personality.

---

[505] Kisfalusi 1995, 24, cf. Diary of Klára Csépe: Vision dates from October 1949: *"The Virgin Mother told me that the archbishop of Eger, Gyula Czapik wants me to be kept in hospital."*
[506] Cf. Jádi – Tüskés 1986, 531: Klára Csépe herself narrates the story in an interview given to Jádi.
[507] Cf. Especially: Ortega y Gasset, José: *La rebelión de las masas*, Obras completas, Tomo IV, sexta edición, Revista de Occidente, Madrid, 1966

According to Varga the source of the perilous religious phenomenon is usually the so-called "inductor", who must be lifted out of one's own environment not to infect the surroundings further more. He supports his view with Russian names like Bechterew and Pavlov. [508] In our case Klára Csépe is pointed out as an inductor who obviously shows the "spiritual world of a primitive personality because of emotive, instinctive motivations instead of intellectual decisions before action." [509] Varga uses the technical terms of psychiatry rendering the condition of Csépe with great firmness, even if not correctly. [510]

## Positive medical empathy and holistic view

The rehabilitation of Klára Csépe took another 20 years. As compared with previous psychiatric treatments, Jádi and Tüskés approach the issue in 1986 [511] with a completely different, rather understanding medical attitude supported by the conviction in the elaborating contents and therefore positive task of human religious manifestations. According to them the central question of psychiatric theories is the characterisation of relation towards reality, namely, the interpretation of the notion "sense of reality". The right diagnosis takes into account the social-cultural differentiation of the psychical condition of the person. If psychiatry as science does not examine the complexity of intrapsychical and interpersonal aspects of the phenomenon, it can easily become a tool of *ideological manipulation*.

The case of Klára Csépe having special abilities shows a strong stigmatising process both in a negative and in a positive direction depending on the socio-cultural judgement. On the one hand the contemporary official state and church authorities describe her as dangerous mental patient to be outcast from society (previously this kind of attitude led to the burning of witches or killing of shamans etc.). On the other hand those who interpret her experiences as signs of heavenly powers have a high respect for her (earlier in the course of church history this type of process often culminated in the person's canonisation).

The psychiatrist Jádi rejects the negative and often malicious medical categorisations regarding the mental condition of Klára Csépe. Instead of hallucinations he speaks about spiritual experiences having reality components for

[508] Cf. Varga 1961, 40–41
[509] Varga 1961, 42
[510] See its criticism in: Jádi – Tüskés 1986, 518
[511] Jádi – Tüskés 1986

the individual that appear in peculiar situations. In the case of Csépe the particular religious experiences coincided with the time of prayer after waking up in the morning or before going to sleep in the evening. Since for Mrs. Sánta these periods were the most intensive moments of being busy with religious themes into which she entered in a kathatym way, it offered her a good atmosphere for meditative state of being. Behind the images of her world of faith there are usually well circumscribable elements of yearnings to be fulfilled that serve as strengthening spiritual tools of self-identity. The figures are never bizarre, self-alien forms, but statue-like representations showing continuous contact with reality. The unalloyed relationship established between mother and children indicates well-ordered personality. She was always able to distinguish her religious experiences from other events of everyday reality.

Strictly speaking she had an inclination to gloss over the unpleasant side of reality with religious contents from childhood. The feeling of being chosen[512] can be the result of certain parental upbringing. Mary the Magna Mater replaced the real figure of the mother. She had no interest in second dogmas about Mary (immaculata, semper virgo) of the Christian tradition. The Happy Woman appearing in the image of the Virgin Mary is rather the good alter-ego of her own mother, to whom she could project her childlike feelings in a ruthless, strictly organised world that had no place for any human emotions. This maternal fellow understands her difficult situation in many ways, in the images of Mater speciosa, Mater dolorosa, Mater misericordiae, Mater amabilis or Regina coeli. Jádi points out a clear continuity of identity between the Christian Madonna and the maternal Goddess of pre-Christianity.

The message of visions could not remain a simply private business in an obviously intense atmosphere of people being in collective emotional-mental regression with similarly receptive inclination to the proclaimed idea of powerful female love. The mystical-transcendent ancient world concept, the individual suggestibility, the low level of development of the self-functions and external social conditions influence propensity altogether. As Jádi claims, this background could effect the crowd to identify oneself with state authorities, but because of strong longing for defence of the local heritage of a certain ancient religious-cultural-economic world, inhabitants of the sur-

---

[512] Cf. e.g. *"The Virgin Mother appeared and [...] told me that She wandered all over the world, but She found only me with an immaculate heart."* In: Diary of Klára Csépe, Vision dated from 1ˢᵗ March 1965

rounding villages had a greater sympathy towards their attacked and oppressed female fellow sufferer. (Table V. / Fig. 16.)[513]

Moreover this deep compassion can cause such a powerful identification that results in similar experiences in large numbers of people [and] leads to a symbiotic bond among previously outsiders. The archetypal Magna Mater offers healing-feeding water (this refers to amniotic fluid) to her children in the form of a source in the forest, which means purification and innocence of paradise to all. This great opportunity inspires then the faithful to build up the chapel, which is basically the materialisation of the receiving Mother (and her parallel, the mater ecclesia), whose existence turns a neutral group of people into a lively-sharing community. Certainly here manifests a group will to change and solve psychological-social problems on another level of their transcendent relations.

According to Jilek *"ritualised modified states of consciousness, whether interpreted as possession-trance or trance according to culture, must be conceptually differentiated from psychopathological conditions. Such conditions do not usually correspond to the behaviour expected in a socially sanctioned ceremonial and are defined as abnormal by indigenous experts. [...] The previously common pathology labelling of modified states of consciousness which were institutionalised in the religious and therapeutic ceremonials of non-western cultures, has led to a distorted view of traditional practitioners, especially shamans, as mentally abnormal deviants. Such views are examples of Eurocentric and positivistic fallacies. "*[514]

Jádi's scientific attitude towards the firm belief represented by Klára Csépe and her followers' witnesses a great sympathy with the ethnopsychiatric significance of socio-cultural differentiation described by Jilek. The radical-revolutionary revival of the holistic, integrative way of doing psychiatric-spiritual research is that culturally sanctioned ritual practices are to be considered as learned behaviour rather than psychopathology. It should never be interpreted as subjects to psychiatric diagnosing.[515] Leavitt lines up sever-

---

[513] The wall-paintings represent events of Mary's life. The small sculpture of the Holy Trinity is set to the side.

[514] Jilek, Wolfgang G.: *Modified States of Consciousness: Their Role in Ethnopsychiatry,* in: Newsletter of Transcultural Psychiatry, December 1994, Vol. XII, No. 2, 5

[515] Jilek, Wolfgang G.: *Normality and psychopatology in the context of culture: Some thoughts on culture-sensitive diagnosing in psychiatry,* in: Newsletter of Transcultural Psychiatry, August 1994, Vol. XII, No.1, 4

al examples from different parts of the world, where trance is a perfectly normal side of religious life. In only a "very few societies are these states identified primarily with madness or other disorder."[516]

## Clerical attitudes[517]

From 1947 in the Hungarian Catholic Church there has been a deep fear of communist reprisal regarding the popularity of the pilgrim place at Fallóskút and of a simple, uneducated woman proclaiming her "dangerous", "reactionary" persuasion openly. The brave message of Lady Klára not only disturbed the state authorities that were pointed out by Csépe as enemies of God and of the working peasantry. The church authorities were similarly in an uncomfortable situation, partly because of state pressure to forbid Csépe's anti-Soviet criticism, and partly because of the appearing female leader whose presence stretched and irritated the frames of the patriarchal church order.

The sight of many followers around the woman made clear that the spiritual "hierarchy" did not necessarily coincide with the prescribed ecclesiastical structural hierarchy. In the long run the latter has usually no efficacy without authentic personal commitment among the faithful. Even peasants see the difference between the shallow, routine-like, burnt out pastors and the seriously understanding, attentive attitude of their female fellow sufferer coming from the same environment and having the same rhythm and view of life. The mass of "renegades" elicited various reactions from the officially appointed priests of the narrower and wider faith community.

---

[516] Leavitt, John: *Are Trance and Possession Disorders?*, in: Transcultural Psychiatric Research Review, 1993, Vol. XXX, No. 1, 51–57, here 52

[517] Most of the following quoted ecclesiastical documents are officially still restricted. I was only able to read them with the help of Klemm, who as a Catholic priest was able to get access to the materials of the blocked episcopal archive in Eger and quickly made photoprints of them – in secret. Even Jádi and Tüskés commented this fact: The ecclesiastical judgement of the issue was quite typical. When they asked about the ecclesiastical documents, the diocesan authorities did not allow them to examine the materials for scientific research, because "the ecclesiastical investigation of the case is still in progress." Jádi – Tüskés 1986, 540; cf. The official ecclesiastical answers to the researchers, Letters Nr. 2274/1980 and Nr. 44/1981.

## Negative sacerdotal aspects effected by political ascendancy

Immediately after the first vision of Klára Csépe followed by communal events, three priestly reports were written to the Episcopal office in Eger, in which we get a real picture of the administrative ecclesiastical attitude towards the questions, which arose around the issue. These accounts witness the mixture of blind obedience, fear of the state- and church-authorities and sarcastic disdain of the simple believers. All of these attitudes seem to originate from the same root, namely, from an inferiority complex hidden behind hypocrisy showing great self-confidence and self-conceit, in reality with massive uncertainty of seriously played priestly roles in the background.

Here in the following few paragraphs I will illustrate the shilly-shally ecclesiastical approach to the theme through quoted paragraphs of reports written to Gyula Czapik (archbishop of Eger) by three priests. These were written almost in the same period of time. Dr. József Takács, parish priest of Bátor, rural dean, professor and expert of Mariology;[518] Dr. László Székely, parish priest of Pásztó (the nearest town to Hasznos, the dwelling place of Klára Csépe) and Episcopal counsellor;[519] József Zakkay, parish priest of Tar near Hasznos.[520] In their reports Székely and Zakkay mention previous Episcopal commissions of Czapik to investigate the issue of the pilgrim place from official clerical aspects,[521] which motivated their inspections. Takács was requested to do the job personally by the archbishop. The following quotations represent the priestly thoughts of the era. The formulation of the idioms and the style of the reports speak for themselves. I will introduce their essence in chronological order.

In his first report[522] to the archbishop Zakkay gives account of his actions carrying out the instructions of the first Episcopal commission[523] regarding

---

[518] Report dates from 18th October 1947

[519] Report dates from 25th October 1947, Nr. 320/1947

[520] Reports date from 25th September 1947, Nr. 229/1947 and from 30th October 1947, Nr. 258/1947

[521] Episcopal commission, Nr 4195/1947. Cf. Report of Zakkay (Tar, 25th September 1947); Episcopal commission, Nr. 5504/1947. Cf. Reports of Székely (Pásztó, 25th October 1947) and Zakkay (Tar, 30th October 1947). The original text of these commissions are not known, because of ecclesiastical freezing of certain documents relating to the case. Nevertheless references of the priestly reports to them draw a more or less clear picture of their content and of the situation interpreted by the official church.

[522] Report dates from 25th September 1947, Nr. 229/1947

[523] Episcopal commission, Nr 4195/1947.

the case of Klára Csépe. In his letter he informs the archbishop that the declaration attached to the prohibitive Episcopal order was read and placarded in Tar and in all its filiae.

"The ecclesiastical order instructs me *to report* all *the faithful* collecting donations[524] for the chapel – *to the police*. I announce with respect that I have immediately made a report to the police of Galyatető. Here I attach the result of the investigation of the police.

While *obeying the instruction* of the order, I follow the events by the spring with attention, but without intervention. [...] Very big crowds visit both the spring and the female visionary of Hasznos. They come *from all over the country*, many even *from Budapest. Intellectuals just as simple people. There are also priests and nuns among them.* Ecclesiastical persons often come to the parish of Tar for information. I inform them about the hitherto valid church order. At Mátraverebély the orator exhorted the faithful *to keep strictly the church* order and *not to go* on pilgrimage to the spring *until the church gives permission to do so.* In spite of this warning crowds go there every day, by all sorts of means of transport. [...]

Since then the female visionary goes to mass every time and receives the sacraments. Her husband is also fervent, and welcomes the strangers with great cordiality. Generally speaking the issue has a very good influence on the faithful. They are consequently annoyed with all for being sceptic. I experienced that even in the railway carriage was this issue intensely discussed, and during these conversations everyone appeared rather to be a believer than a non-believer. [...] In front of the parish I often see *women, young people, sick persons, miners and other working men, but also intelligent men and women,* going with jugs to the spring for water. Reading the ecclesiastical prohibitive order in the surrounding villages to keep the people away from the spring until the official ecclesiastical investigation is in progress,[525] seems to be *insufficient.* From now on only a *general prohibition* would be *expedient,* because there is a keen interest in the spring. Everyone would like to know about it and to get there, especially since the daily papers also deal with the visions of Hasznos. [...]"[526]

---

[524] Those who collected money for the chapel or for themselves made Lady Klára very angry: "Nobody has the right to ask for money from the faithful. The Blessed Virgin Mother wants no money, but prayer and love. I do not let anyone speculate." Cf. Kelemen (ed.) 2001, 22

[525] According to Jádi – Tüskés the official ecclesiastical investigation is *still* in progress *in 1982.* Cf. Jádi – Tüskés 1986, 540

[526] Italics mine

The letter witnesses a great ecclesiastical anxiety with regard to the totally promiscuous, growing crowd of the faithful going on pilgrimage to
Fallóskút and to the uneducated peasant woman to find hope and understanding in the era of terror, when clerics and policemen have the same interest in silencing uncomfortable voices of the margin. The only alternative
seems to be the authoritative, prohibiting, but basically helpless, impotent
official declarations to solve "the problem".

Takács puts his thoughts in the following way:

"[…] I ask *Your Most Reverend with filial homage* to take steps so that the
clergy *keeps serious distance*, especially those who have no experience
about the issue: the deluge has started and *it is very powerful.* We must not
swim with the tide, because *it does not come from God.* We are not able *to
stand up against it;* we would have very little positive outcome with greater
bad consequences. Not our *best* faithful strive after the source; if the priests
are against them, they believe for all that. We must assume an *expectant
attitude* […] *Our well-intentioned* believers will have the opportunity to
congregate *around us* and to wait for events to calm down with us.
We must not deny *openly* the rumours connected with the spring. The
atmosphere is already anti-clerical enough. *They attack us* in different
ways: *in their opinion we are the unbelievers;* obviously the priests are the
biggest sinners. The communists had already argued in this way: the
priests do not go there [to the pilgrim place[527]], because they have to go
there on foot, without car or coach, therefore they prefer to leave the people alone, although they could read the mass at a field-altar.
I cannot keep back *my worry* that came to mind during the night I spent
by the spring: the Mariavitans. There is a great respect for Mary, for the
Holy Eucharist, and *great hostility towards Catholicism. If these ones get
a foothold here, they could cause a lot of trouble.* But it is only a sudden
thought of mine at the moment.
Anyway, now it is raining, the weather has turned cold, the chilly winter
is falling. The life around the source will be *surely less intensive.* The
springtime might change the interests. […]
*Finally I make mention of why I find it very useful for the clergy to prac-
tise* a careful and non-committal attitude. *[…] We can easily be slandered
as* reactionary priests *who instigate rebellion among the people. The simple human beings understand the pressure weighing heavily on the*

---

[527] My remark

*Hungarians better than we do and they tolerate it even more hardly. They break out into angry words more easily, but they are lightly forgiven. Nevertheless* it would be bad, if the priests were blamed by the present police and by its friends.
*While kissing your consecrated hand, I am the obedient priest of Your Most Reverend with rendering respect [...]* "[528]

This letter written in a particularly ornate language mirrors a kind of unconditional servile obedience existing in the church hierarchy. In contradistinction to his clerical fellow quoted above Takács assumes an expectant attitude. In his opinion keeping a distance is the only chance for the clergy to have a narrow escape of the situation without conflict. Similarly to Zakkay his words show the same fear, but instead of aggression suggested by Zakkay his solution is rather regressive withdrawal of the enraged people. He hopes to avoid the ever-louder marginal voices criticising the authoritative clerical forces with the help of this new type of tactics. Székely's interpretation runs as follows:

"[...] I found it necessary to look around the spring when not too many believers were there. I must be able to calm my faithful who see the marching pilgrim groups, the lorries decked out with flowers, not rarely the buses decorated with flags in the national[529] and red[530] colours everyday, and especially the people at large arriving by train on Friday evenings (On the 17th October 1700 passengers arrived). Here I represent my following observations:
[...] I *do not know* the wife[531] of László Sánta. I *did not talk to her*, because I did not find her at home. [...] All the faithful of Hasznos are involved in the events, who are very proud of becoming famous in this way. It is quite understandable, why they are threatening all those who do not believe the authenticity of the happenings. I also almost became the victim of the

---

[528] Italics mine
[529] red-white-green
[530] Visibly the new possessive political ideology appears as an understanding friend of the oppressed people in 1947, even if Klára Csépe speaks against communism (and against church authority interpreted incorrectly) from the beginning. Religious and communist ideas seem to get on well together at this time. The faithful see no difference between the saving message of Mary mediated by Csépe and the communist ideologist promising prosperity for everyone built on equality. The contradictions only later come to the forefront. It takes time for the simple people to understand that the new regime is not at all better for them than the previous one.
[531] = Klára Csépe

rational enlightening. I know their excellent business sense [...]. *They go about in fear of their business occasions.* [...]

Visions are the most frequent. Whole crowds see the figure of the cross, the Eucharist, the Virgin Mother with the little Jesus, the Great Lady of Hungarians,[532] the Holy Family etc. in the Sun [...] The visions are totally unreliable, because everyone sees different things. [...]

The miraculous spring has *very annoying* aspects. The pilgrims returning from Szentkút[533] dropped in by the shrine at Fallóskút and neglected the holy mass at home. It is said that there were about 7000 people. When I stayed by the spring I noticed one of my faithful of Pásztó as chief organiser there. The doctor says he is epileptic, but *greater blemish* is that he has already lived with his fiancée for months *without getting married.* I had also to see a group of pious pilgrims cooking a big kettle of goulash[534] on Friday. I have other, yet not controlled news about the source where wine was sold for 14 forints per litre. In short at the spring *a whole lot of sins are interwoven by breaking the mass and fasting rules, fornication, cheating and usury.* I reproached all those present with these things. I heard *no word of protest. My faithful were molested* only on the following day at the market place by saying that *their priest was a non-believer.* I can keep back neither the unhealthy conditions around the spring. [...]

By way of *compensation* however there is a large number of cases of conversion, in sede confessionali. Individuals, who were not even attracted by the mission of last year, come to confessional. [...]"[535]

Székely does not take the trouble to get to know Mrs. Sánta personally, but he seems extremely self-confident to judge the ritual events occurring around the woman unilaterally in a negative way. His only aspect is to keep the rules declared by the church authorities. He can see only business in the happenings at Fallóskút, and the faithful are purely sinful souls in his eyes. Statistical data have particular significance in his letter that witness for him the spreading of dangerous popular ideas permitted by the cult of the Virgin Mother accompanied by anticlerical feel. In his second report[536] Zakkay takes the following notes:

---

[532] = The Happy Woman
[533] Centuries old pilgrim place near Fallóskút.
[534] Goulash is a kind of Hungarian one-course meal with meat that is forbidden to eat on Friday, which is the day of the week set aside for fasting.
[535] Italics mine
[536] Report dates from 30 October 1947, Nr. 258/1947

"On the 22<sup>nd</sup> inst. I received a *commission nr. 5504* to search in detail the personal and family circumstances of the seer of Hasznos, Klára Csépe, to talk with the more *serious, elderly, reliable and rational* believers, to describe the *mental condition* of the parents, sisters and brothers of Klára Csépe, to see if anyone among them was previously *neurotic,* to examine the *degree* of her religious attitude and to answer the following questions: *Did she receive the sacraments in the church? Did she change after the asserted visions? Does she go to church at the moment? When did she receive the Holy Eucharist for the last time?* I had to register the names of all the witnesses who provided the information.

I announce with great respect that I acted *in the proper sense of the received instructions.* [...]

As your parish priest, I can tell the following about her: I have known her for five years. She regularly went to the church on Sundays and feast days. She received the sacraments several times during the year. Since her visions she receives the sacraments almost at every turn, when the holy mass is celebrated in Hasznos.[537]

*I see her* always in the church on Sundays and feast days. At last *I have seen her* receiving the Eucharist on the 28<sup>th</sup> October. At the same time *I report* that they plan to build up a chapel; the bricks are already carried to the spring.

[...] After her eyes had been healed a resident of Budapest sent a beautiful *statute* of Mary to Hasznos, which *is in the house of the female visionary* at the moment.

On the 5<sup>th</sup> November a retired parish priest from Budapest [...] asked for permission to stay with a huge number of pilgrims in Hasznos and to carry out priestly functions in the local church. *I informed him* immediately that the priestly direction of the pilgrims is *forbidden,* and *I am permitted to give permission.* At the same time *I made known to him the main points of the Episcopal order.* [...]

My bell-ringer mentioned the bailiff of Eger who permitted 2000 copies of the booklet about the visions and miracles, which are already sold out, according to the bell-ringer.

Since the weather turns to cooler autumn, the number of pilgrims decrease, even in the church of Hasznos *I see no more strangers* at present.

After the *reverential representation* of the above mentioned things I remain with deep respect [...]."[538]

---

[537] Because of the many tasks parish priests have to fulfil in several villages at the same time, Zakkay probably rarely reads weekday-mass in Hasznos, filia of Tar.

[538] Italics mine

At this time Zakkay follows Székely's method of focusing on purely quantitative questions. It seems that the helpless church authorities are stuck to forms instead of content. For them the most important point is *regularity*. Lady Klára can be preserved from the negative judgement of the church only if she participates in ecclesiastical ceremonies regularly enough. In the following decades there have been continuous vain official attempts to set the female seer out of way. The increasing number of pilgrims at Fallóskút did not allow any real official intervention in the events. Only in 1987 did the official Catholic Church, remaining unappropriated after the death of Klára Csépe, have full play at the pilgrim place.

### Positive priestly voice from the margin

In 1978 Nándor Klemm a parish priest in Budapest, began to take an interest in the issue in detail. He interviewed numerous eyewitnesses and other believers to get a better picture of the happenings at the source. He began his job without any prejudice, but with great empathy accompanied with a circumspection, deeply understanding attitude towards the simple souls. In 1982 he wrote his perceptions to the archbishop of Eger. He puts the following questions:

"I see many things clearly, but I do not get answers to certain questions. *The church staff does not reply to* my letters, *a parish priest refused* to make a report of a healing process, *others give me evasive answers.* A *high-ranking church officer* wrote to me that the issue belongs to the competence of the archbishop of Eger. This is why I have the courage to turn directly to you, Sir Archbishop, with my questions. [...]
All my problems concern the events after the circular letter of the archbishop dated from the autumn of 1947.[539] [...]
The fact is that since then Fallóskút is a place *"de iure" prohibited by the church,* but *"de facto" it has been a well-attended pilgrim place for 35 years.* It is more frequented than any other pilgrim places in Hungary being much easier to reach and being acknowledged by the church. [...]
There are always fresh flowers on its altar [...], its flowery decoration could rival many of our churches in the capital. Its visitors are not only the

---

[539] Circular written by Gyula Czapik, the archbishop of Eger of the time, 1947.

pious Palóc folk,[540] but [...] people also come from Czecho-Slovakia, Szeged, Budapest and even Veszprém[541].

[...] If the events of Fallóskút belong to the "world of fantasy", as archbishop Czapik put it in 1948, *why did he not prevent the building of the chapel?* Or if it had already been built, *why did he not close it?* In this way he and his successor also offered an *opportunity of 'falsa cultus'* to the faithful. [...] If nothing happened at Fallóskút, why does the archbishop swallow this 'cultus'? Or supposing something happened there?

[...] How is it possible that *in the summer of 1948 the police accepted the interpretation of Mrs. Sánta according to which she got permission for building from heaven?*[542] [...]

What is the explanation of letting Mrs. Sánta out from the hospital to listen to mass in the town in 1949, in the middle of the Rákosi-era?[543] [...]

I read the following statements about the mental conditions of Mrs. Sánta: [...] 'She has a defective memory, reasoning and critical power...'

I can confirm the short memory of Mrs. Sánta. But how is it interpretable that she speaks about the visions of 1947 in the same way and says the same things even in 1979?

If her reasoning power is weak [...], and if she has only completed the sixth form of the primary school [...], where did she take the *devotion of the Holy Trinity* that, according to my experiences, *is not usual among the laity?*

Why is she *quite self-confident in substantial questions regarding the visions,* while at the same time seems very uncertain in other questions? [...] Even the electric shocks were not able to destroy her 'fixed ideas'. She is so sure of them that she even takes the trial for them. [...]

In my student years I was taught by Professor Rajeczky to get to the bottom of all my doubt concerning faith. This is what has motivated me to investigate the events in Hasznos and at Fallóskút so intensely, and this is what has encouraged me to write to you, Sir Archbishop. [...]

Based on my research I am afraid that the Episcopal *circular* of 1947 is *outworn,* the *events are more than fairy tales.*"[544]

---

[540] Hungarian ethnic group with special dialect and traditions. They live in North-Hungary, in the wider area of the Mountain Mátra. Hasznos (the birth place of Lady Klára) and Fallóskút (the pilgrim place come into being after the visions of Lady Klára) both belong to this region.

[541] Veszprém is a Hungarian Trans-Danubian town far away from Fallóskút.

[542] Notice that in this time the political atmosphere was extremely rigorous, to which many people fell victim in Hungary.

[543] Mátyás Rákosi, the most notorious communist minister president of the period in Hungary.

[544] Letter of Nándor Klemm to the archbishop of Eger in November 1982, manuscript, italics mine

Klemm queries the ambiguous ecclesiastical practice of causing conflict between church rules and personal conviction of the faithful. Through his questions he points out the failure of church authorities regarding the issue of Lady Klára. As a cleric however, he shows an honest interest in the case of the simple peasant woman followed by many believers. Instead of automatic refusal he tries to get a fuller picture of the phenomenon before forming an opinion about the people involved in the theme. He goes beyond the surface questions of formalities and catches a deeper essence of the traditional cult focusing on Mary's maternal figure.

*Continuous rebirth of the Goddess –*
*in the midst of patriarchal oppression*

After all we realise an intensified conflict of ideologies, among which it is usually the representatives of the popular belief whose ritual actions turn to be the real point of attacks. In reality it is an endless invalidating process of the praised female figure, the ancient-pagan Happy Woman hidden behind the baptised image of the Virgin Mother throughout the centuries. Most scientific experts judging the phenomenon remain on the surface of the problem. In their eyes the products of imagination of the "simple souls" are ridiculous and should not be taken seriously from a scientific point of view. None of these judgements attempt to honestly answer the question WHY these people need such a powerful female character in their world of belief. This trend of the religious folk tradition manifesting mainly in the magic devotion to the principal female figure of Christianity seems to be a general phenomenon all over the Christian world that goes back to the ancient worship of a female divine figure whose character usually offers quite a different quality than that of her male equivalent

Csépe's image of God the Father mirrors medieval characteristics: He appears as a dignified, authoritative forefather with white hair, a beard and the inevitable stick in his right hand.[545] This description moulds strict parental attitude, in which the stick symbolises a kind of physical privilege opposite to the child, but it also demonstrates the generally legitimised male force in society.

---

[545] Cf. Diary of Klára Csépe, e.g. Vision dates from 7th December 1974

## Answering the aspersions through female visions

The peasant Klára Csépe being a woman, uneducated and lay – therefore having no real power facing the church authorities – gives the words describing her thoughts and feelings into the mouth of her solely understanding divine Mother. She needs to be hidden beyond the image of the heavenly female figure who empowers Lady Klára to express her female being in a male-centred society self-confidently enough. For Klára the filial character of Jesus, the Son of the Virgin Mother symbolises the gentle counterpart of the violent male society. He *"is the only one who knows the holy mystery. It is unknown to both the church and state authorities, nevertheless this mystery will be realised.*"[546]

Mrs. Sánta takes the role of real priesthood seriously. In one of her visions she drinks bitter liquid left over by male clerics. In contradiction to the reality of ecclesiastical oppression in the visions her position is strongly established and even bishops ask for her help.

"I saw a man with a chalice. *I also held a chalice.* He poured its content into his, and left *only a little* liquid for me that *I have drunk off. It was bitter.* […] Then I saw a bishop wearing a *high cup* with a *long stick* in his hand. I asked him: *'What do you want from me?'* He replied: *'I beg you to request the clergy to do penance.*'"[547]

She realises with the assistance of the Virgin Mother that the only priest to be followed and represented is Her Son who has nothing to do with the clerics bothering the peasant woman.

"The Virgin Mother said: 'You must not follow the *hideous ones.*[548] There *is* a real pontiff, who is my Son.'"[549]

Lady Klára receives satisfaction directly from God who guarantees the rehabilitation of the woman with divine supremacy.

"The Good God told me: *'Those who are above now, will be down and out.*'"[550]

---

[546] Cf. Diary of Klára Csépe: Vision dates from the 9th February 1963
[547] Cf. Diary of Klára Csépe: Vision dates from 14th February 1973, italics mine
[548] = priests
[549] Diary of Klára Csépe, Vision dates from 5th January 1974, italics mine
[550] Cf. Diary of Klára Csépe: Vision dates from 4th October 1974

The woman suffering a lot of pontifical molestation is finally reconciled at least in her visions. After the death of archbishop Czapik justice is realised in the following vision of Klára: On another occasion:

"I was praying when I saw a big *black* orb with a human figure in it. In his right hand he had a *stick* that he *raised in the darkness.* I asked him: 'Who are you? *I do not know you.'* He replied: 'I am Archbishop Gyula Czapik. *Forgive me, because I have done a lot of harm to you.'* I said: *'Go to the priests who should remedy all that you have damaged. They do not want to believe me.'''* [551]

The next section of Lady Klára's diary mirrors the experienced general hostile clerical attitude towards the cult of Mary and Her female representatives:

"The Virgin Mother stood in front of me, her face was serious. Brightness radiated from Her hands. She told me: 'Ask the *priests not to stab my* holy *heart* with their daggers all the time, because disaster comes if they are not converted.'" [552]

"The Virgin Mother asked me to *tell the priests* that She is the *Mother of God* and the *Queen of Heaven. Why are you against Her?*" [553] (Table V. / Fig. 17.) [554]

Nevertheless the Virgin Mother Herself assures the rural happy woman of Her divine female strength that encourages Mrs. Sánta to stand up against the state and church authorities.

The Virgin Mother appears to her as "Queen in the colour of glory". She calms her with the following fact: *She Herself has the power* above the staff of church and state, therefore *'Do not let them to push you about.'''* [555]

---

[551] Cf. Diary of Klára Csépe: Vision dates from the 20th September 1975, italics mine
[552] Cf. Diary of Klára Csépe: Vision dates from 3rd January 1976, italics mine; similar visions on 7th December 1977, 20th February 1978, 8th July 1978
[553] Cf. Diary of Klára Csépe: Vision dates from 7th January 1976, italics mine
[554] The female figure is placed under a shelter, which is in the shape of the Hungarian crown implying that She is the real king of Hungary.
[555] Cf. Diary of Klára Csépe: Vision dates from 4th March 1976, italics mine

Not even the pope is saved from facing the question of female authority within the Catholic Church. Both the oppressed cult of Mary and the prohibited activity of Her female earthly representatives in the church bring the two women, the Virgin Mother and Klára, into close female alliance to gain over the pope himself for the sake of the cause.

"The Virgin Mother asked me: 'What will you tell *the pope?*' I replied: 'Whatever you ask me to say, Virgin Mother.' She said: 'Convey to him *regards from the Virgin Mother,* who *asks him* to confirm the place of Her appearance.' [...]"[556]

After all the inspiring Holy Spirit is blowing high, blowing low – and transcends the competence of rules declared by church and state authorities.

"I was praying when the Holy Spirit in the image of a white dove told me: *'Permission is not needed* to build up the house of God. The church of God will be built up.'"[557]

The connection between the religion of Hungarians and the figure of the Virgin Mary is unambiguously manifested in Klára's visions. These images obviously refer to the pagan cult of the Happy Woman who is above all other gods in rural Hungarian communities:

"I have seen the Virgin Mother climbing the stairs and accompanied by an angel who said: *'In Hungary the Virgin Mother is on the highest stage.'*"[558]

Lady Klára, the so-called happy woman is measured differently from earthly hierarchy by supernatural forces. Her status is restored in the transcendent sphere, which means that she basically goes through the process of identifying herself with the divine Happy Woman who in Christianity becomes the Queen of heaven, the crowned Virgin Mary.

"I was praying when two angels held a crown above me. I was surprised. They said: *'You are crowned, you are holy in the eyes of the powers above.'*"[559]

---

[556] Cf. Diary of Klára Csépe: Vision dates from 13th May 1976, italics mine

[557] Cf. Diary of Klára Csépe: Vision dates from 15th May 1978, italics by author

[558] Cf. Diary of Klára Csépe. Vision dates from 20th April 1974, italics by author

[559] Cf. Diary of Klára Csépe: Vision dates from 6th May 1976, italics by author; powers above = divine persons

After long decades of ecclesiastical refusal the restricted clerical position slowly becomes friendlier. Persisting in devotion to the Virgin Mother bore good results for the steady rural community. In a vision in 1947 God asks Lady Klára to visit the local parish priest and to request him to proclaim the good news instead of preaching the ideas coming from the contemporary Hungarian media. According to Mrs. Sánta: "he strongly held onto my arm to throw me out into the garden of the church. But I could not move, and he could neither. [...] Then he never hurt me again."[560] Many years later, in 1980 she told the parish priest that on the day of the Great Happy Woman[561] she would like to visit the little chapel of Fallóskút instead of going to the official mass in Hasznos. He did not resist, because he was no longer opposed to the events of Fallóskút.[562] (Table VI. / Fig. 18.)

In 1982 the last note of her visions was taken, when the Virgin Mother appeared and asked her to start building the church. This instruction motivated Lady Klára to write a letter to the archbishop Kádár for an audience. In his answer the archbishop asked her to apply for an appointment in the following July. As we know she never had the opportunity to meet the archbishop. Nevertheless after her death the church immediately took over the pilgrim place and legitimised it on the 3rd October 1987. Since then the former devoted faithful have no right to intervene in the issue on behalf of keeping the original popular religious atmosphere built up during long decades of suffering.

Although in 1990 the believers expressed their hope to finally get into good, co-operative relationship with the ecclesiastical authorities.[563] In the same year the archbishop of Eger, István Seregély consecrated in honour of the *"Queen of Forests"* the new chapel built very quickly by the official church in the place of the previous, destroyed chapel built by simple believers. The new naming of the pilgrim place still shows strong insistence on nature and its "queen", the Magna Mater or the Earth Mother.[564] (Table VI. / Fig. 19.)

Nevertheless the bishop stresses in front of the celebrating faithful that he is not at all convinced of the authenticity of the pilgrim place. He only con-

---

[560] Kelemen (ed.) 2001, 33

[561] 15th August

[562] Cf. Jádi – Tüskés 1986, 521

[563] "We have been waiting for this day for a long time. We are prepared, and this is the reason our joy. This day is really given by God, let us rejoice in it. This is a day of happiness for us, because our little chapel is a real church consecrated to God. It will be the earthly dwelling place of the Virgin Mother. We proclaim with Jacob: 'This is the house of God and the door of heaven.' [...]", Words of welcome at the pilgrim place of Fallóskút, told by József Dér, on 22nd September 1990, on the day of consecrating the chapel by the archbishop

[564] "The Virgin Mother stopped at the spring. I kissed the earth where the Virgin Mother stood [...]." In: Diary of Klára Csépe, Vision dated from 10th July 1947

secrated the chapel because there were too many people visiting it. Furthermore in 1994 the ecclesiastical authorities reject any help from the long-standing believers. *"The parish priest lays no claim to your service. Consequently in the future abstain from intervening in the administration of the pilgrim place* "[565] – writes the vicar-general of Eger to the neglected, but still enthusiastic faithful. (Table VII. / Fig. 20.)


Ancient spiritual power manifested in the healing presence of Klára Csépe

"Hundreds of people gather together at the miraculous place, but in the church of the village only a sparse group of native believers attend the religious ceremony."[566] Judging mystical experiences is always problematic, especially for a simple, uneducated peasant woman. Klára Csépe did not get any real exterior help to examine the events. At the beginning her parish priest refused her the sacraments. Besides being outcast from the church she was full of cares in her family. The curious visitors also absorbed her energy. She was busy with numerous tasks that needed to be done. She lived just as her fellow sufferers. She slept very little, because – besides bringing up three children, keeping the house, baking bread early every morning and working in the fields – she prayed a lot. When the first chapel was built near to the source of Fallóskút, she spent all her free time there.[567]

The increasing number of believers around Lady Klára confirmed the authenticity and legitimacy of the growing popular religious movement focusing on the figure of the Virgin Mother, existing beside and often in opposition to man-centred sacred images of the official church. Even scholars describe scenes in which certain peoples' ambition is only to touch the clothes of Klára,[568] who is the messenger of the heavenly good news of caring maternal love. The belief in the healing power of purely touching the spiritual leader having magic power is a well-known usual religious phenomenon, also in Christianity.[569] Klára drew a little cross with her right thumb on the forehead of the faithful. She was convinced that the

---

[565] Cf. Letter of the ecclesiastical authority of Eger with the signature of the vicar-general of Eger – to a faithful; dates from Eger, 15th December 1994, Nr. 2257/1994

[566] Quotation from László Zakupszky, retired president of the local council of Hasznos, in: Kerekes (ed.) 2001, 23

[567] Cf. Klemm 1999, 49

[568] Manga 1962, 373

[569] Cf. Mt 9:20–22

Virgin Mother Herself blessed her right thumb and informed her that this "right thumb will heal."[570] Some did not get this sign because they were not purified. According to Lady Klára's narrative she had a sense of recognising and distinguishing the evil spirits occupying certain people from the grace of God.[571] One of her confidants told Klemm that Lady Klára suffered a lot by not being understood. Therefore she was always glad when she could speak to people open to her visions involving her whole personality and everyday life. She also suffered in spirit because she was in the other world, but she was busy with secular issues most often regarding the chapel.[572]

Some visions mirror characteristics of Yahweh of the Old Testament represented in the female figure of the Virgin Mother of Hasznos. Pilgrims with the same religious background produce the same kind of syncretism turning up from time to time in their world of faith. One female faithful for example cured from cancer reports her healing process as follows: Suddenly she felt the hand of the Virgin Mother on her head. After Her blessing touch the Virgin Mother smiled at the sick woman and Her figure was gradually covered by fog descending from the top of the church.[573] In the Old Testament the image of fog or cloud usually symbolised the mysterious greatness of God whose powerful presence was simply impossible to see and comprehend by the human being. Therefore Yahweh wrapped Himself up in thick fog both to gently preserve the faithful from the shock of theophany and to stress the *divine distance* from the human sphere.[574] This type of syncretism was possibly shaped by the faithful themselves hearing and re-combining the readings of the Old Testament in the holy mass. These texts went through further interpretations by people replacing Yahweh's distant figure with the *more personal* and informal female character of Mary being principally in natural relationship with the believers and in this way understanding everyday problems of fallible human beings.[575]

Most of the Hungarian religious symbols however point back to an even earlier cultural era than that of Yahweh of the Old Testament. Our national consciousness rather keeps in mind the memory of shamanic elements shap-

---

[570] Cf. Klemm 1999, 57

[571] Cf. Kelemen (ed.) 2001, 85

[572] Cf. Kelemen (ed.) 2001, 96

[573] Klemm 1999, 40

[574] Cf. e.g. Ex 16:10

[575] Cf. The examples of re-interpreting biblical stories and characters e.g. in the Peasant Bible

ing the way Hungarians think.[576] The scraps of this influence can be explored for example in the following vision of Klára Csépe:

> "I had a vision: I was out in the chapel, where I saw *a riddle* and wheat. The wheat had to be riddled by me. There was chaff among the grains of wheat. I had *to riddle* all of them. The wheat remained clean, the chaff fell out of the riddle. There was more clean wheat than chaff. And then *a voice* said to me: 'There is a great *mystery* left to you. This mystery will become real.'"[577]

The riddle refers to one of the most important tools of shamanic healing rituals. The magic drum of the shaman survives in the form of a sifter or riddle, both are used for predictions in the more isolated and therefore more archaic groups of Hungarian-speaking native of Moldavia even today.[578] Among other utensils the riddle also has particular significance in less segregated regions. In fact, it is kept in secret and interpreted as taboo by the folk tradition. Out of the house it must be covered, not even researchers are allowed to see it.[579]

The riddle symbolises the mental and spiritual ability to distinguish between good and evil spirits and to harmonise and integrate the different forces of the soul. In this way to heal the ill pieces of the personality and to restore the intra- and interpersonal aspects of the individual puts the arising problems into a wider context of the invisible sphere of life. The rhythmical movement of riddling recalls the ecstatic shamanic dance that leads the dancer into communication with the spirits of the other world. Even if the shamans themselves disappeared from our culture, fragmentarily their knowledge survived in the rituals of wise women and men, and it is still alive in Hungarian children's songs well-known to all Hungarian children, that refers to the era of the Turkish occupation of Hungary:

---

[576] Diószegi, Vilmos: *A sámánhit emlékei a magyar népi műveltségben* [The tokens of shamanic belief in the Hungarian popular cultivation], Akadémiai Kiadó, Budapest, 1998 (Reprint), 34–37, 171–227

[577] Cf. Diary of Klára Csépe: Vision dates from the 16th March 1979

[578] Jankovics, Marcell: *Archaikus világkép a szibériai sámándobokon* [Archaic world concept represented on Siberian shamanic drums], in.: Jankovics, Marcell: Ahol a madár se jár [Out-of-the-way place; literal translation of the Hungarian title: Where even a bird has not passed yet], Pontifex Kiadó, Budapest, 1996, 9–25, cf. Diószegi (Reprint) 1998, 178, 205–215

[579] Makoldi, Sándor – Makoldi, Sándorné: *Síppal – dobbal, avagy rosta lyukával?* [With whistle and drum, or else with the hole of the riddle], in: Végvár, József (ed.): "Kiálts telyes torokal" [Shout at the top of your voice], Polar Alapítvány, Budapest, 2000, 203–214, here: 208, 203

*"Stork, stork, turtle-dove,*
*Why is your leg covered with blood?*
*Turkish child cut it,*
*Hungarian child cured it*
*With whistle, drum and reed-violin. "*[580]

Besides the magic drum other elements of ancient rites can be found in the following short rhymed saying. Both the reversed listing of the names of weekdays and the linking up of sifter, love and drum represent the storehouse of ancient magical resources of our ancestry:

*"Let God give us slow rain,*
*Let God wash them together.*
*Sifter, sifter Friday,*
*Love Thursday,*
*Drum Wednesday. "*[581]

Accordingly the riddle of Klára's vision involves a wide range of meanings referring to the rich religious-cultural heritage being alive even today. Symbols known to all rural people, attributed with divine forces by the visionary, makes Mrs. Sánta the mastress of the local language. Language is a dynamic reality going beyond purely words and their grammar. It involves dreams, attitudes, and practical experiences of a whole community and unites the tradition of the past with the matter of life and death of the contemporary human being. Its metaphors are, at the literal level, absurd, but obviously they intend serious meaning.[582] Lady Klára spoke the "language of the people" of her environment, this is, why she became a central figure of the Hungarian popular belief. Among the rural people her wholly involved simple personality in religion was evaluated more authentically than the distant religious behaviour of the official church hierarchy.

---

[580] *"Gólya, gólya, gilice,*
*Mitől véres a lábad?*
*Török gyerek megvágta,*
*Magyar gyerek gyógyítja*
*Síppal, dobbal, nádi hegedűvel. "*
[581] *"Adjon Isten lassú esőt,*
*Mossa össze mind a kettőt,*
*Szita, szita péntek,*
*Szerelem csütörtök,*
*Dob szerda. "*
[582] Cf. McFague, Sallie: *Metaphorical Theology: Models of God in Religious Language,* Fortress Press, Philadelphia, 1982, 31–42

Lady Klára represented the female power of the Happy Woman well-known in the Hungarian rural religious communities for long centuries. It seems that the usually rigorous images of God the Father proclaimed by most clerics did not so intensively attract the peasantry being continuously in everyday close connection with the *Mother Earth* and Her divine representative in the christianised figure of the *Virgin Mother*. The ancient female images of centuries-old Hungarian folk prayers live down any kind of conscious brainwashing attacks of the officially prescribed ritual habit. The cult of the Happy Woman allows local spontaneous dynamic contemporary reinterpretations of the religious tradition that survives through constantly supplementing self-experiences of all believers. (Table VII. / Fig. 21.)

One of the best illustrations of this culturally enriching process is the story of vicissitudes of the life-sized statue of Mary dominating the inner space of the little chapel at Fallóskút. The restoration of the sculpture, getting damaged several times, was financed by donations from the believers who felt usually empowered to add their individual characteristics to the original form of the figure during the renovation. In this way Mary's face expresses various manifestations of liveliness depending on the character of the actual person taking charge of the restoration. (Table VIII. / Fig. 22.)

The last restored version of the statue was obviously aided by a gypsy believer. This believer "made Mary a gypsy: her hair is longer, her eyes are brighter, lipstick is put on her mouth, her cheeks are sprinkled with powder, her clothes are more colourful, her original form is unrecognisable."[583] (Table VIII. / Fig. 23.)

The female heritage of the earlier represented ancient Hungarian folk prayers survives through the unbroken bequeathing of cultural-religious elements of the old tradition reinterpreted and accordingly enriched by a new generation. This continuity maintains a particular formation of religious ballad extant in certain communal aspects of faith.

In these rhymed chronicles the contemporary prominent female religious leader becomes an unforgettable legendary figure of the popular religion whose co-operation with the female divine figure of the Virgin Mother is immortalised for ever in the living local religious community. In this way the seer of Fallóskút is also transfigured. One of the most popular religious songs eternising the character of Klára Csépe and the divine power of the Virgin Mary or of the Happy Woman accompanying her activity runs as follows:

---

[583] Cf. Interview with the hermit on the 22nd October 2002

"Come here, Christians, near to Hasznos,
Mary appeared there in the valley of Gallya,
There is a little source there by the stock of the bush,
Mary glitters there in her pink wrap.

She has chosen the day of the Reaping Happy Woman,[584]
Mary appeared on this day.
She saw a woman praying in the wheat,
Exactly when the peal of bells in the village could be heard.

The woman mumbles, Hail Mary,
Blessed are you among the women, holy mother of God.
She saw a great brightness in front of herself,
Oh, what can this bright spectacle mean my Virgin Mother?

A voice begins to speak, it is Mary's voice.
Come with me, good woman, follow the light.
And the woman starts out with clasped hands,
Through ditch and bush, why am I worthy of it?

The brightness stopped at the foot of a shrub,
The Virgin Mary stood there in plain pink,
Her ornamented crown shone, glistened,
And She pointed to the source with Her arm.

The good woman fell on her knees before this sight,
Oh, my Virgin Mother, what does this vision mean?
I shall tell you then, good woman,
You will get to know the mystery of this little source.

The right hand of My Son is on this little source,
He heals the cripples and sick people.
Therefore I ask you, good woman, to proclaim it to the people,
Because you are the only worthy one to see this beautiful vision.

Oh, my dear Virgin Mother, take my heart into your mercy,
I shall proclaim your holy place to the people.

---

[584] 2 July

*Proclaim, proclaim, good woman, ask also your husband*
*Not to be an unbeliever, but to come to me.*

*And the woman went home, praying fervidly,*
*And her husband waited for her and asked:*
*Oh, you, woman, where were you, why are you so pious?*
*Do you pray, because you are maybe sinful?*

*Oh, you, my dear good husband, come and listen to me,*
*Do not be angry with me, but forgive me.*
*Oh, if you knew where I was with the Virgin Mary,*
*I was there by the source with the Mother of God.*

*She told her husband the happenings,*
*Come if you do not believe it, she also asked you to come.*
*She proclaims the source of healing to the people,*
*Here all the mute, crippled and sick people are cured.*

*The inhabitants of the village gather together,*
*And hurry with the good woman to the source.*
*And the brightness, the miracle of miracles appears,*
*And the light of the sky foretells the great thunder.*

*Thereupon all the Christian faithful fell on their knees,*
*And prayed faithfully with clasped hands.*
*Their lips stopped speaking, because they heard a song,*
*Oh, my Virgin Mother, Mary, star of the source.*

*Thereupon the faithful started to have a wash,*
*They felt the healing power of the holy spring-water.*
*And the mute, blind, crippled people rejoiced,*
*Because you, oh, my beautiful Virgin Mother, gave it to us.*

*Whoever trusts in Her, will never be disappointed,*
*But can carry off the prize of the hope of healing.*
*Therefore come now here, Christian believers,*
*And sing a song to the beautiful Virgin Mary.*

*Hail Virgin Mary, holy Mother of God,*
*Blessed are you among the women, beautiful Virgin Mary,*
*And the glorious crown of Jesus Christ. Amen.* "[585]

## A "NEW MARY" GIVES BIRTH TO A SECOND FEMALE REDEEMER: THE CASE OF MÁRIA KATONA, PROPHET OF SOMOSKŐÚJFALU

After the change of regime Limbacher, ethnographer and director of the Museum of Balassagyarmat explored a female healer called Mária Katona, endued with special abilities, in a little Hungarian village by the Slovakian border, near to the pilgrim place of Fallóskút. There is an obvious spiritual connection between her and the seer of Fallóskút, even if through many years the relationship between the two spiritual leaders culminated in an irreversible conflict.

### BIOGRAPHICAL DATA

The healer Mária Katona was born in Dorogháza on 7th May 1922. She originates from a Hungarian peasant family taking on bourgeois habits. She herself mentions particular circumstances of her birth like being born exactly at midnight and having a penetrating look from infancy, both emphasising special abilities, according to the popular belief.[586] Several times throughout her childhood she visited the surrounding Marian pilgrim places of Mátraverebély-Szentkút and the Mount Karancs and later the near devotional place of Fallóskút with her mother. Once they went to a seer who had contact with the soul of the dead. However she knew nothing about the Wise Woman previously active in *her* native village in the second half of the 19th century.[587] (Table IX. / Fig. 24.)

She first experienced her supernatural gifted ability at the age of seven, which was consistently hindered by her authoritarian father. In the 1940s she

---

[585] Mrs. Kalla, Emil and her husband (editors and publishers): *A hasznosi Szűzanya története és búcsú énekek* [The story of the Virgin Mother of Hasznos and pilgrim songs], Kovács Nyomda, Jászberény, 1948

[586] Pócs, Éva: *Néphit* [Popular belief], in: Dömötör, Tekla (ed.): Népszokás, néphit, népi vallásosság. Magyar Néprajz VII [Popular custom, popular belief, folk religion. Hungarian Ethnography VII], Akadémiai Kiadó, Budapest, 1990, 527–692

[587] Limbacher, Gábor: *Gyógyítóasszony Nógrádban a XX. század végén* [Healing woman in Nógrád at the end of the 20th century], in: Ethnographia CVI, 1995, 787–829, here 792

married a railway employee nearby, in Somoskőújfalu, who tolerated her later spiritual activity but at the same time always warned his wife by saying, "it is not a game".[588] Since the age of 9 until the decisive vision in 1975 she was sickly weak, therefore she was not able to bear offspring.

In the form of three male figures dressed priestly the Holy Trinity called her to fulfil a noble heavenly task and provided her with healing power. After this event she was shortly put into the neurological nursing home of Salgótarján, where István Samu was a medical doctor. Besides curing she is a teacher, religious leader and prophet, who takes care of the souls of the faithful and can speak with people who are in the next world. In brief she is a Wise Woman, who looks like a priest, while wearing a white dress by every religious events led by herself. (Table IX. / Fig. 25.)

Since her initiation she acts with the help of heavenly instructions. After the death of Klára Csépe and after the change of regime in 1989 and becoming a widow at the same time and after buying her tenement as private property the zone of her attraction suddenly grew beyond the borders.[589]

## FEMALE RELIGIOUS IDENTITY

From springtime until autumn thousands of people visited the little old woman in her home coming from all over the country. Many of them were intellectuals, principally women, but men also came. They seemed to honestly be devoted to the message mediated by Aunt Mária.

On the 2nd May 1975 Mária Katona dropped in at the Roman Catholic Church on the way to say one tenth of the rosary, before returning home from the etiologist of Salgótarján, a town nearby. Three men dressed in white waited for her in the sanctuary; this meeting made her very frightened. They looked like "earthly priests", but when they started to talk to her, she gradually recognised the Holy Trinity. The Father or the so-called "Lord of Heaven" and the Holy Spirit or the so-called "My Little God the Holy Spirit" wore golden crowns. On the crown of "My Little God the Holy Spirit" there was a *lion*, while the crown of the "Lord of Heaven" represented the form of a *tiger*. "My Little Jesus" did not have a crown, and His hair was naturally let down. "My Little God" was 202 centimetres, the "Lord of Heaven" was 185 centimetres and "My Little Lord Jesus" was 200 centimetres.[590]

---

[588] Cf. Interview with Mária Katona on the 1st May 2003
[589] Cf. Limbacher 1994; Limbacher 1995, 793
[590] Cf. Interview with Mária Katona 1st May 2003

According to Mária Katona the men started their conversation in the following way: "Come closer! Do not be afraid! Be brave!" Mária thought: "Me and the bravery?" But they continued by saying that she was the one who would save the whole world. Before she left the church the "tall one" asked her to pluck three boughs of silver fir and to make tea from it against her headache that had already lasted for nine years. The pain that could be cured by no "earthly medical doctor" in the past, at this time disappeared from her head after a few days.

She was aware of her old age, but, as she has narrated, after the one week she had been given by the heavenly figures to think about the heavenly task, she accepted everything, because she realised that if she took up the mission, the world would really be saved. Before accepting her mission she was subjected to several dangers: a taxi-driver almost knocked her over; a machine working on the street almost struck her dead; at the railway station a drunken man pulled her under the spring-buffer just before the train was departing, which was then quickly stopped by the engine-driver; two women attacked her and suspected her of stealing their lovers. She only later found out that her husband once danced with these women in his bachelorhood, but he soon realised that both were just "whores". "What a day, my God!", she thought, "I am saved all the time, but this situation is still awful." In opposition to the case of Lady Klára the husband of Aunt Mária seemed to be a lot more tolerant towards his wife being awakened to her new vocation. Many years after his death she still shows great affection for the memory of her husband.

They themselves had no children, but she brought up ten other little ones of neighbouring families instead who were actually thankful for the great help. Probably the strong yearning to have her own children established her conviction to be the mother of the second redeemer of the world called *Christa*. In the imagination of the faithful surrounding Aunt Mária this redeeming figure appears as a *female* character.[591] The seer has continuous contact with the Holy Trinity and the Virgin Mary, but also St. Anne, the mother of Mary visits her regularly. According to her narrative the Virgin Mother kissed her hand and gave thanks to Mária for the brave decision.[592]

---

[591] Cf. Interview with the Dér couple, Törökbálint 16th November 2002. Although they mention this female redeeming figure in a rather negative, rejecting way, because they are basically devoted to Klára Csépe who is the summit for them. If they accepted Aunt Mária as the Mother of God, they would query the position of Klára Csépe, who actually also always acted in the name of the Virgin Mother, that shows quite obviously her ambition for complete identification with the Mother of God. It seems that Aunt Mária further developed the religious ideas of Lady Klára.

[592] Cf. Interview with Mária Katona 1st May 2003

It seems that both the heavenly and the earthly woman understand each other very well, because they both fulfil the divine will, as Aunt Mária told me. Her ambition to realise the dream of motherhood being already physically impossible finally culminates in total identification of the self with the heavenly mother having divine characteristics. (Table X. / Fig. 26.)

In the company of her female fellows of common destiny it is easier to accept the unacceptable. The female genealogy is even more accented, if Christa, the redeemer is female. The whole story recalls and reinterprets the "Saint Anne Trinitarian" features of the archaic Hungarian folk prayers. In the version of Aunt Mária, independently from having intense communication with a male dominant Trinity there has been built up a Trinitarian form representing strong female communion. (Fig. 7.)

Fig. 7. Heures a l'Usage d'Angers: Saint Anne Trinitarian (16th C.), printed by Simon Vostre, Estampes, Bibliotheque Nationale, Paris[593]

---

[593] Representations of female Trinitarian forms are not a uniquely Hungarian speciality. See one of the most expressive illustrations of the generally known "Saint Anne Trinitarian" reproduced by Ashley, Kathleen – Sheingorn, Pamela (eds.): *Interpreting Cultural Symbols. Saint Anne in Late Medieval Society*, The University of Georgia Press, Athen – London. 1994, 79. *Fig. 26*. Heures a l'Usage d'Angers: *Saint Anne Trinitarian* (16th C.), printed by Simon Vostre, Estampes, Bibliothèque Nationale, Paris.

The figure of Christa reminds us that divine redemption must happen "in carne" and therefore must be realised "as if bodies matter".[594] The symbolic Christa invites women of different cultures to share their personal practical experiences of trouble and joy, crucifixion and resurrection, and to reflect on them from a female perspective. It is a visible sign of the christomorph nature of women having the ability to realise their saving-redeeming quality. Christa incarnates not a particular kind of womanhood but contextual variety of female life stories. (Table X. / Fig. 27.)[595]

She does not represent the image of any single woman but involves all female characteristics. She is never the same, but is in continuous dynamic change who occasionally takes shape of black or white, old or young, thin or fat, etc. Nevertheless her complex versatility goes far beyond these surface features and queries the absolutisation of any female character.[596] The image of Christa is by no means a final solution, but an attempt, anyway, to realise

---

[594] McFague, Sallie: *The Body of God. An Ecological Theology*, Fortress Press, Minneapolis, 1993, viii, cf. McFague, Sallie: *Models of God. Theology for an Ecological, Nuclear Age*, Fortress Press, Philadelphia, 1987. McFague connects Christology with erotic love, healing ethic and saving activity to benefit the whole world that is basically God's body.

[595] Christ Sophia with the maternal heritage of the solid figure of Venus of Willendorf, painted by Robert Lentz, 1989, New Mexico. "Christ Sophia: Various names are used for God in the Jewish Scriptures. 'Wisdom' is among the names used most frequently, and God is always feminine when she is called Wisdom. 'She is a reflection of the eternal light, untarnished mirror of God's active power, image of his goodness' [Wisdom 7:26]. It is Wisdom who creates and orders the world, making manifest the divine will. And it is Wisdom who delights to be among the human race, teaching us her ways.

In the Byzantine Church, these references to Wisdom are considered references to Christ. Churches like Hagia Sophia in Istanbul are dedicated to Christ. From the Middle Ages on, icons depicting Christ as an androgynous figure, flanked by Mary and John the Baptist, have been painted in Russia and elsewhere. [...]

Looking honestly at our ancient tradition, it is clear that the mystery of Christ cannot be described in masculine terms alone. Because of historical and cultural circumstances, the Second Person of the Trinity became a male human being. Before the Incarnation, however, that person was described as 'she'. As the incarnation continues to unfold after Christ's resurrection and ascension, it is again the feminine Sophia who expresses the mystery – as pointed out by the Russian theologian Soloviev.

Christ Sophia is depicted in this icon in an egg-shaped mandala. The inscription in her halo is Greek for 'I am who I am', the divine name given Moses at the burning bush on Sinai. The Greek inscriptions in the upper corners are abbreviations for 'Jesus Christ', her historical manifestation. She holds the ancient statue called 'Venus of Willendorf', and points to herself as if to say, 'I am she. Know me now more *fully*.'" Lentz, Robert: *Christ Sophia*, Bridge Building, Burlington, 1989.

[596] Cf. Kalsky, Manuela: *Christaphanien. Die Re-Vision der Christologie aus der Sicht von Frauen in unterschiedlichen Kulturen*, Gütersloher Verlagshaus, Gütersloh, 2000, 322–325

the various aspects of the existing female dimension hidden behind all type of biographies of women.[597]

## Sanctified profanity: Continuity and reinterpretation of female religious traditions in a secularised world

Mária Katona was instinctively inspired to restore sanctity in the profane, as it has generally been normal in the time of her ancestry. In opposition to Klára Csépe she did not pay too much attention to official ecclesiastical judgement, but went her own way. Her ritual has many interesting new elements compared with the practice of Fallóskút.

Although at the beginning she tried to legitimise her particular abilities to heal through water carried home regularly from the spring of Fallóskút by herself. It was symbolising the continuity of female power. During those years she also attempted to "occupy" a chapel near to her home.[598] (Table XI. / Fig. 28.)

Nevertheless she gradually took a quite distinguishable direction of developing her own ritual rules. This ambition was probably influenced by circumstances created by those believers who visited her unceasingly. The devoted faithful presented her with many sacred Christian icons and statues representing most often Mary or Jesus.[599]

Instead of building a chapel in the forest the increasing number of these images offered the opportunity to turn the pantry of her own flat into a little chapel. (Table XI. / Fig. 29.) Slowly, but especially after the death of the seer of Fallóskút, she became accepted as an expert of the forces of the other world, independently from the character of Klára Csépe whose figure earlier played a significant background supporting role in the events of Somoskőújfalu. Her affirmed position empowered Aunt Mária to continue the sanctifying process in her own profane environment.

Her activity, just like that of Lady Klára, is also connected with the spring-water of Fallóskút; The study of Limbacher from 1995 describes the spring-water of Fallóskút as a welcoming refreshment for all the visitors of Aunt Mária.[600] (Table XII. / Fig. 30.)

---

[597] Cf. Strahm Bernet, Silvia: *Jesa Christa*, in: Strahm, Doris – Storbel, Regula (eds.): Vom Verlangen nach Heilwerden. Christologie in feministisch-theologischer Sicht, Exodus, Fribourg/Luzern, 1991, 172–181

[598] As she says "Mátraverebély-Szentkút belongs to the Franciscan friars, Fallóskút belongs to Aunt Klára and Karancs belongs to me." Cf. interview with Mária Katona 1ˢᵗ May 2003

[599] The central figure among other women is conspicuous because of the special way she is dressed.

[600] Cf. Limbacher 1995, 807

By 2003 this habit gradually disappeared from the flat of the old woman. She consciously cut any mental and spiritual connection with the seer of Fallóskút that would diminish the validity of her own ritual.

As she explained she does not use the spring-water of Fallóskút anymore because the official church taking over the authority above the chapel at Fallóskút made the source dirty and the water coming from it is spoiled. Nowadays the healing-refreshing liquid comes directly from the tap in her own kitchen. (Table XII. / Fig. 31.)

She also heals with the aid of photos of the modern world taken of the sick persons willing to be cured. An interesting point to mention is that none of Limbacher's published photos about the furnished flat of the old woman represent the most expressive recent tendency of Aunt Mária's spirituality, namely, that she defines herself suitable to the portrayals of heavenly characters. (Table XIII. / Fig. 32.)

Her proper place is the divine sphere, photos of herself get on well with the statue representing the Virgin Mother and the paintings of Jesus on the wall of the kitchen or of the pantry turned already into a sanctuary in her flat.

Her spiritual power is represented even in the so-called "manna".[601] This is basically a feeding movement of her right hand in front of the opened mouth of the faithful[602] who usually get three pieces of manna or its multiple after a long recited prayer most often built up of sentences repeated three times again. The numbering plays a particular magical role in the healing process. Only the movement of the hand shows how many pieces of manna the believer exactly received. According to Aunt Mária this manna is invisible, because it comes from heaven. She stresses that the priests also give manna to the faithful in the form of the Eucharist, but it is only earthly manna.

Sometimes she herself also goes to hear mass of the official church, because in her opinion God did not forbid it. "If you like to be there with the other faithful, just go."[603] Being in the church is basically a kind of social life for her. While continuously being in the presence of God she has built up her own rituals (Table XIII. / Fig. 33.), therefore religious ceremonies offered by the church are not really extra opportunities for her to meet God. She has her own opinion about many religious questions that can be quite well differentiated from the official viewpoint.

---

[601] See its origin according to the Old Testament, in: Ex 16:31
[602] See its representations in: Limbacher 1995, 800 (fig. 8), 819 (fig. 25). When I visited Aunt Mária on the 1st May 2003, she gave me nine mannas. According to her they are enough for ten years.
[603] Cf. interview with Mária Katona 1st May 2003

The 81-year old woman confirmed that marriage is sanctified not by church authorities, but by love existing between a woman and a man. When love is over in a relationship, divorce, as consequence is not questionable. In her opinion it is better to separate than to stay together[604] if it causes only hatred for both partners in the marriage. You can never judge a couple for getting into a gap of communication, because you do not know the background of their motives. The only sure thing is that hatred does not come from God, therefore God does not certify this kind of relationship. Hate itself already involves divorce of the souls.[605] Aunt Mária is also convinced that Catholic priests should be allowed to marry because, as she points out, "they are made of the same blood as any other human beings. The real sin is when they are not allowed to get married."[606]

She queries the divine legitimisation of confession. In her opinion it is totally unnecessary because God is in continuous dialogue with us and it is God who forgives the sins without any mediator. She herself never asks about the sins, but rather about family circumstances and about the spheres of activity. She manifests great empathy towards the believer. She diagnoses if someone has bad legs, eyes, etc. and besides touching the sick person with healing attitude she gives further realistic suggestions to solve the problem. Considering her age the worldview of the old lady shows surprisingly a quite modern model of life. It is however also possible that her up-to-datedness is rather the manifestation of her ancient being that points back to the archaic era of total integrity based on holistic view. Nowadays all the sciences try to

---

[604] Aunt Mária lived in a very harmonious relationship with her husband. On the other hand her predecessor, Mrs. Sánta tolerated the violence of her husband for a long time. Nevertheless strangely it is Lady Klára who is strictly against divorce in contradistinction to Mária Katona's opinion, when she declares that "God ordered only one woman to the man." In: Diary of Klára Csépe, Vision dated from 3rd October 1961. Although she suffered a lot from her husband, she continuously tried to avoid her rejecting feelings towards her husband. She probably wanted to be suitable for the social expectations of her direct surroundings. Even if she had conflicts with church authorities, from childhood she had enough time to be permitted by the prohibitions of the church law that often leaves out of consideration the person's biography. Klára tried to find an answer for herself that legitimised her sufferings by the divine will: "God ordered only one woman to the man." This statement allows no deviation, even if the woman is constantly threatened by her husband. The religious conviction of Aunt Mária seems however independent from church authorities.

[605] Cf. similar view about relationship in: Moore, Robert: *Care of the Soul – How to add depth and meaning to your everyday life*, Piatkus, London, 1992; Moore, Robert: *Soul Mates – Honouring the mysteries of love and relationship*, Element, London, 1994

[606] Cf. Interview with Mária Katona 1st May 2003

re-explore and re-evaluate this holistic attitude leading beyond the order of human rules to a higher, integrating-uniting ambition.

The believers pay the generous help of Aunt Mária in kind. She receives various types of food which she never keeps for herself but shares with the people who are poorer than she is. She uses only as much as she needs. As she says God tells her what to eat. When she is ill, God suggests to her a diet.[607]

God also determines the period of her consulting hours with the faithful. As she points out God accepts the visitors only between 10 a.m. and 4 p.m. every day in her home. Before and after that she prays and has important conversation with the powers above. The Virgin Mother walks through her flat in any optional times; she basically lives together with her old female fellow, as Aunt Mária narrates. While I was present at her flat I asked her to take photographs of the little chapel, she immediately turned to God for permission. During the time of our conversation she asked God's divine opinion and suggestion several times. Every moment of her life is permitted by the believed presence of divine persons.

Recently she bought a pram for Christa who is soon to be born. The highly valued pram is kept in her room like a sacrament. Not even a photo can be taken of the perambulator until Christa will outgrow it, she says. The pram symbolises her right to motherhood that is even more exalted by the powers above than the position of other mothers.

According to Sered *"women's religious behaviour is often trivialised either through being labelled magic or superstitious, or through being interpreted as the outcome of women's psychopathology."*[608] Instead Sered shows how the loss of a child influences the position of the mother in the family and in the wider society. The case of Aunt Mária confirms that not only the death, but also the hopeless want "of a child tends to have a greater impact upon women than upon men. [...] the mother is blamed for angering the spirits [...]"[609]

A good example of the endless female struggle and hopeless want of child-bearing can be found in the *Kalevala – The Finnish national epic, rune I.* (Translated by John Martin Crawford, 1888):

---

[607] The icons of divine persons together with Aunt Mária's daily meal and toiletries like talcum powder and a bottle of spirit of salt (Table XIV. / Fig. 34.)

[608] Cf. Sered, Susan Starr: *Mother Love, Child Death and Religious Innovation,* in: Journal of Feminist Studies in Religion, 1996, Nr. 12, 5

[609] Cf. Sered 1996, 6

## RUNE I.
### *BIRTH OF WÄINÄMÖINEN*

In primeval times, a maiden,
Beauteous Daughter of the Ether,
Passed for ages her existence
In the great expanse of heaven,
O'er the prairies yet enfolded.
Wearisome the maiden growing,
Her existence sad and hopeless,
Thus alone to live for ages
In the infinite expanses
Of the air above the sea-foam,
In the far outstretching spaces,
In a solitude of ether,
She descended to the ocean,
Waves her coach, and waves her pillow.
Thereupon the rising storm-wind
Flying from the East in fierceness,
Whips the ocean into surges,
Strikes the stars with sprays of ocean
Till the waves are white with fervor.
To and fro they toss the maiden,
Storm-encircled, hapless maiden;
With her sport the rolling billows,
With her play the storm-wind forces,
On the blue back of the waters;
On the white-wreathed waves of ocean,
Play the forces of the salt-sea,
With the lone and helpless maiden;
Till at last in full conception,
Union now of force and beauty,
Sink the storm-winds into slumber;
Overburdened now the maiden
Cannot rise above the surface;
Seven hundred years she wandered,
Ages nine of man's existence,
Swam the ocean hither, thither,
Could not rise above the waters,

Conscious only of her travail;
Seven hundred years she labored
Ere her first-born was delivered.
Thus she swam as water-mother,
Toward the east, and also southward,
Toward the west, and also northward;
Swam the sea in all directions,
Frightened at the strife of storm-winds,
Swam in travail, swam unceasing,
Ere her first-born was delivered.
Then began she gently weeping,
Spake these measures, heavy-hearted:
"Woe is me, my life hard-fated!
Woe is me, in this my travail!
Into what have I now fallen?
Woe is me, that I unhappy,
Left my home in subtle ether,
Came to dwell amid the sea-foam,
To be tossed by rolling billows,
To be rocked by winds and waters,
On the far outstretching waters,
In the salt-sea's vast expanses,
Knowing only pain and trouble!
Better far for me, O Ukko!
Were I maiden in the Ether,
Than within these ocean-spaces,
To become a water-mother!
All this life is cold and dreary,
Painful here is every motion,
As I linger in the waters,
As I wander through the ocean.
Ukko, thou O God, up yonder,
Thou the ruler of the heavens,
Come thou hither, thou art needed,
Come thou hither, I implore thee,
To deliver me from trouble,
To deliver me in travail.
Come I pray thee, hither hasten,
Hasten more that thou art needed,

Haste and help this helpless maiden!"
When she ceased her supplications,
Scarce a moment onward passes,
Ere a beauteous duck descending,
Hastens toward the water-mother,
Comes a-flying hither, thither,
Seeks herself a place for nesting.
Flies she eastward, flies she westward,
Circles northward, circles southward,
Cannot find a grassy hillock,
Not the smallest bit of verdure;
Cannot find a spot protected,
Cannot find a place befitting,
Where to make her nest in safety.
Flying slowly, looking round her,
She descries no place for resting,
Thinking loud and long debating,
And her words are such as follow:
"Build I in the winds my dwelling,
On the floods my place of nesting?
Surely would the winds destroy it,
Far away the waves would wash it."
Then the daughter of the Ether,
Now the hapless water-mother,
Raised her shoulders out of water,
Raised her knees above the ocean,
That the duck might build her dwelling,
Build her nesting-place in safety.
Thereupon the duck in beauty,
Flying slowly, looking round her,
Spies the shoulders of the maiden,
Sees the knees of Ether's daughter,
Now the hapless water-mother,
Thinks them to be grassy hillocks,
On the blue back of the ocean.
Thence she flies and hovers slowly,
Lightly on the knee she settles,
Finds a nesting-place befitting,
Where to lay her eggs in safety.

Here she builds her humble dwelling,
Lays her eggs within, at pleasure,
Six, the golden eggs she lays there,
Then a seventh, an egg of iron;
Sits upon her eggs to hatch them,
Quickly warms them on the knee-cap
Of the hapless water-mother;
Hatches one day, then a second,
Then a third day sits and hatches.
Warmer grows the water round her,
Warmer is her bed in ocean,
While her knee with fire is kindled,
And her shoulders too are burning,
Fire in every vein is coursing.
Quick the maiden moves her shoulders,
Shakes her members in succession,
Shakes the nest from its foundation,
And the eggs fall into ocean,
Dash in pieces on the bottom
Of the deep and boundless waters.
In the sand they do not perish,
Not the pieces in the ocean;
But transformed, in wondrous beauty
All the fragments come together
Forming pieces two in number,
One the upper, one the lower,
Equal to the one, the other.
From one half the egg, the lower,
Grows the nether vault of Terra:
From the upper half remaining,
Grows the upper vault of Heaven;
From the white part come the moonbeams,
From the yellow part the sunshine,
From the motley part the starlight,
From the dark part grows the cloudage;
And the days speed onward swiftly,
Quickly do the years fly over,
From the shining of the new sun
From the lighting of the full moon.

Still the daughter of the Ether,
Swims the sea as water-mother,
With the floods outstretched before her,
And behind her sky and ocean.
Finally about the ninth year,
In the summer of the tenth year,
Lifts her head above the surface,
Lifts her forehead from the waters,
And begins at last her workings,
Now commences her creations,
On the azure water-ridges,
On the mighty waste before her.
Where her hand she turned in water,
There arose a fertile hillock;
Wheresoe'er her foot she rested,
There she made a hole for fishes;
Where she dived beneath the waters,
Fell the many deeps of ocean;
Where upon her side she turned her,
There the level banks have risen;
Where her head was pointed landward,
There appeared wide bays and inlets;
When from shore she swam a distance,
And upon her back she rested,
There the rocks she made and fashioned,
And the hidden reefs created,
Where the ships are wrecked so often,
Where so many lives have perished.
Thus created were the islands,
Rocks were fastened in the ocean,
Pillars of the sky were planted,
Fields and forests were created,
Checkered stones of many colors,
Gleaming in the silver sunlight,
All the rocks stood well established;
But the singer, Wainamoinen,
Had not yet beheld the sunshine,
Had not seen the golden moonlight,
Still remaining undelivered.

Wainamoinen, old and trusty,
Lingering within his dungeon
Thirty summers altogether,
And of winters, also thirty,
Peaceful on the waste of waters,
On the broad-sea's yielding bosom,
Well reflected, long considered,
How unborn to live and flourish
In the spaces wrapped in darkness,
In uncomfortable limits,
Where he had not seen the moonlight,
Had not seen the silver sunshine.
Thereupon these words be uttered,
Let himself be heard in this wise:
"Take, O Moon, I pray thee, take me,
Take me, thou, O Sun above me,
Take me, thou O Bear of heaven,
From this dark and dreary prison,
From these unbefitting portals,
From this narrow place of resting,
From this dark and gloomy dwelling,
Hence to wander from the ocean,
Hence to walk upon the islands,
On the dry land walk and wander,
Like an ancient hero wander,
Walk in open air and breathe it,
Thus to see the moon at evening,
Thus to see the silver sunlight,
Thus to see the Bear in heaven,
That the stars I may consider."
Since the Moon refused to free him,
And the Sun would not deliver,
Nor the Great Bear give assistance,
His existence growing weary,
And his life but an annoyance,
Bursts he then the outer portals
Of his dark and dismal fortress;
With his strong, but unnamed finger,
Opens he the lock resisting;

With the toes upon his left foot,
With the fingers of his right hand,
Creeps he through the yielding portals
To the threshold of his dwelling;
On his knees across the threshold,
Throws himself head foremost, forward
Plunges into deeps of ocean,
Plunges hither, plunges thither,
Turning with his hands the water;
Swims he northward, swims he southward,
Swims he eastward, swims he westward,
Studying his new surroundings.
Thus our hero reached the water,
Rested five years in the ocean,
Six long years, and even seven years,
Till the autumn of the eighth year,
When at last he leaves the waters,
Stops upon a promontory,
On a coast bereft of verdure;
On his knees he leaves the ocean,
On the land he plants his right foot,
On the solid ground his left foot,
Quickly turns his hands about him,
Stands erect to see the sunshine,
Stands to see the golden moonlight,
That he may behold the Great Bear,
That he may the stars consider.
Thus our hero, Wainamoinen,
Thus the wonderful enchanter
Was delivered from his mother,
Ilmatar, the Ether's daughter.

In the cult of fertility unproductivity was considered as shameful. Even today it is often seen as punishment of the improperly behaved woman, or at least purely, as the result of female infertility. Probably Aunt Mária also had to face this problem several times in her environment. This fact can be one of the reasons of her ambition to legitimise and confirm her motherhood – as the only normal and accepted condition of womanhood in her archaic circumstances – strongly by divine forces.

The phenomenon could be described as "phantom child syndrome"[610] that is used by the psychologist Rubin for mothers losing, but psychically still developing their deceased child. In our case the "permanent presence of the child in the maternal experience"[611] regards a still unconceived, unborn, but wanted phantom child. Women being judged for the lack or death of a child are often more encouraged to re-evaluate existential questions.

This psychical elaboration often turns them into founders or leaders of religion. As compared with the officially legitimised and institutionalised "high" religions dealing with the elements of life on a so-called "higher" abstract level, the popular belief dealing with the aspects of life on the level of the individual is mostly associated with magic that is seen systematically less estimable.[612]

The fact that both women and men can be barren, is pointed out only by the newest scientific researches, which finally exhorts the public to be slower in their judgement of women for being childless.[613] The opposite is just as valid in the extreme feminist infertility cult of the modern era announcing for women revolutionary equality with the society of men. It seems that both the misapprehension and misconstruction of the ancient fertility cult and the forced maintaining infertility cult of the modern era have inhuman expectations towards all being exception to certain rules. In large families again purely the woman is disdained for being "too fertile" in the age of building merely the individual career and for being less responsive to the liberating ideas and actions of certain feminist movements. The modern society based on the economics of achievements no longer takes motherhood into consideration. It offers much less chance and respect for mothers than for single women in public.

Aunt Mária experienced the former viewpoint regarding female fertility forcing childbirth and disdaining unproductivity shifting the blame purely to the woman. Her biography is a good example for building up self-consciously a positive, acceptable, loveable, even highly respectable character, often against the stream of unrealisable social expectations. She attempted to find her

---

[610] Cf. Rubin, Simon Shimshon: *Maternal Attachment and Child Death. On Adjustment, Relationship, and Resolution,* Omega 15, Nr. 4, 1984–1985, 347–352, quoted also by Sered 1996, 17

[611] Rubin 1984–1985, 351

[612] Sered 1996, 17–20

[613] Cf. Almási, Tamás: *Sejtjeink* [Our cells], 2002, documentary about the programme of in vitro fertilisation in Hungary

roots in the female sphere of the Magna Mater offering valuable life for all Her daughters. Defining a strong-minded self-need really provides a lot of encouragement for a woman of the margin in many ways. Aunt Mária, the childless simple woman living in the back of beyond, in the last village by the northern border of Hungary, similarly to Klára Csépe became a legendary figure of the region. Prayers narrating her story are well-known among the people:

*"Aunt Mária visits the mount Mátra*
*In the circle of believers.*
*The Virgin Mary and the big crowd of ill people*
*Wait for her there.*

*She falls on her knees with opened arms*
*By the cross of the Lord and asks the Holy Father:*
*Help, Lord, the many sick people,*
*They trust in You who never allows them to be lost.*

*She mediates between the Lord and the people,*
*On the faces love shines.*
*She asks the Lord of heaven*
*To listen to the words of the faithful.*

*The Virgin Mary bustles,*
*She begs the Father for mercy.*
*Come here, you will be healed here,*
*God the Lord will help you all."*

*"My medical woman in the little house,*
*Aunt Mária in her home,*
*Heals the many sick people,*
*Longs for true souls.*

*The little shelter is packed,*
*I fall on my knees in the sanctuary,*
*Aunt Mária is the most beloved daughter of the Lord,*
*Who waits for her children with the Good God.*

*When the lost child drops in,*
*One will find consolation and the soul purified.*

*The heavenly Father and his beloved Son*
*Welcome you with great joy. "*

*"Bless the inhabitant of this house, my God,*
*She takes the trouble, she does not spare herself.*
*Let Your charitable hand take her one,*
*Lead her and bless her life for long.*

*Her dear old body is unceasingly active,*
*Her little house waits for many people,*
*Come, faithful souls, here you will be healed,*
*God the Lord will relieve you of the burden.*

*That dear woman is the mediator,*
*And many cured people return home.*
*Bless her, my Lord, hundred and thousand times,*
*So that even more ones will receive healing. "*

Mária néni a hívek körében
Ellátogat a Mátra hegyére.
Ott várja Őt a szép Szűz Mária
És betegek nagy-nagy sokasága.

Kitárt kézzel az Úr keresztjénél
Leborulva a Szent Atyát kéri:
Segíts Uram a sok betegen,
Benned bíznak, nehogy elvesszenek.

Közvetít Ő az Úr és nép között ,
Az arcokon szeretet tündököl.
Imádkozva kéri Egek Urát
Hallgassa meg a hívőknek szavát.

Szűz Mária azon szorgoskodik ,
Az Atyától irgalmat esdekli.
Gyertek ide , itt gyógyulást nyertek ,
Az Úr Isten megsegít titeket.

Az én orvosom kicsi házban,
Mária néni hajlékában,
Gyógyítja a sok beteget,
Áhítja az igaz lelkeket.


Zsúfolt a kis hajlék,
A szentéjben térdet hajték,
Mária néni az Úr legkedvesebb leánya,
Ki a Jóistennel gyermekeit várja.


Ha betér az eltévelyedett gyermek,
Vigaszt talál és megtisztul a lélek.
Örömmel fogad a mennyei Atya,
És az ő szeretett, egyetlen Fia.

### Kérés az Úrhoz Mária néniért

Áldd meg Úr Istenem e háznak lakóját ,
Ki értünk fárad , nem kímélve magát .
A jóságos kezed fogja meg az övét ,
Vezesse még soká , ádja meg életét .


Drága öreg teste szüntelenül tesz , vesz ,
Várja kicsiny háza a sok embert .
Hívő lelkek gyertek , itt gyógyulást nyertek ,
Az Úr Isten maga veszi le a terhet .


Az a drága asszony , Ő az ki közvetít ,
És az a sok ember gyógyulva hazatér .
Áldd meg Uram százszor meg ezerszer ,
Hogy még nagyon sokan gyógyulást nyerjenek .

# WOMEN'S RELIGION: INTERPERSONAL ORIENTATION AND NONTRANSCENDENT VIEW OF DIVINITY

In the following table I have compared the basic elements of the above examined religious world of the two female visionaries, I have illustrated a trend of re-establishing the sacred sphere in our secularised, profane world that addresses the human being of the modern age easier.

| | *Klára Csépe* | *Mária Katona* |
|---|---|---|
| *Leading religious functions* | – Spiritual leader<br>– Healer<br>– Mediator | – Spiritual leader<br>– Healer<br>– Co-efficient co-operator<br>– Priestess<br>– Mother of a Female Redeemer |
| *Attitude towards church representatives* | – Continuous conflict<br>– Official legalisation of her activity seems to be important | – Partly negative<br>– Partly neutral |
| *Attitude towards church doctrine* | – Sacraments are valid<br>– Divorce is not allowed | – In human relationship love's priority is above church rules<br>– Sacraments for themselves have no significance<br>– Marriage ceremony is an unnecessary formality<br>– When marriage does not function divorce is allowed<br>– Obligatory celibacy does not come from God<br>– The heavenly manna offered by herself is above the earthly Eucharist offered by earthly priests |

|  | *Klára Csépe* | *Mária Katona* |
|---|---|---|
| *Frequency of communication with divine characters* | – Usually in the time of the morning and evening prayer <br> – Ecstatic state | – Continuous detailed communication all day just like any other human conversation <br> – Reflection on every small happening |
| *Performers of the religious communication* | – The most frequently appearing figure is the Virgin Mother | – The persons of the Holy Trinity named in a peculiar individual way, parallel with: Saint Anne Trinitarian in which Anne appears as dominating female fig ure, Mary is manifested as a thankful fellow sufferer |
| *Localisation of the self in relation to the divine sphere* | – Belonging to the other-world <br> – Partial identification with Mary <br> – Though subordinate position | – Partnership <br> – Mutuality <br> – Mother of God: <br> – Full identification with Mary <br> – In fact exceeding Mary's character |
| *Localisation of the ritual* | – Chapel in the forest <br> – Uninhabited area (16 km from the village) <br> – Determined by the localisation of the healing spring-water | – Chapel in the flat <br> – Replacing the former pantry of the flat |
| *Localisation of the healing water as stressed symbol of the ritual* | – Coming from a spring in the forest, uninhabited area, next to the chapel <br> – Nature-worship (Mary = Queen of Forests) | – Coming from a spring nearby, but accessible through the tap of the kitchen |

Similarly to the results of Sered's general scientific investigation about women's religions[614] the following can be said about the religion of specific Hungarian women:

Although surrounded by a patriarchal organised society they live in the heritage of matrifocality that provides them with a sense that their roles in the community are particularly significant. While the accentuated role of motherhood being ritually elaborated, their role as mother obviously seems to be more important than their role as wife. The responsibility for the lives of children, but also welcoming change and fostering growth are central themes of women's religion. Male resistance to this ritualised motherhood is understandable in the mirror of the fact that male dominated religions recognise: motherhood gives women special power.

Since women as primary caretakers have to raise children being able to adopt themselves to the surrounding social environment, for the benefit of the success of the new generation they still tend to take on the values of the dominantly patriarchal ideologised culture in which women's religion is often located. It seems that women represent rather concrete thinking that roots in motherhood with its particularity, connection, complexity and ambiguity. The abstract thinking of men however incline to generalise, sharply define and simplify. It is best illustrated by the fact that women usually stress shared responsibility rather than pure commitment rights. Nevertheless concreteness does not exclude but strengthens the holistic view manifested in the multiplicity of female healing procedures.

Women's religion is deeply engaged with cure. On the one hand they are already practising domestic healing in the family circle, on the other hand "as subordinate members of sexist societies, women more than men suffer from persistent and recurrent conditions. In addition, women bear the brunt of culturally assigned responsibility for infertility and all the physical consequences of pregnancy and childbirth."[615] It calls forth automatic feminisation of suffering that often becomes a supportive basis for legitimising female religious leadership.

---

[614] Sered, Susan Starr: *Priestess, Mother, Sacred Sister. Religions Dominated by Women,* Oxford University Press, Oxford, 1994. 66. 71–72, 78, 83–84, 121, 145, 152, 155, 169, 171, 216, 225, 238, 243, 285

[615] Sered 1994, 103. Cf. Kiev, Ari: *The Study of Folk Psychiatry,* in: International Journal of Psychiatry, Vol 1, No. 4, 1965, 524–550, here 539: "*[...] perforations of ulcers in young women occured frequently in the beginning of the nineteenth century but diminished at the beginning of the twentieth century. What was once principally a female disorder has predominantly become a male disorder. [...] this shift can be understood in terms of altered*

Rituals executed by women usually sacralise profane female experiences and reflect the "interpersonal orientation"[616] of their profane activities. In this way one another mutually permit sacred ritual and the profane aspects of life. In contradiction to the good religious man whose main task is to perform rituals properly, the good religious woman is expected rather to help the poor, the sick, the neighbour. The religion of women being involved in intimate-personal aspects of life, far away from dogmas or moral doctrines produces a "nontranscendent view of divinity"[617] who deals with persons rather than rules.

Women's religion allows interaction with numerous supernatural beings like ancestors, spirits and gods. Scholars pointed out close connection between male dominance and monotheism in contradistinction to women's religion tending to be rather polydeistic[618] As we have seen this phenomenon has clear relation to gender based social status. Public deities mainly support the more or less rich, educated male society, while women's scope of activities limited the both materially and mentally poorer-narrower familiar sphere suggests rather the development of personal spirits, who allow "endless possibilities for explaining, dealing with, and (hopefully) healing suffering and illness."[619]

Female religious leaders, unlike men being in distance of authority, are personally known by their followers. Although no system of women's religion is totally non-hierarchical, their religious practice shows clear absence of centralised authority, their identity is better expressed locally. Women's religions serve basically their own secular interests, as they attempt to accentuate their significance in the society from a marginalised position.

---

*relationship between sexes, reflected, for example, by a change of women's role in society and the family and a corresponding change in attitude toward men following urbanisation. Increasing emancipation of women has lessened their dependence on men, while the increasing confusion of the male role has placed increased stress on men afforded them few opportunities to satisfy the dependency needs that previously could be satisfied under cover of their "dominant" role.*

[16] Sered 1994, 121

[617] Sered 1994, 158

[618] Stover, Ronald – Hope, Christine: *Monotheism and Gender Status. A Corss-Societal Study*, in: Social Forces 63 (2) 1984, 335–348

[619] Sered 1994, 171

# Conclusion

Being opposed to centuries old, essentially exotic portrayals of people my aim was to offer more than a fascinating description of Hungarian religious popular customs. While drawing the sketch of peculiar phenomena in a certain epoch, I intended "to reach beyond the frontiers of our usual way of thinking".[620]

For a better understanding of the issue I attached great importance to the outgrowth of modern ethnopsychiatric researches. Although the altered states of consciousness (ASC) meet a massive lack of comprehension and therefore have been obstacled with malicious negative judgement in the western civilisation since the Renaissance, several experts of the area tried to turn to these unusual human manifestations with at least scientific openness.

Many of them soon took at the beginning of their scholarly career the measure of the "matter of embarrassment for our Western society that traditions of other cultures have often been looked down upon with condescension as the curious behavioural oddities of underdeveloped people who should learn something from us – rather than we from them"[621].

The forced and artificial adaptation of our "Euro-American" notions of the "natural science" to a phenomenon completely alien to our cultural sphere easily leads to a sort of superiority complex of "ethnocentralisation". On the other hand, when we enter into the inheritance of the examined cultural community and use their own developed cultural concepts, while being unnoticeably assimilated to them, we can slowly and easily lose sight of the wholeness of reality, the complexity of certain examined cultural-religious phenomena.[622]

---

[620] Quotation from Manfred Bleuler, in: Jilek, Wolfgang G.: *Indian Healing. Shamanic Ceremonialism in the Pacific Northwest Today*, Hancock House Publishers Ltd., Surrey, 1982, 6

[621] Jilek 1982, 5

[622] Grynaeus, Tamás: *Az ethnopsychiatria egyes kérdései* [Questions of ethnopsychiatry], JATE Néprajzi Tanszék, Szeged, 2000, 35–56

As Jilek points out "the criteria of normality deduced from a statistical norm are valid only for the population in which they have been established and cannot be assumed to be valid for populations in other socio-cultural or historical situations."[623]

The same question arises in gender studies of religion. Developing the scientific results of ethnopsychiatry, scholars examining religious rituals and rules from gender perspectives maintain that normality controlling cultural-religious attitudes are dictated not simply by developed Western religious systems, but by systems dominated by educated male representatives of Western patriarchal religions taking shape in rituals offered exclusively to images of male divine characters.

This trend undervalues not only the cultural characteristics of so-called "underdeveloped people", but also the belief of women (belonging often to the social strata of uneducated, poor people) expressed in different female ways. Women's religion does not suit the requirements of normality defined by the "developed" Western male society.

Their belief fell victim not merely to ethnocentralisation, but to the centralisation of religion that tends to specify women's religion as "magic" sharply differentiated from "religion" as collectively recognised norm-giving authority. Although today's science of religion attempts to avoid this kind of categorisation, the traditional distinction still reflects established power-relations between higher and lower religious systems.[624]

All those who interpret themselves as representatives of a certain traditional community perform a cultural task that is continuously enriched by individual elements in an unbroken interactive process. According to Jádi and Tüskés being involved in religious-cultural happenings defines and motivates the homo religiosus (the religious human being preserving tradition) to become homo tradens[625] who oneself forms tradition through integrating all cultural effects influencing identity.[626]

The obsolete idea of "homo religiosus" however bears witness to earlier studies of religion handling women as externalised objects of researches rather than religious subjects. The so-called "homo religiosus" implied generally exclusively male characteristics and the notion was basically interpret-

---

[623] Jilek August 1994, 3

[624] Cf. Pahnke, Donate: *Religion and Magic in the Modern Cults of the Great Goddess*, in: King. Ursula (ed.): Religion and Gender, Blackwell, Oxford, 1995, 165–176

[625] The expression *tradens* comes from the Latin verb *trādō* which means among others "entrust", "yield", "report", "bequeath", "teach" etc.

[626] Cf. Jádi – Tüskés 1986, 549

ed as "vir religiosus". Furthermore it assumes a "complicated interaction between economic, political, and cultural dimensions in the development of human societies."[627]

The attempt to define and strongly over-simplify female religious positions and roles is a general-systematic tendency in world religions. Similarly gender attitudes of the Hungarian popular belief also effected primarily by early and patristic Christian interpretations of sharply shaping male-centred world-views is well illustrated among others by Jerome's idea to derive the notion "virgo" from "vir".[628]

It postulates a primitive "husband/monarch system of power related to divine Fatherly rule",[629] in which women are totally condemned for their "physical" nature. The pureness of genealogy is to be guaranteed through the father's, husband's, brother's and son's control over woman legitimised by certain type, male-centred religious orders.[630]

According to Göttner-Abendroth, while the patriarchal system is most often associated with the civilised world of culture, female spirituality is not a religion of a super-mother in heaven as counterpart to God the Father but rather "magical-spiritual capacity within each woman herself"[631] to express reconciliation, harmonious inclusiveness and solidarity between the natural and the super-natural. "The problem is that Western religious studies [...] have constructed conceptual categories and developmental schemes in which the specific is less valued than the abstract, and in which women − associated with private or personal rather than public concerns − are automatically substandard."[632]

Heide Göttner-Abendroth outlines well distinguishable elements of patriarchal-abstract and matriarchal-concrete/tangible cult systems:[633]

---

[627] Turner, Bryan S.: *The Body in Western Society*, in: Coakley, Sarah (ed.): Religion and the Body, Cambridge University Press, Cambridge, 1997, 15–41, here 26

[628] Cf. Louth, Andrew: *The Body in Western Catholic Christianity*, in: Coakley (ed.) 1997, 111–130, here 116. See also: Jerome: Epistles 49:2

[629] Turner 1997, 26

[630] Cf. Heller, Birgit: *Revision des homo religiosus: Religion und Geschlecht*, in: Becker, R. − Kortendieck, B. (eds.): Handbuch Frauen- und Geschlechterforschung, Leverkusen, 2003 (in press)

[631] Göttner-Abendroth, Heide: *Matriarchale Ästhetik, ein ganzheitlicher Prozess*, in: Lutz, Rüdiger (ed.): Frauenzukünfte. Ökologbuch 3, Beltz, Weinheim, 1984, 166–175, here 171

[632] Sered 1996, 22

[633] See the summing up of Heide Göttner-Abendroth's (researcher of matriarchy and leader of the Hagia Academy for Critical Matriarchal Research and Experience) scientific consequences by Pahnke, in: Pahnke 1995, 168–169

| Patriarchal cult system | Matriarchal cult system |
|---|---|
| Monotheism with exclusive pretension | A threefold great Goddess who includes all others, with many names |
| The godhead is something distant, high, extraneous, transcendent | The godhead is near, present |
| God the Father/Lord *creates* heaven and earth and man | The Goddess *is* the world, heaven, earth, Me |
| Institutionalised state-religion | Locally different variations (place-religion) |
| Centralised hierarchical order | Multiplicity with certain hierarchical order |
| Monopoly of male priestly caste for sacred actions | Priestesses/queens and priests/kings Both woman and men have the right to perform sacred actions |
| Priests are interpreters and mediators of the relation of God-man | Female and male priests are performers of female and male principles |
| Dogmas | No generally prescribed dogmas |
| Subordination and obedience to God | Integration and obedience to the natural laws |
| Political imperialism and mission | No imperialism, no mission |
| Linear comprehension of time and cult | Cyclic-spiral comprehension of time and cult |
| Repetitive character: Spiritual experiences of the founders are tried to be repeated | Present character, with reflection on the tradition. Spiritual experiences are central |
| *Dualistic* view of world:<br>1. Heaven and earth are divided<br>2. Man and woman are basically and completely different<br>3. Man stands above nature<br>4. God-devil<br>5. Split between body and spirit<br>6. Life-death-the beyond | *Holistic* view of world:<br>1. Heaven and earth are one<br>2. Man and woman are different aspects of the one<br>3. Wo/man is part of nature<br>4. The Goddess is good as well as evil<br>5. Integration of body and spirit<br>6. Life-death-survival in the sense of rebirth |

However, as Heller[634] points out, in reality the sharp distinction between patriarchal and matriarchal systems is a scientifically outworn conception. We must be careful about the scientific language we use. Dualistic and hierarchical systems of conceptions describing gender roles in culture and religion do not properly express the diversity and complexity of human reality. Though as we have seen, the Mother Goddess is mostly associated with fertility, this maternal role of being the source, ruler and transmitter of life does not universally characterise other, more combined figures of goddesses, like the Sumerian Inanna or the Babylonian-Assyrian Ishtar.

Even though the maternal divine figure is a sign of the so-called matrifocal cultures, and elder sociological interpretations postulate a direct contact between the worship of the Mother Goddess and matriarchal formed society, there is not an automatically establishable relation between the existent Great Mother and social dominance of women.

The attempts to divide the history of religion into two groups of maternal and paternal religion neglect religious reality and the socio-cultural variety of female and male roles.[635] The religious symbolism of motherhood is in combined mutuality with the human mother. Its images represented by women mirror the diverse experiences of mothers and at the same time offer models of imitation for women.

Nevertheless in patriarchal religious traditions the symbol of the divine Mother often illustrates a kind of religious message of praised motherhood of the woman that can easily lead to legitimisation of hierarchically interpreted gender roles. Women's religious significance is based essentially on their mother role, more precisely, mothering definitely sons.[636]

In this context the role of the grandmother as an extension of the mother's role has a remarkable significance in the history of representing the powerful leading character of the Great Mother, who most often appears in the christianised Europe as Saint Anne, the mother of the Virgin Mary and grandmother of the Redeemer, represented in fascinating textual and visual images of Saint Anne Trinitarian form.[637] In women's religion mothers are primarily

---

[634] Cf. Heller, Birgit: Art. *Muttergottheiten, religionswissenschaftlich*, in: Betz, D. et al. (eds.): Religion in Geschichte und Gegenwart, Vol. 5, Tübingen, ⁴2002 (revised edition), 1630f

[635] Cf. Risman, Barbara J.: *Intimate Relationships from a Microstructural Perspective. Men Who Mother*, in: Gender and Society I, 1987, 6–32. By comparing the personality characteristics of married parents, single mothers and single fathers Risman proves that single fathers being primarily responsible for childcare rather show maternal traits than features of married fathers.

[636] Cf. Heller 2003

[637] Cf. textual examples in: Erdélyi 1999; textual and visual examples e.g. in: Beattie 1999

participants, grandmothers however tend to take leadership in the religious community.

This phenomenon is ideologically based on the postmenopausal state that protects elderly women from being excluded from sacred activities because of menstrual impurity.[638] Pragmatically these women have already gone through the slow process of self-recognition and simply have more autonomy and spare time to practise leading religious roles.[639] Grandmothers know that "which is not celebrated, [...] not ritualised, goes unnoticed, and in the long run [...] will be devalued."[640]

History as a matter of interpretations shaped by power relations of certain time and space rather than facts overshadows Goddess symbolism rooted in prehistoric eras. New methodologies and frameworks of scientific interpretation are needed to reveal the undermined reality of Goddess-like characteristics in different cultural traditions. For being able to investigate the story of the Goddess and her female representatives we must be aware of the continuous effort to ignore the fact of female existence in the heritage of human culture.

Christ describes several scientific methods[641] focusing on distorting women's significance in the course of history: For example (1) not even mentioning explored data referring to female activities and existence of female divine figure(s), (2) presenting some of the evidence of Goddess history only "within the framework of androcentric theories"[642], (3) representing the Goddess as purely the product of the unconscious feminine in opposition to consciousness identified with masculine ego. These attempts expect women to unconditionally support male social-cultural order.

Gimbutas warns us that we "are still living under the sway of that aggressive male invasion and only beginning to discover our long alienation from our authentic European Heritage – gylanic, non-violent, earth-centred culture."[643] The image of the Mother Earth or the female divine figure representing earthly fertility and creativity queries traditional abstract interpretations of gender roles that manifest the female body as a frail, vulnerable entity in contradistinction to the earliest portrayals of solid and strong divine female characteristics reflected in earth-like maternal features.

---

[638] Cf. Heller 2003

[639] Sered 1994, 78, cf. Sered, Susan Starr: *Women as Ritual Experts. The Religious Lives of Elderly Jewish Women in Jerusalem*, Oxford University Press, New York, 1992

[640] Budapest, Zsuzsanna E.: *The Grandmother of Time*, Harper and Row, San Francisco, 1989, xxi

[641] Christ, Carol P.: *Rebirth of the Goddess*, Routledge, New York, 1997, 79–88

[642] Christ 1997, 80

[643] Gimbutas 1989, xxi

When the power of naming and reshaping symbols is "shared by women and men, then biological or other differences between women and men do not have to be interpreted to define one sex as subordinate to the other. Indeed, anthropologists are coming to the conclusion that in many traditional cultures, sex roles are distinguished without giving one sex control over the other."[644]

Human life is expressed bodily, as incarnated entity being relational and interdependent as well as relationally independent at the same time.[645] It depends on the contemporary mythos of culturally shaped rituals and symbols how the ethos of everyday activities develops. Only "the ethos of genderised domination"[646] distorts relational human embodiment. According to this anti-corporal system bodily limitation and vulnerability are seen as weakness that is best represented in "primitive" ancient Goddess cultures.

Nevertheless the vision of Goddess religion about the connectedness and consequently respect of all lively entities challenges the illusion of domination-theory.[647] While recognising the importance of often destructively treated but actually culturally independent female physical realities, Budapest does not see her own bodily experience as "something I am going to keep quiet about. It is what women do, we make people."[648]

Women's religion reflects a significant psychological aspect of female identity. Being in close connection with their mothers, the primary caretaker of children, girls grow up in the midst of continuous intimate personal familiar relationships that helps developing less rigid, accordingly more permeable female ego boundaries for women that is also seen in their particularly empathetic and intuitive religious activities.[649] At the same time "women typically become leaders through a slow process of self-recognition, [...] the life histories of many women leaders involve years of illness, visions and struggling with the call of spirits – a process that often begins in early childhood and only ends in old age."[650]

---

[644] Christ 1997, 93

[645] Cf. Moltmann-Wendel, Elisabeth: *Mein Körper bin Ich. Neue Wege zur Leiblichkeit*, Gütersloher Verlagshaus, Gütersloh, 1994

[646] Christ 1997, 161

[647] Cf. Ywahoo, Dhyani: *Renewing the Sacred Hoop*, in: Plaskow, Judith – Christ, Carol P. (eds.): Weaving the Visions, Harper and Row, San Francisco, 1989, 275

[648] Budapest, Zsuzsanna E.: *Self-Blessing Ritual*, in: Christ, Carol P. – Plaskow, Judith (eds.): Womanspirit Rising, Harper and Row, San Francisco, 1979, 271

[649] Gudorf 1987, 304, cf. Rubin, Lillian B.: *Intimate Strangers. Men and Women Together*, Harper and Row, New York, 1983, 58–59

[650] Sered 1994, 237

Instead of the model of objective thinking women follow the model of *embodied* thinking that maintains the significance of individual actions that have powerful influence and consequences even for the next coming generations.[651] (Table XIV. / Fig. 35.)

---

[651] Christ 1997, 173

# Bibliography

Achterberg, Jeanne: *Die Frau als Heilerin. Die schöpferische Rolle der heilkundigen Frau in Geschichte und Gegenwart,* Scherz, Bern, 1990

Almási, Tamás: *Sejtjeink* [Our cells], 2002, documentary

Ashley, Kathleen – Sheingorn, Pamela (eds.): *Interpreting Cultural Symbols. Saint Anne in Late Medieval Society,* The University of Georgia Press, Athen – London, 1994

Avalon, Arthur: *Shakti and Shakta,* Dover, New York, 1978

Badiny, Ferenc Jós: *The Sumerian Wonder,* School for Oriental Studies, University of Salvador, Buenos Aires, 1974

Balázs, György: *The Magyars,* Corvina, Budapest, 1989

Bálint, Sándor: *Népünk imádságai* [Prayers of our people], in: Regnum, Budapest, 1937

Bálint, Sándor: *A magyar vallásos népélet kutatása* [The examination of the Hungarian popular belief], in: Dankó, Imre – Küllős, Imola (ed.): Vallási néprajz III. – Módszerek és történeti adatok [Religious ethnography 3. – Methods and historical data], Budapest, ELTE Folklore Tanszék, 1987, 8–65

Balz-Cochois, Helgard: *Inanna. Wesenbild und Kult einer unmütterlichen Göttin,* Gütersloher Verlagshaus Gerd Mohn, Gütersloh, 1992

Barna, Ferdinánd: *Ősvallásunk főistenei* [The principal gods of our ancient religion], MTA, Budapest, 1881, 70

Baum, William Wakefield – Magistris, Luigi De: *Decree of the Sacred Penitentiary on the Conditions for Gaining the Jubilee Indulgence,* Rome, 29 November 1998

Beattie, Tina: *Mary, the Virgin Priest?,* in: The Month 257, December 1996, 485–493

Becker-Cantarino, Barbara: *Der lange Weg zur Mündigkeit. Frau und Literatur (1500–1800),* Metzler, Stuttgart, 1987

Beinert, Wolfgang: *Theologische Information über Marienerscheinungen,* in: Anzeiger für die Seelsorge, Herder, Freiburg, 5/1997, 250–258

Benedek, Elek: *Világszép Nádszálkisasszony* [The most beautiful reed-miss, Hungarian fairy tales], Móra, Budapest, 1976

Bihari, Anna (ed.): *Magyar Hiedelemmonda Katalógus* [Catalogue of the Hungarian myths of belief] , MTA Néprajzi Kutatócsoport, Budapest 1980

Bly, Robert – Woodmann, Marion: *The Maiden King: The Reunion of Masculine and Feminine*, Henry Holt, NY, 1998

Bobula, Ida: *Origin of the Hungarian Nation*, Danubian Press, Astor, Fla., 1982

Boehmer, R. M.: *Die Entwicklung der Glyptik während der Akkad-Zeit*, Untersuchungen zur Assyriologie und Vorderasiatischen Archäologie 4, Berlin, 1965

*Book of the Dead* (revised edition: Wallis Budge), Bell, New York, 1960, 518

Børresen, Kari Elisabeth: *Subordination and Equivalence – The Nature and Role of Woman in Augustine and Thomas Aquinas*, Kok Pharos Publishing House, Kampen, 1995 (first edition: 1968)

Bosnyák, Sándor: *A világ teremtése a moldvai magyarok mondáiban* [The creation of the world in the legends of Hungarians coming from Moldva], in: Dankó, Imre – Küllős, Imola (ed.): *Vallási néprajz III. – Módszerek és történeti adatok* [Religious ethnography 3. – Methods and historical data], Budapest, ELTE Folklore Tanszék, 1987, 348–354

Bosnyák, Sándor: *Magyar biblia* [Hungarian Bible], Európai Folklór Intézet – L'Harmattan, Budapest, 2001

Bourguignon, Erika (ed.): *Religion. Altered States of Consciousness and Social Change*. Ohio University Press, Columbus, 1973

Braulik, Georg: *Die Ablehnung der Göttin Aschera in Israel*, in: Wacker, Marie-Theres – Zenger, Erich (eds.): Der eine Gott und die Göttin. Herder, Freiburg, 1991, 106–136

Buckland, Jill Theresa: *Multiple Interests and Powers*, in: Felföldi, László – Buckland, J. Theresa (eds.): *Authenticity. Whose tradition?*, European Folklore Institute, Budapest, 2002, 70–78

Budapest, Zsuzsanna E.: *Self-Blessing Ritual*, in: Christ, Carol P. – Plaskow, Judith (eds.): Womanspirit Rising, Harper and Row, San Francisco, 1979

Budapest, Zsuzsanna E.: *The Grandmother of Time*, Harper and Row, San Francisco, 1989

Bynum, Caroline Walker: *Jesus as Mother. Studies in the Spirituality of the High Middle Ages*, University of California Press, Berkeley, 1982

Campbell, Joseph: *The Masks of God. Primitive Mythology*, Viking, New York, 1959

Campbell, Joseph: *The Masks of God. Occidental Mythology*, Viking, New York, 1964

Campbell, Joseph: *The Masks of God. Creative Mythology*, Viking, New York, 1970

Christ, Carol P.: *Rebirth of the Goddess*, Routledge, New York, 1997

Chung, Hyun Kyung: *Schamanin im Bauch – Christin im Kopf. Frauen Asiens im Aufbruch*, Kreuz Verlag, Stuttgart 1992

Cirlot, Juan Eduardo: *A Dictionary of Symbols*, Philosophical Library, New York, 1962

Congar, Yves: *The Meaning of Tradition*, Hawthorne, NY, 1964

Courtenay, William J.: *Between Despair and Love – Some Late Medieval Modifications of Augustine's Teaching on Fruition and Psychic States*, in: Hagen, Kenneth (ed.):

Augustine, the Harvest, and Theology (1300–1650) – Essays Dedicated to Heiko Augustinus Oberman in Honour of his Sixtieth Birthday, E.J. Brill, Leiden, 1990, 5–19

Csonka-Takács, Eszter: *Női tisztátalansági tabuk a magyar néphitben* [The taboos of female impurity in Hungarian folk belief], in: Küllős, Imola: Hagyományos női szerepek – Nők a populáris kultúrában és a folklórban [Traditional female roles – Women in popular culture and in folklore], MNT – SZCSM NT, Budapest, 1999

Cs. Varga, István: *Szent művészet II – Tanulmányok költészetünk szakrális vonulatából* [Holy art 2 – Studies from the sacred range of our poetry], Székesfehérvár, 2000

Daczó, Árpád: *Népünk hitvilága* [The world of our folk's belief], Kolozsvár/Cluj, 1992

Daczó, Árpád: *Csíksomlyó titka. Mária-tisztelet a néphagyományban* [The mystery of Csíksomlyó. The reputation of Mary in the folk tradition], Pallas-Akadémia, Csíkszereda 2000

Daly, Mary: *Beyond God the Father – Toward a Philosophy of Women's Liberation*, Boston, Beacon Press, 1973

Danthine, Hélène: *Le palmier-dattier et les arbres sacrées dans l'iconographie de l'asie occidentale ancienne*, 2 vol. (Texts and Plates), Geuthner, Paris, 1937

Derlon, Pierre: *Die Gärten der Einweihung. Und andere Geheimnisse der Zigeuner*, Hugendubel, München, 1991

Dienst, Heide: *Männerarbeit und Frauenarbeit im Mittelalter*, in: Beiträge zur historischen Sozialkunde, 1981, Heft 3, 88–90

Diószegi, Vilmos: *A sámánhit emlékei a magyar népi műveltségben* [The tokens of shamanic belief in the Hungarian popular cultivation], Akadémiai Kiadó, Budapest, 1998 (Reprint)

Douglas, Mary: *Purity and Danger. An Analysis of Concepts of Pollution and Taboo*, London-Hanley, 1966

Durand, Gilbert: *Les structure anthropologiques de l'imaginaire. Introduction à l'archétypologie générale*, Bordas, Paris, 1969

Dümmerth, Dezső: *Az Árpádok nyomában* [On the track of the Árpáds], Panoráma, Budapest, ²1977

Dürr, Hans Peter: *Traumzeit über die Grenzen zwischen Wildnis und Zivilisation*, Suhrkamp, Frankfurt am Main, 1985

Egg, Markus – Pase, Christopher: *Die Metallzeiten in Europa und im Vorderen Orient. Die Abteilung Vorgeschichte im Römisch-Germanistischen Zentralmuseum*, Kataloge Vor- und Frühgeschichtlicher Altertümer, Band 26, Verlag des Römisch-Germanistischen Zentralmuseums, Mainz, 1995

Ehlert, Trude: *Die Rolle von "Hausherr" und "Hausfrau" in der spätmittelalterlichen volkssprachigen Ökonomik*, in: Ehlert, Trude (ed.): Haushalt und Familie in Mittelalter und früher Neuzeit, Jan Thorbecke Verlag, Sigmaringen, 1991, 153–166

Eliade, Mircea: *Das Heilige und das Profane. Vom Wessen der Religiösen*, Rowohlt, Hamburg, 1957

El-Safadi, H. *Die Entstehung der syrischen Glyptik und ihre Entwicklung in der Zeit von Zimrilim bis Amitaquamma*, UF 6, 1975, 313–352

Ennen, Edith: *Frauen im Mittelalter*, Verlag Beck, München, [4]1991

Erdélyi, István – Sugár, Lajos: *Ázsiai lovas nomádok* [Equestrian Nomads from Asia], Gondolat, Budapest, 1982

Erdélyi, Zsuzsanna: *Modern szinkretizmus* [Modern syncretism], in: Horváth, Pál (ed.): Néphit, népi vallásosság ma Magyarországon [Popular belief, folk religion in Hungary today], MTA Filozófiai Intézet, Budapest, 1990

Erdélyi, Zsuzsanna (ed.): *Boldogasszony ága – Tanulmányok a népi vallásosság köréből* [The bough of the Happy Woman – Studies on the folk belief], SzIT, Budapest, 1992

Erdélyi, Zsuzsanna: *A látomásformulák szerepe az archaikus népi imádságokban* [The role of the formulae of vision in archaic Hungarian folk prayers], in: Pócs, Éva (ed.): Eksztázis, álom, látomás – Vallásetnológiai fogalmak tudományközi megközelítésben [Ecstasy, dream, vision – An interdisciplinary approach of religious-ethnological concepts], Balassi, Budapest, 1998, 405–433

Erdélyi, Zsuzsanna: *Hegyet hágék, lőtőt lépék – archaikus népi imádságok* [~ Up to hill, down to vale – archaic folk prayers], Kalligram, Pozsony, [3]1999

Érszegi, Géza (ed.): *Árpád-kori legendák és intelmek* [Legends and exhortations of the age of the Árpád-house], Budapest, 1983

Falvay, Károly: *A sámánszertartások szimbolizmusához* [To the symbolism of shamanic rituals], Új Magyarország Magazin, Budapest, July 10th 1993

Falvay, Károly: *Boldogasszony – A női szerep a magyar hitvilág tükrében* [Happy Woman – The female role in the mirror of the world of the Hungarian belief], Tertia, Budapest, 2001

Feldtkeller, Andreas: *Im Reich der syrischen Göttin – Eine religiös plurale Kultur als Umwelt des frühen Christentum*, Studien zum Verstehen fremder Religionen, Band 8., Gütersloher Verlagshaus, Gütersloh, 1994

Felföldi, László – Buckland, J. Theresa (eds.): *Authenticity. Whose tradition?*, European Folklore Institute, Budapest, 2002

Fettich, Nándor: *Vallásos jellegű varázs-szövegek a magyar néphitben* [Religious magic texts of the Hungarian folk belief], in: *Ethnographia*, LXXXII, Budapest, 1971

Frankfort, H.: *A Note on the Lady of Birth*, Journal of Near Eastern Studies 3, 1944, 198–200

Franz, Marie-Louise von: *Női mesealakok* [Hungarian translation of "The Feminine in Fairy Tales"], Európa, Budapest, 1992

Frazer, James: *Az Aranyág* [Hungarian translation of "The Golden Bough"], Gondolat, Budapest, 1965

Gimbutas, Marija: *The Language of the Goddess*, Harper & Row, San Francisco, 1989

Göttner-Abendroth, Heide: *Matriarchale Ästhetik, ein ganzheitlicher Prozess*, in: Lutz, Rüdiger (ed.): Frauenzukünfte. Ökologbuch 3, Beltz, Weinheim, 1984, 166–175

Graves, Robert: *The Greek Myths*, 2 Vol., Penguin Books, New York, 1955, Vol. 1

Green, Miranda: *The Gods of the Celts*, Barnes & Noble, Totowa, 1986

Grey, Mary: *Introducing Feminist Images of God*, Sheffield Academic Press, Sheffield, 2001

Grynaeus, Tamás: *Sozialpsychologische Aspekte der ungarischen Hexenprozesse und des Hexenglaubens*, Acta Ethnographica Acad. Sci. Hung., Budapest, 1991–1992, 37 (1–4) 479–488

Grynaeus, Tamás: *Az ethnopsychiatria egyes kérdései* [Questions of ethnopsychiatry], JATE Néprajzi Tanszék, Szeged, 2000

Gudorf, Christine: *The Power to Create: Sacraments and Men's Need to Birth*, in: Horizons 14, 1987, 296–309

Gulyás, Ernő: *Miben sántikál Klára asszony?* [Is Lady Klára up to some mischief?], in: Nógrád Megyei Napló, Balassagyarmat, 1966 (series)

Gunda, Béla: *Szépasszonyok kútja* [The well of the beautiful women], in: Ethnographia, Magyar Néprajzi Társaság, Budapest, 1947, 281–282

Heller, Birgit: Art. *Muttergottheiten, religionswissenschaftlich*, in: Betz, D. et al. (eds.): Religion in Geschichte und Gegenwart, Vol. 5, Tübingen, ⁴2002 (revised edition), 1630f

Heller, Birgit: *Revision des homo religiosus: Religion und Geschlecht*, in: Becker, R. – Kortendieck, B. (eds.): Handbuch Frauen- und Geschlechterforschung, Leverkusen, 2003

Herodot: *Historien*, Kröner, Stuttgart, 1971

Hoffmann-Krayer, Eduard – Bächtold-Stäubli, Hanns: *Handwörterbuch des Deutschen Aberglaubens*, 10 Volumes, Vol. 2, Walter de Gruyter & Co., Berlin und Leipzig, 1929/1930

Hoppál, Mihály: *A meztelenség mint az erósz tagadása* [Nakedness as the denial of eros], in: Hoppál, Mihály – Szepes, Erika (eds.): A szerelem kertjében. Erotikus jelképek a müvészetben [In the garden of love. Erotic symbols in the art], Budapest, 1987, 223–239

Hoppál, Mihály – Jankovics, Marcell – Nagy, András – Szemadám, György (eds.): *Jelképtár* [Collection of symbols], Helikon, Budapest, 1990

Hoppál, Mihály: *Sámánok. Lelkek és jelképek* [Shamans. Spirits and symbols], Helikon, Budapest, 1994

Hoppál, Mihály: *Hiedelemrendszerünkről* [About the system of our folk beliefs], in: Bali, János – Jávor, Kata: Merítés. Néprajzi tanulmányok Szilágyi Miklós tiszteletére [Immertion. Ethnographical studies in honour of Miklós Szilágyi], Budapest, 2001, 433–440

Hoppál, Mihály: *Tradition, Value System and Identity: Notes on Local Cultures*, in: Felföldi, László – Buckland, J. Theresa (eds.): *Authenticity. Whose tradition?*, European Folklore Institute, Budapest, 2002, 1–18

Howell, Signe – Melhuus, Marit: *The study of kinship; the study of person; a study of gender?*, in: del Valle, Teresa (ed.): Gendered Anthropology, Routledge, London, 1993, 38–53

Hufnagel, Alfons: *"Die Bewertung der Frau bei Thomas von Aquin"*, Theologische Quartelschrift 156 (1976) 132–165

*Inter Insigniores*, in: Origins 6:33, February 3, 1977

Ipolyi, Arnold: *Magyar mythologia* [Hungarian mythology], Heckenast, Pest, 1854

Ipolyvölgyi Németh, Krizosztom: *Szívet keres a Szeretetláng a Kármelhegyi Boldogasszonnyal* [The Flame of Love looks for hearts with the Happy Woman of the Mount Carmel], booklet, Balassagyarmat, 1992

Irigaray, Luce: *Sexes and Genealogies*, Columbia University Press, NY, 1993

Jacobsen, Thorkild: *The Treasures of Darkness. A History of Mesopotamian Religion.* Yale University Press, New Haven, 1976

Jádi, Ferenc – Tüskés, Gábor: *A népi vallásosság pszichopatológiája. Egy hasznosi parasztasszony látomásai* [The psychopathology of the popular belief. The visions of a peasant woman from Hasznos], in: Tüskés, Gábor (ed.): "Mert ezt Isten hagyta...". Tanulmányok a népi vallásosság köréből ["Because it was devised by God...". Studies from the world of popular belief], Magvető, Budapest, 1986, 516–556

Jankovics, Marcell: *Archaikus világkép a szibériai sámándobokon* [Archaic world concept represented on Siberian shamanic drums], in.: Jankovics, Marcell: Ahol a madár se jár [Out-of-the-way place], Pontifex Kiadó, Budapest, 1996

Jilek, Wolfgang G.: *Indian Healing. Shamanic Ceremonialism in the Pacific Northwest Today*, Hancock House Publishers Ltd., Surrey, 1982

Jilek, Wolfgang G.: *Normality and psychopathology in the context of culture: Some thoughts on culture-sensitive diagnosing in psychiatry*, in: Newsletter of Transcultural Psychiatry, August 1994, Vol. XII, No.1

Jilek, Wolfgang G.: *Modified States of Consciousness: Their Role in Ethnopsychiatry*, in: Newsletter of Transcultural Psychiatry, December 1994, Vol. XII, No. 2

Johnson, Elizabeth: *Mary and the Female Face of God*, in: Theological Studies 50, no. 3, 1989, 500–526

Johnson, Robert A.: *The Fisher King and the Handless Maiden: Understanding the Wounded Feeling Function in Masculine and Feminine Psychology*, HarperSanFrancisco, NY, 1993

Jung, Carl Gustav: *Man and His Symbol*, Doubleday, New York, 1964

Jung, Károly: *Köznapok és legendák – Tanulmányok a népi kultúra köréből* [Weekdays and legends – Studies from the area of the popular culture], Forum, Novi Sad, 1992

Kalla Mrs., Emil and her husband (editors and publishers): *A hasznosi Szűzanya története és búcsú énekek* [The story of the Virgin Mother of Hasznos and pilgrim songs], Jászberény, 1948

Kállay, Ferencz: *A pogány magyarok vallása* [Religion of pagan Hungarians], Lauffer and Stolp, Pest, 1861, reprinted by Püski, Budapest, 1999

Kálmány, Lajos: *Boldogasszony, ősvallásunk istenasszonya* [The Happy Woman, the goddess of our ancient religion], in: Diószegi, Vilmos (ed.): *Az ősi magyar hitvilág* [The ancient world of the Hungarian belief], Gondolat, Budapest, 1971

Kalsky, Manuela: *Christaphanien. Die Re-Vision der Christologie aus der Sicht von Frauen in unterschiedlichen Kulturen*, Gütersloher Verlagshaus, Gütersloh, 2000

Kapitány, Ágnes – Kapitány, Gábor: *Értékrendszereink* [Our value systems], Kossuth, Budapest, 1983

Kassel, Maria: *Trauma, Symbol, Religion – Tiefenpsychologie und feministische Analyse*, Herder, Freiburg, 1991

Kassel, Maria: *Biblische Urbilder*, Herder, Freiburg, 1992

Keel, Othmar – Uehlinger, Christoph: *Göttinnen, Götter und Gottessymbole*, Herder, Freiburg, 1992

Kerekes, József (ed.): *Egy zarándokhely kialakulása. Hasznos – Fallóskút* [The evolution of a pilgrim place. Hasznos – Fallóskút], Kerekes, Budapest, 2001

Keszeg, Vilmos: *A kör szemantikája és szerkezete* [The semantics and structure of the circle], in: Művelődés L. 4., 1997, 34–37

Keszeg, Vilmos: *Jóslások a Mezőségen. Etnomantikai elemzés.* [Predictions in the Mezőség. Ethnomantic analysis], Bon-Ami, Sepsiszentgyörgy, 1997

Kiev, Ari: *The Study of Folk Psychiatry*, in: International Journal of Psychiatry, Vol 1, No. 4, 1965, 524–550

King, Herbert: *Die Bedeutung der Marienerscheinungen im kirchlichen Leben der Neuzeit*, in: Ziegenaus, A. (ed.): Marienerscheinungen, Ihre Echtheit und Bedeutung im Leben der Kirche, Mariologische Studien X, Pustet, Regensburg, 1995, 119–120

Kisfalusi János (ed.): *A fallóskúti (hasznosi) Mária-kápolna* [The chapel of Mary in Fallóskút (Hasznos)], booklet, private edition, 1995

Kiškūnaitė, Laimė: *About a Moonwoman – Giving birth*, Part II, Klubas "Gimtis", Vilnius, 1997, documentary (video, 42')

Kleinheyer, Bruno: *Marienfeiern im Kirchenjahr*, in: Beinert, Wolfgang – Petri, Heinrich (eds.): Handbuch der Marienkunde, Verlag Friedrich Pustet, Regensburg, 1984

Klemm, Nándor (ed.): *Fallóskút 50 éves* [Fallóskút is 50 years old], booklet, private edition, 1997

Klemm, Nándor (ed.): *Így történt. Fallóskút története* [The way it happened. The story of Fallóskút], private edition, 1999

Komjáthy, István: *Mondák könyve* [The book of myths], Móra, Budapest, 1955

Kontler, László: *Millennium in Central Europe: A History of Hungary*, Atlantisz, Budapest, 1999

Korompay, Bertalan: *Finn nyomokon I–II.* [On Finnish tracks, vol. 1–2], private edition, Budapest, 1989

Kristeva, Iulia: *Powers of Horror - An Essay on Abjection*, Columbia University Press, NY, 1982

Kríza, Ildikó: *Az Anasztázia-monda magyar vonatkozásai* [The Hungarian relations of the legend of Anastasia], in: Barna (ed.) 2001, 49–64

Kutter, Erni: *Der Kult der drei Jungfrauen. Eine Kraftquelle weiblicher Spiritualität neu entdeckt*, Kösel, München, 1997

LaCugna, Catherine Mowry (ed.): *Freeing Theology - The Essentials of Theology in Feminist Perspective*, HarperCollins, N. Y., 1993

Laing, Ronald David: *Wisdom, Madness and Folly. The Making of a Psychiatrist*, McGraw-Hill Book Company, New York, 1985

Lammel, Annamária – Nagy, Ilona (ed.): *Parasztbiblia – Magyar népi biblikus történetek* [Peasantbible – Hungarian biblical folk stories], Osiris, Budapest, $^{2}$1995

László, Gyula: *A népvándorláskor művészete Magyarországon* [The art of the period of great migrations in Hungary], Corvina, Budapest

Lázár, István: *Hungary. A Brief History*, Corvina, Budapest 1993

Leavitt, John: *Are Trance and Possession Disorders?*, in: Transcultural Psychiatric Research Review, 1993, Vol. XXX, No. 1, 51–57

Leibovitch, J.: *Kent et Qadech*, Syria 38 (1961) 23–34

Lengyel, Dénes: *Régi magyar mondák* [Old Hungarian myths], Móra, Budapest, 1974

Lentz, Robert: *Christ Sophia*, Bridge Building, Burlington, 1989

Limbacher, Gábor: *Máriácska Káponkája* [The chapel of Mary], in: A Nógrád Megyei Múzeumok Évkönyve [The yearbook of museums of the county Nógrád], Balassagyarmat, 1991

Limbacher, Gábor: *Egy nógrádi javasasszony életútja és gyógyítóvá válása* [The path of life of a wise-woman from the county Nógrád and her becoming healer], in: A Nógrád Megyei Múzeumok Évkönyve [The yearbook of the museums of the county Nógrád], Balassagyarmat, 1994

Limbacher, Gábor: *Gyógyítóasszony Nógrádban a XX. század végén* [Healing woman in Nógrád at the end of the 20th century], in: Ethnographia CVI, 1995, 787–829

Liszka, József: *Ágas-bogas fa* [Branchy tree], Dunaszerdahely, Lilium Aurum, 1992

Livius, Thomas: *The Blessed Virgin in the Fathers of the First Six Centuries*, Burns & Oates Ltd., London, 1893

Louth, Andrew: *The Body in Western Catholic Christianity*, in: Coakley, Sarah (ed.): Religion and the Body, Cambridge University Press, Cambridge, 1997, 111–130

Lovász, Irén: *Oral Christianity in Hungary: Interpreting Interpretations*, in: Davis, Jon – Wollaston, Isabel (eds.): *The Sociology of Sacred Texts*, Sheffield Academic Press, Sheffield, 1993, 72-82

Lovász, Irén: *Az imádkozásról – Nyelvészeti-pragmatikai és a kulturális antropológiai megközelítés* [About praying – Linguistic-pragmatical and cultural anthropological approach], 3, in: Barna, Gábor (ed.): „Nyisd meg, Uram, szent ajtódat..." – Köszöntő kötet Erdélyi Zsuzsanna 80. születésnapjára ["Open your holy door, my Lord..." – Congratulatory volume for the 80th birthday of Zsuzsanna Erdélyi], SzIT, Budapest, 2001, 3–27

Lükő, Gábor: *Feleim*, in: Medvigy Endre (ed.): Válasz [Reply], Püski, Budapest, 1989, 122–136

Lükő, Gábor: *A magyar lélek formái* [The forms of the Hungarian Soul], Táton, Budapest, 2001

Lys, Claudia de: *The Giant Book of Superstitions*, Citadel Press, Secaucus, 1979

MacHaffie, Barbara J.: *Her Story. Women in Christian Tradition*, Fortress Press, Philadelphia, 1986

Madas, Edit: *Szöveggyűjtemény a régi magyar irodalom történetéhez. Középkor* [Reader to the history of old Hungarian literature. The Middle Ages], Tankönyvkiadó, Budapest, 1992

Makoldi, Sándor – Makoldi Mrs., Sándor: *Síppal – dobbal, avagy rosta lyukával?* [With whistle and drum, or else with the hole of the riddle], in: Végvár, József (ed.): "Kiálts teljes torokal" [Shout at the top of your voice], Polar Alapítvány, Budapest, 2000, 203–214

Manga, János: *Hasznos. Egy vallási tömegpszichózis története a néprajzkutató szemével* [Hasznos. The story of a religious mass psychosis interpreted by the ethnographer], in: Világosság, Nr. 7, 1961, 44–48

Manga, János: *A hasznosi tömegpszichózis. A búcsújáróhelyek és a "hasznosi csoda" összefüggései* [The mass psychosis of Hasznos. The relations of the shrines and the "miracle of Hasznos"], Ethnographia, Nr. 3, 1962, 353–388

Marosi, Ernő: *A középkori művészet történetének olvasókönyve XI–XV. század* [The reader of the history of medieval art, 11–15th century], Budapest, 1997

McFague, Sallie: *Metaphorical Theology: Models of God in Religious Language*, Fortress Press, Philadelphia, 1982

McFague, Sallie: *Models of God. Theology for an Ecological, Nuclear Age*, Fortress Press, Philadelphia, 1987

McFague, Sallie: *The Body of God. An Ecological Theology*, Fortress Press, Minneapolis, 1993

McLaughlin, Eleonor C.: *Equality of Souls, Inequality of Sexes: Women in Medieval Theology*, in: Ruether, Rosemary Radford (ed.): Religion and Sexism, Simon and Schuster, NY, 1974, 213–266

Meier-Seethaler, Carola: *Von der göttlichen Löwin zum Wahrzeichen männlicher Macht. Ursprung und Wandel großer Symbole*, Kreuz, Zürich, 1993

Mészáros, István: *Az iskolaügy története Magyarországon 966–1777 között* [The History of Educational Affairs in Hungary between 966–1777], Budapest, 1981

Moltmann-Wendel, Elisabeth: *Mein Körper bin Ich. Neue Wege zur Leiblichkeit,* Gütersloher Verlagshaus, Gütersloh, 1994

Moore, Robert: *Care of the Soul – How to add depth and meaning to your everyday life,* Piatkus, London, 1992

Moore, Robert: *Soul Mates – Honouring the mysteries of love and relationship,* Element, London, 1994

Morvay, Judit: *Asszonyok a nagycsaládban* [Women in the larger family], Akadémiai Kiadó, Budapest, ²1981

Mulack, Christa: *Maria – Die geheime Göttin im Christentum,* Kreuz, Stuttgart, 1985

Nemeshegyi, Péter: *A Szép Szűz Mária Japánban* [The Beautiful Virgin Mary in Japan], in: Szolgálat, Eisenstadt (1975) Nr. 24, 73–80

Nettl, Bruno: *Arrows and Circles.* Yearbook for Traditional Music, ICTM, 1998

Neumann, Erich: *Die Große Mutter,* Olten, 1974

Orosz, György: *Nézzetek rám szemetekkel, hallgassatok fületekkel* [Look at me with your eyes, listen to me with your ears], Nyíregyháza, 1996

Ortega y Gasset, José: *La rebelión de las masas,* Obras completas, Tomo IV, sexta edición, Revista de Occidente, Madrid, 1966

Ortutay, Gyula (ed.): *Magyar Néprajzi Lexikon* [Hungarian ethnographical encyclopedia] I–V. Akadémiai Kiadó, Budapest, 1977–1982

Pahnke, Donate: *Ethik und Geschlecht. Menschenbild und Religion in Patriarchat und Feminismus.* Diagonal, Marburg, 1991

Pahnke, Donate: *Religion and Magic in the Modern Cults of the Great Goddess,* in: King, Ursula (ed.): Religion and Gender, Blackwell, Oxford, 1995, 165–176

Pásztory, János: *Hasznosi Mária* [Mary of Hasznos], MTV, Budapest 1966, documentary

Piankoff, Alexandre – Rambova, Natacha: *Mythological Papyri,* 2 vol., (Egyptian Religious Texts and representations III), NY, 1957

Pócs, Éva: *Szem meglátott, szív megvert. Magyar ráolvasások* [Eye had seen, heart had cursed. Hungarian incantations], Helikon, Budapest, 1986

Pócs, Éva: *Néphit* [Popular belief], in: Dömötör, Tekla (ed.): Népszokás, néphit, népi vallásosság. Magyar Néprajz VII [Popular custom, popular belief, folk religion. Hungarian Ethnography VII], Akadémiai Kiadó, Budapest, 1990, 527–692

Pócs, Éva: *Transz és látomás Európa népi kultúráiban* [Trance and vision in the folk culture of Europe] in: Pócs, Éva (ed.): Eksztázis, álom, látomás – Vallásetnológiai fogalmak tudományközi megközelítésben [Ecstasy, dream, vision – An interdisciplinary approach of religious-ethnological concepts], Balassi, Budapest, 1998, 15–55

Pongrátz, Ester: *Igaz Isteni Szeretetnek Harmattyából Nevelkedett. Drága Kövekkel ki-rakott Arany Korona* [Golden crown brought up by the dew of the true divine love, trimmed with precious stones], with characters of the Royal University, Buda, 1808

Posener, Georges – Sauneron, Serge – Yoyotte, Jean (eds.): *Knaurs Lexikon der ägyptischen Kultur*, Droemersche Verlagsanstalt Th. Knaur Nachf., Munnich, 1960

Rahner, K. – Modehn, Ch – Göpfert, M. (eds.): *Népi vallásosság* [Folk religion], OMC, Vienna, 1987

Risman, Barbara J.: *Intimate Relationships from a Microstructural Perspective. Men Who Mother*, in: Gender and Society I, 1987

Rubin, Lillian B.: *Intimate Strangers. Men and Women Together*, Harper and Row, New York, 1983

Rubin, Simon Shimshon: *Maternal Attachment and Child Death. On Adjustment, Relationship, and Resolution*, Omega 15, Nr. 4, 1984–1985, 347–352

Ruether, Rosemary Radford: *Sexism and God-Talk: Toward a Feminist Theology*, Beacon Press, Boston, 1983

Ruether, Rosemary Radford: *Gaia and God. An ecofeminist theology of earth healing*, Harper, San Francisco, 1992

Sartory, Gertrude and Thomas: *Maria von Ägypten – Allmacht der Buße*, Herderbücherei 977, Freiburg-Basel-Wien, 1982

Scherf, Dagmar: *Der Teufel und das Weib. Eine kulturgeschichtliche Spurensuche*, Fischer Taschenbuch V., Frankfurt am Main, 1990

Schöll, Hans Christoph: *Die Drei Ewigen. Eine Untersuchung über den germanischen Baiernglauben*, Jena, 1936

Schramm, Albert: Der Bilderschmuck der Frühdrucke, 23 volumes, Leipzig, 1920–1940, vol. 3

Schroer, Silvia: *Die Zweiggöttin in Palästina/Israel. Von der Mittelbronze II B-Zeit bis zu Jesus Sirach*, in: Küchler, M. – Uehlinger, Ch. (eds.): Jerusalem. Texte – Bilder – Steine, Novum Testamentum et Orbis Antiquus 6, Freiburg Schweiz u. Göttingen, 1987, 201–225

Sered, Susan Starr: *Women as Ritual Experts. The Religious Lives of Elderly Jewish Women in Jerusalem*, Oxford University Press, New York, 1992

Sered, Susan Starr: *Priestess, Mother, Sacred Sister. Religions Dominated by Women*, Oxford University Press, Oxford, 1994

Sered, Susan Starr: *Mother Love. Child Death and Religious Innovation*, in: Journal of Feminist Studies in Religion, 1996, Nr. 12

Sisa, Stephen: *The Spirit of Hungary. A Panorama of Hungarian History and Culture*, Vista Books, New Jersey, 1995

Soskice, Janet Martin: *Blood and Defilement*, in: ET: Journal of the European Society for Catholic Theology, Tübingen, booklet 2, 1994

Spinetoli, Ortensio da: *Luca*, Cittadella Editrice, Assisi, ²1986

Stone, Merlin: *Ancient Mirrors of Womanhood. Our Goddess and Heroine Heritage*, 2 Volumes, New Sibylline, New York, 1979, vol. 2

Stover, Ronald – Hope, Christine: *Monotheism and Gender Status. A Cross-Societal Study*, in: Social Forces 63 (2) 1984, 335–348

Strahm Bernet, Silvia: *Jesa Christa*, in: Strahm, Doris – Storbel, Regula (eds.): Vom Verlangen nach Heilwerden. Christologie in feministisch-theologischer Sicht, Exodus, Fribourg/Luzern, 1991, 172–181

Székely, Orsolya: *Fallóskút – Hasznos*, DunaTV, Budapest 2002, documentary

Székely, Orsolya: *Hittörténeti archívum-búcsújáróhelyek* [Archives of the history of divinity-places of pilgrimage], DunaTV-Ikon Stúdió 2002, documentary, 40'

Székely, Orsolya: *Gondolatok a vallásos világkép női princípiumáról* [Thinking about the female principle of the religious worldview], DunaTV-Ikon Stúdió 2003, documentary, 55'

Szenti, Tibor: *A nők társadalmi és szexuális kiszolgáltatottsága a magyar feudalizmus utolsó másfélszáz évében a Dél-Alföldön* [The social and sexual defencelessness of women in the last 150 years of Hungarian feudalism in the South of the Hungarian Great Plain], in: Küllős, Imola: Hagyományos női szerepek – Nők a populáris kultúrában és a folklórban [Traditional female roles – Women in popular culture and in folklore], MNT – SZCSM NT, Budapest, 1999, 27–45

Tánczos, Vilmos: *Eleven ostya, szép virág – A moldvai csángó népi imák képei* [Live host, beautiful flower – The images of folk prayers of the Hungarian-speaking native of Moldavia], Pro-Print, Csíkszereda, 2000

Thuróczy, János: *A magyarok krónikája* [The chronicle of Hungarians], Európa, Budapest, 1980

Tomisa, Ilona: *A Magyar Növendékpapság Néprajzi Munkaközössége* [The ethnographical co-operation of the Hungarian Seminarists], in: Dankó, Imre – Küllős, Imola (ed.): Vallási néprajz III. – Módszerek és történeti adatok [Religious ethnography 3. – Methods and historical data], Budapest, ELTE Folklore Tanszék, 1987, 66–79

Tomka, Ferenc: *Intézmény és karizma az egyházban* [Institution and charisma in the church], Országos Lelkipásztori Intézet, Budapest, 1991, 18–69

Torjesen, Karen Jo: *Als Frauen noch Priesterinnen waren*, Zweitausendeins, Frankfurt am Main, 1995

Toschi, Paolo: *La poesia religiosa del popolo italiano*, Firenze, 1922

Tóth, Melinda: *Árpád-kori falfestészet* [Wall-painting in the Arpadian age], Budapest, 1974 (Művészettörténeti Füzetek 9)

Tóth, Péter Pál – Molnár V., József: *Aranyfűrész. Fallóskút 50 esztendeje* [Golden saw. Fallóskút for 50 years], Duna TV, Budapest 1998, documentary

Trigg, Elwood B.: *Gypsy Demons and Divinities*, Citadel Press, Secaucus, 1973

Turner, Bryan S.: *The Body in Western Society*, in: Coakley, Sarah (ed.): Religion and the Body, Cambridge University Press, Cambridge, 1997, 15–41

Varga, Lajos: *Hasznos. Egy vallási tömegpszichózis története, ahogy az ideggyógyász látja* [Hasznos. The story of a religious mass psychosis as it is seen by the neurologist], in:

Világosság, Nr. 7, 1961, 40–44

Volly, István: *Karácsonyi és Mária énekek* [Christmas- and Mary-chants], SzIT, Budapest, 1982

Walker, G. Barbara: *Die geheimen Symbole der Frauen. Lexikon der weiblichen Spiritualität*, Hugendubel, München, 1997

Watzlawick, Paul – Weakland, John H. – Fisch, Richard: *Change. Principles of Problem Formation and Resolution*, Norton, New York, 1974

Weiler, Gerda: *Der enteignete Mythos. Eine feministische Revision der Archetypenlehre C.G. Jungs und Erich Neumanns*, Campus, Frankfurt am Main, 1991

Wijngaards, John: *The priesthood of Mary*, in: The Tablet, vol. 253, 4 Dec/1999

Wild, Henri: *Geb*, in: *Lexikon der Ägyptologie*, vol. 2, Otto Harrassowitz, Wiesbaden, 1980

Winter, Urs: *Frau und Göttin. Exegetische und ikonographische Studien zum weiblichen Gottesbild im Alten Israel und in dessen Umwelt*, Vandenhoeck & Ruprecht, Göttingen, 1983

Ywahoo, Dhyani: *Renewing the Sacred Hoop*, in: Plaskow, Judith – Christ, Carol P. (eds.): Weaving the Visions, Harper and Row, San Francisco, 1989

Zohary, Michael: *Pflanzen der Bibel*, Calver Verlag, Stuttgart, 1983

Table I.

# *Illustrations*

Fig. 8. The Miraculous Stag from Mezőkeresztes-Zöldhalompuszta (p. 35)

Fig. 9. Lucas Cranach: Madonna lactans, 1528, Kapuzinerklaster, Innsbruck (p. 40)
The painting before (1901-1968) and after (1968) its restoration

Fig. 10. The breast-feeding tree, Egypt, 18th dynasty, 1540-1295 BC (p. 77)

Fig. 11. Emese with twigs in her hands symbolising fertility, falcon in the
background (p. 100, footnote 331)

Table III.                                                    223

Fig. 12. Fence hiding Klára Csépe's house built by her son to exlude curious visitors
(p. 136, footnote 456)

Fig. 13. Anna and József Dér (p. 138.)

Table IV.

Fig. 14. The first chapel built by the faithful in 1948 (p. 141)

Fig. 15. The house of Klára Csépe in Hasznos with a statue of Mary built into the front wall
(p. 144)

Table V.                                                                225

Fig. 16. Interior of the chapel of Fallóskút with Mary's statue in the centre (p. 153)

Fig. 17. An open-air statue of Mary at Fallóskút's spring with welcoming hands (p. 165)

Table VI.

Fig. 18. The first official mass was celebrated in October 1987 (p. 167)

Fig. 19. The new chapel built after the death of Klára Csépe, in 1990 (p. 167)

Table VII.                                                                 227

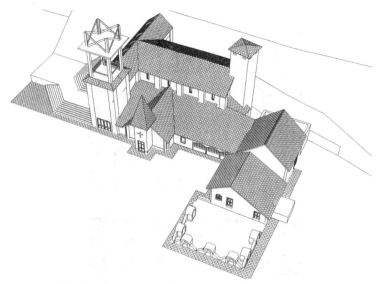

Fig. 20. The design for the future cathedral at Fallóskút (p. 168)

Fig. 21. The first variation of the statue of Mary dated from 1948 (p. 172)

Fig. 22. The newest, restored "gypsy" version of the statue of Mary with long hair (p. 172)

Fig. 23. The "gypsy" Mary with lipstick and other make-up on her face (p. 172)

Table IX.                                                      229

Fig. 24. The house belonging to the local railway, where Aunt Mária officially resides in
Somoskőújfalu (p. 175)

Fig. 25. Aunt Mária praises divine entities together with the faithful (p. 176)

Fig. 26. A statue of Mary in the pantry-chapel, with the photo
of Aunt Mária in the background (p. 178)

Fig. 27. Christ Sophia: Female genealogy deriving from the Magna Mater (p. 179)

Table XI. 231

Fig. 28. Aunt Mária surrounded by faithful at the chapel of Karancs (p. 180)

Fig. 29. Mary, in different forms situated in the centre of the pantry-chapel,
representing female divine dominance of the ritual (p. 180)

Fig. 30. The welcoming "holy water" in the kitchen (p. 180)

Fig. 31. The tap in the kitchen providing "healing holy water" (p. 181)

Table XIII.                                                  233

Fig. 32. The photo of Aunt Mária among icons of divine characters (p. 181)

Fig. 33. Aunt Mária practises her own ritual out in the open air (p. 181)

Fig. 34. The kitchen table as a mixture of sacred and profane (p. 183, footnote 607)

Fig. 35. "The Earth Has Given Birth to the Sky..."
*Earth-Order* [Földgolyó-rend], Gobelin made by the Hungarian artist, Flóra Remsey (p. 205)